Victor Turner's work has helped pave the way for a new understanding of performance, ritual, and the study of cultures. At the time of his death in 1983, he was the William R. Kenan, Jr. Professor of Anthropology at the University of Virginia, Charlottesville. Among his many books are *The Forest of Symbols, Dramas, Fields and Metaphors,* and *From Ritual to Theatre: The Human Seriousness of Play,* also a PAJ Publications title.

ON *THE ANTHROPOLOGY OF PERFORMANCE*

"In this posthumous collection, Turner continues his quest for 'a liberated anthropology,' a cause helped in part by the recent postmodern consciousness."
—*American Theatre*

ON *FROM RITUAL TO THEATRE*

"Turner looked beyond his routinized discipline to an anthropology of experience. . . . We must admire him for this."
—*The Times Literary Supplement* (London)

"One of the outstanding recent books in educational studies."
—*American Educational Studies Association*

"A hallmark of this little volume is the contemporaneity of his approach."
—*Choice*

"Such irrepressible intellectual elan is rare among social scientists."
—*Journal for the Scientific Study of Religion*

THE ANTHROPOLOGY OF PERFORMANCE

Published by PAJ Publications
Box 532, Village Station
New York, NY 10014

Library of Congress Cataloging in Publication Data
The Anthropology of Performance
Library of Congress Catalog Card No.: 86-62159
ISBN: 1-55554-000-7 (cloth)
ISBN: 1-55554-001-5 (paper)

Printed in the United States of America on acid-free paper

Publication of this book has been made possible in part by grants received from the National Endowment for the Arts, Washington, D.C., a federal agency, and the New York State Council on the Arts.

The publication of this edition has been made possible in part by a grant from the Rockefeller Foundation, whose support is gratefully acknowledged.

A catalog record for this book is available from the British Library.

Acknowledgments:

"Rokujo's Jealousy: Liminality and the Performative Genres" first appeared in *Studies in Symbolic and Cultural Communication*, Lawrence: University of Kansas Publications in Anthropology, 1982. "*Carnaval* in Rio: Dionysian Drama in an Industrializing Society" appeared in *The Celebration of Society*, ed. Frank Manning, London, Canada: University of Western Ontario, Congress of Social and Humanistic Studies, 1983. "Performing Ethnography" appeared in *The Drama Review*, 26, 2 (T94), 1982. "Body, Brain, and Culture" appeared in *Zygon* 18, 3, 1983.

The Anthropology of Performance

Victor Turner

Preface by Richard Schechner

PAJ Publications
(A Division of Performing Arts Journal, Inc.)
New York

This is the fourth volume of the Performance Studies Series edited by Richard Schechner. The Series is published by PAJ Publications. Other titles include: *The End of Humanism* by Richard Schechner; *From Ritual to Theatre: The Human Seriousness of Play* by Victor Turner; *American Popular Entertainments* by Brooks McNamara.

GENERAL INTRODUCTION TO THE PERFORMANCE STUDIES SERIES

What is a performance? A play? Dancers dancing? A concert? What you see on TV? Circus and Carnival? A press conference by whoever is President? The shooting of the Pope as portrayed by media—or the instant replays of Lee Harvey Oswald being shot? And do these events have anything to do with ritual, a week with Grotowski in the woods outside of Wroclaw, or a Topeng masked dance drama as performed in Peliatan, Bali? Performance is no longer easy to define or locate: the concept and structure has spread all over the place. It is ethnic and intercultural, historical and ahistorical, aesthetic and ritual, sociological and political. Performance is a mode of behavior, an approach to experience; it is play, sport, aesthetics, popular entertainments, experimental theatre, and more. But in order for this broad perspective to develop, performance must be written about with precision and in full detail. This series is designed as a forum for investigating what performance is, how it works, and what its place in postmodern society may be. Performance Studies is not properly theatrical, cinematic, anthropological, historical, or artistic—though any of the monographs in the series incorporate one or more of these disciplines. Because of this new approach to the study of performance, the series has been left open-ended in order to incorporate new work. The series, I hope, will measure the depth and breadth of the field—and its fertility: from circus to Mabou Mines, rodeo to healing rites, Black performance in South Africa to the Union City Passion Play. Performance Studies will be valuable for scholars in all areas of performance as well as for theatre workers who want to expand and deepen their notions of performance.

Richard Schechner

Contents

VICTOR TURNER'S LAST ADVENTURE   7
Richard Schechner

IMAGES AND REFLECTIONS: RITUAL, DRAMA,   21
CARNIVAL, FILM, AND SPECTACLE IN
CULTURAL PERFORMANCE

SOCIAL DRAMAS IN BRAZILIAN UMBANDA   33
THE DIALECTICS OF MEANING

THE ANTHROPOLOGY OF PERFORMANCE   72

ROKUJO'S JEALOUSY: LIMINALITY AND   99
THE PERFORMATIVE GENRES

CARNAVAL IN RIO: DIONYSIAN DRAMA   123
IN AN INDUSTRIALIZING SOCIETY

PERFORMING ETHNOGRAPHY   139
(with Edie Turner)

BODY, BRAIN, AND CULTURE   156

INDEX   179

Victor Turner's Last Adventure

Richard Schechner

Victor Turner in his late work brought up some very troublesome questions. It is the mark of his generous genius that he never stepped back from thinking into a problem merely because he had no clear way out. I admire his "notyetness," his "unfinishedness" which forces those who get into his work to wrestle through the whole night, as Jacob did with-and-against his angel. Or, more mundanely, the ways Turner, his wife and collaborator, Edith, and I—and whoever else was there, and often there were others—sat around their kitchen table in Charlottesville Talmudically arguing the hours away.

Turner, throughout his career, investigated ritual. He found it in social process, especially in the ways people resolved crises. Soon enough Turner realized that social process was performative. Thus began his detailed and exhilarating explorations into the multiplex, multivocal relationships between ritual and theatre. Turner developed his theories of social drama (1974) and later collected much of his thinking on performance in *From Ritual to Theatre*.

Turner sought to integrate the notion of liminality—the threshold, the betwixt and between—so decisive to his grasp and experience of ritual as anti-structural, creative, often carnivalesque and playful—with his emerging understanding of the relationship between social drama and aesthetic drama. Performance is central to Turner's thinking because the performative genres are living examples of ritual in/as action. And not only when performance is overtly "ritualistic"—as in a Mass, a healing ceremony, a shamanic journey, or a Grotowskian poor theatre or paratheatrical event: all performance has at its core a ritual action, a "restoration of behavior" (see Schechner, 1985).

Turner's passionate impulse, both personally and professionally, was to integrate, to include, to make and seek the links, the networks. In August 1982, as part of a world conference on ritual and theatre that he and I co-chaired, Turner, one epiphanous afternoon, went to the blackboard and drew a map of "the evolution of cultural genres of performance: from 'Liminal' to 'Liminoid' " (figure 1). He wanted to show the planners of the conference just how traditional, modern, and postmodern performative genres interconnect. Later this model was the keystone of one of Turner's last writings, "Are There Universals of Performance in Myth, Ritual, and Drama" (1985).

Turner's gifts were many and he spent them generously. He gave himself with enthusiasm. His importance to people working in the theatre—as theorists, practitioners, or critics—cannot be over-emphasized. He taught that there was a continuous, dynamic process linking performative behavior—art, sports, ritual, play—with social and ethical structure: the way people think about and organize their lives and specify individual and group values. Turner, who specialized in the liminal, the in-between, lived in a house that was all doors: every idea led to new ideas, every proposition was a network of possibilities. I think he was so long interested in performance—theatre, dance, music, ritual, and social drama—because performance is the art that is open, unfinished, decentered, liminal. Performance is a paradigm of process.

Turner also insisted that life be lived, that experience be given its rightful cognitive and emotional place. Here, too, his work and the intensity of his thinking—the passion of his intellect—was brightly performative. For if performance is a paradigm of process it is also the art where experience as such is prized. In the Western post-Renaissance traditions of art the product is valued: works are hung, "museumed," taped, filmed, "videoed"—as if they could be rescued from time. But in other cultures, and at other periods of Western culture, a better balance has been achieved between the "being in" of art and its material products. The "working" is as important, maybe more so, than the "work." Turner prized the working, the doing, the experiential exhilaration of "being in." During the years of our friendship Turner grew more and more deeply interested in the preparatory phases of performance—workshops, rehearsals, training—how people made ready for performances-to-be. He was seeking to specify the ways in which experience and liminality, ritual process and artistic ecstasy coincided. In this active searching he went wherever his ideas and body took him—finally, to the workings of the brain. But although this may appear to be a stopping place—it was one of the places Turner was when he died—such an end-point is illusory, and untrue to Turner's own dynamic process of seeking. What I will miss about Victor most is the loving way he helped me go on: urging me through one more door, across one more threshold.

In this present "introduction" I won't be so far-ranging. I want to concentrate here on what was preoccupying Turner at the moment of his sudden death, from a heart attack, in 1983. He was wondering about ritual, about the connections among body, brain, and culture—the title of the final essay in this current

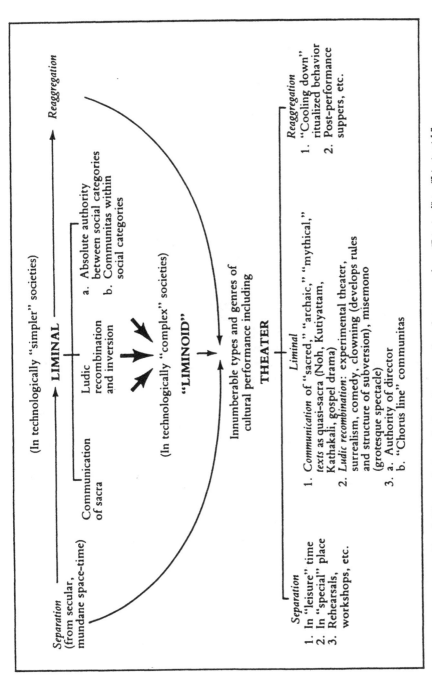

Fig. 1: The evolution of cultural genres of performance: from "Liminal" to "Liminoid."

collection.

Even to say it in one word, ritual, is asking for trouble. Ritual has been so variously defined—as concept, praxis, process, ideology, yearning, religious experience, function—that it means very little because it can mean too much.

Reviewing some of the literature about ritual—the details of which I will spare you—shows that ritual can be looked at five different ways: 1) as part of the evolutionary development of organisms—including, but not limited to, the development of the brain; 2) as a structure, something with formal qualities and relationships; 3) as a performance process, a dynamic system or action, with both diachronic and synchronic rhythms and/or scenarios; 4) as experience, as what a person individually or as part of a collective feels; 5) as a set of operations in human social and religious life.

These categories yield not testable hypotheses so much as opinions belonging mostly to the domain of social and/or artistic criticism. But as Derrida and the second line of deconstructionists remind us, the boundaries between scientific thought, poetry, theatre, and literary criticism are fuzzy. In our emergent neomedieval world a species of religious-artistic thought is, if not replacing, then standing side-by-side with, what used to be called pure science.

Ethologists use the word ritual without quotation marks. But if there are similarities between animal rituals and human arts there are important differences also. The patterned "waggle dance" of bees may look like dancing to Jerome Robbins but the bees are not dancing "emically" speaking. Where everything is genetically determined there can be no learning or improvisation. And where there is no contingency there can be no lying, only deceit: the difference being precisely the player's consciousness concerning her/his range of choice. Even a ballet dancer can choose one night simply not to go up on point though the choreography tells her to do so. She may lose the role, or even her job, but still she can go flatfooted. Not so with the "dancing" bees. If they go wrong look into their screwed-up DNA. Human performance is paradoxical, a practiced fixedness founded on pure contingency: the weird delight people have in going up on point, or watching a trained trapezist make three-and-a-half somersaults, or even applauding the choreographed ineptitutde of the clowns.

The development of ritual among the species can be diagrammed as a tree (figure 2). In this figure I show how the specific functions and properties of human rituals are built on, but are different from those of other animals. It was this link and those differences—this participation of ritual in the evolutionary process—that drew Turner's focused attention during the last years of his life. It might seem to those who followed Turner's earlier work on "ritual process" to be an odd turn. For why should someone who put so much stock in ritual's antistructure, its creative and generative force, suddenly seem to embrace sociobiologists?

Turner laid out his evolutionary approach to ritual only once, in "Body, Brain, and Culture," while his work on ritual process, liminality, communitas,

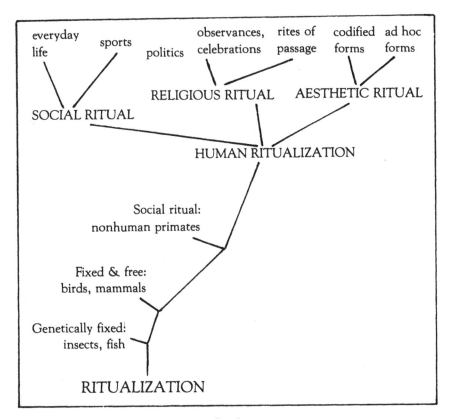

Fig. 2

and antistructure populate most of his writing since *The Forest of Symbols* (1967). Still, had he lived, I think Turner would have gone on with what he started in "Body, etc." because that line of investigation was leading to the crisis (= crux, cross, crossing, decisive meeting place) of ritual, religion, and science, a subject of great importance to social scientists and performance theorists alike.

Surely Turner was aware of this crisis. In "Body, Brain, and Culture" he restates his position that "ritual is not necessarily a bastion of social conservatism; its symbols do not merely condense cherished sociocultural values. Rather, through its liminal processes, it holds the generating source of culture and structure." But these "liminal processes" are precisely those the ethological view undercuts.

Turner sees that his position is apparently contradicted by the classical ethological one where, again in Turner's words, ritual is treated as "genetically programed behavior." Turner reconciles these contrasting views by applying the notion of liminality to the brain itself. For him the human brain is a liminal organ operating somewhere between the genetically fixed and the radically free. The development of the neocortex in humans—with its extreme bilaterality and its complicated interactions with the brain stem and limbic system—seems to enable humans, Turner says, to step outside of ordinary evolutionary constraints, almost.

He outlines the "triune" brain proposed by neuroanatomist Paul MacLean, who asserts that there is an old "reptilian" brain controlling movement, a newer "limbic" brain concerned basically with emotions, and a relatively very recent "cerebral neocortex" brain of cognitive thought. This last is itself divided into left and right lobes, each with distinct functions. These three brains are interdependent. "The highest and newest portion of the cerebral cortex has by no means detached itself from an ancient 'primitive' region, but functions as it does precisely 'by virtue of its relationship to the old emotional circuitry.' " Then Turner poses the decisive question:

> What is the role of the brain as an organ for the appropriate mixing of genetic and cultural information in the production of mental, verbal, or organic behavior? [. . .] To what extent is the upper brain, especially the neocortex, which is the area responsible in mammals for coordination and for higher mental abilities, on a longer leash in terms of control by the genotype or genome, the fundamental constitution of the organism in terms of its hereditary factors? Does socioculturally transmitted information *take over* control in humankind, and, if so, what are the limits, if any, to its control? Does the genotype take a permanent back seat, and is social conditioning now all in all. The picture thus built up for me was of a kind of *dual control* leading to [. . .] a series of symbiotic coadaptations between what might be called culturetypes and genotypes.

Here Turner seems to beg the question. He says that humans have evolved a brain that has all but freed itself from genetic restraints. That humans are in effect genetically determined to be free or at least genetically determined to be "coadaptive." That all people live in the condition and circumstance of being artists. The idea puts into scientific language a fundamentally religious idea classically stated by John Milton in *Paradise Lost* as: "sufficient to stand but free to fall"—standing and falling referring to divine grace and the ultimate destination, in Christian terms, of each individual soul. In its contemporary guise this idea asserts that human behavior is "to a degree" genetically determined. The sociobiologists think this is a high degree and the humanists a low degree. Turner resolves the contradiction between the ethological (sociobiological) viewpoint and his own earlier work with:

[. . .] if ritualization, as discussed by Huxley, Lorenz, and other ethologists, has a biogenetic foundation, while meaning has a neocortical learned base, does this mean that creative processes, those which generate new cultural knowledge, might result from a coadaptation, perhaps in the ritual process itself, of genetic and cultural information?

Movement and feeling (the first two of MacLean's triunity) are mostly genetically based, while cognitive functions are less so. The special kind of performance called "ritual" is the interface between these—the cultural arena where the reptilian and old-mammalian brains meet the neocortex. Not only is the contradiction healed, but Turner's "ritual process" is firmly strapped into the driver's seat of evolution—an evolution in which humans will co-determine what is to happen to them not only socially but biologically. Furthermore, the main arena of evolutionary development is displaced from within individual human beings—the genotype—to collective human cultural action—the ritual process.

As a theatre director I ought to like this model, if I want my art to be central to the future of humankind. For those who understand the ritual/performance process are at the hub of coadaptive evolutionary development.

It seems to me that the fate or future of the collective—of humans as a species, and probably of many of our sister species as well—may depend on the kind of "coadaptation" Turner speaks of. Experiments in the areas of recombinant DNA, cloning, and artifical intelligence are yielding precise methods of elaborating on, and maybe even controlling evolution. It is still an open question whether this represents an advance in freedom or a deep kind of mindlessness posing as free choice. Surely humans—both positively and negatively, both consciously and without forethought—are influencing evolutionary patterns everywhere on the globe. Norman Myers estimates that human intervention will result in the extinction of "at least one-quarter of all species [. . .] possibly a third, and conceivably even more. With so many plants and animals gone, there will be a fundamental shift in evolution itself, as evolutionary processes go to work on a vastly reduced pool of species and as a few new species arise to fill in the gaps" (1985:2).

This is "coadaptation" with a vengeance. But it is not the kind Turner is talking about. Or at least the outcome is radically different than the one Turner is hoping for. In fact, Turner's idea of how the brain works in relation to evolution has two different scenarios. In one, he focuses on the collective, coming close to embracing a notion of a super-brain, an over-brain, "a global population of brains [. . .] whose members are incessantly communicating with one another through every physical and mental instrumentality." In the other, he follows a more conventional evolutionary theory in which variation in the genotype, working on a strictly individual basis, accumulates changes in enough individuals to alter the species.

14

It is also not exactly clear why Turner speaks of a triune brain when there are really four, or even five, brains in his model: the three of MacLean's, plus an extra for the lateralized neocortex, plus the over-brain of the "global population of brains." Thus each human has, or participates in the following brains: 1) reptilian 2) old mammalian 3) right frontal lobe 4) left frontal lobe 5) collective over-brain. As for the attraction of the metaphor of the triune brain, I wonder how many parts there would be in the brain of certain Native Americans whose sacred number is not three but four. Or ought Christianity seriously consider a Trinity plus two: say the traditional Father, Son, Holy Ghost, plus Virgin, plus. . . ?

However many brains there are, Turner's evolutionary process is fundamentally the orthodox one in which accumulating individual changes lead to a change in the species. The question is, why should this change be positive, as Turner assumes it will be? The answer may be in Turner's acceptance of traditional Christian values. Without saying so in so many words, Turner hopes that each individual will love his/her neighbor as him/herself and, when abused, be able to turn the other cheek. . . . Thus for the evolutionary emancipation of the brain to work constructively and not destructively people's day-to-day values as lived will have to approximate the values preached by and to them. But the tendency of modernism—especially in its nineteenth and twentieth century phase of extreme nationalism and materialism—has been anything but loving. Not to mention the long and often bloody history of Christianity.

And, finally, there is in my mind at least the dark shadow of Hitler's "eugenics"—including the unspeakable experiments of Mengele—threatening any positive outcome of coadaptation. For if we are to "improve" our species at the genetic level who will determine what is good and what bad, and how? Again the only answers would appear to be religious: that is, in the realm of consciously articulated ethics founded on some acknowledged scheme of superhuman authority (God, science, the collective, you name it). It is the yearning for this kind of authority by so many people in so many cultures that has given rise to such a variety of "fundamentalisms" in Christianity, Islam, Hinduism, and—a few years back, let's not forget—Maoism and its most crazed offshoot, the Khmer Rouge emptying Cambodia's cities.

Turner was no fundamentalist, he was neither dogmatic nor tolerant of dogmatists. As I knew him, he always prized the fluid, the dynamic, the processual antistructural; he lived to generate, and help others generate new ideas and new ways. So I am talking here not about what Turner himself felt or thought, but about a dark twist that could be put on some of his ideas. Intrigued as I am by coadaptation, when I turn over its implications—as if arguing with Turner around that Charlottesville kitchen table—I think that maybe coadaptation is his utopian wish—a wish that I, a left-handed person through and through, can't help but see the sinister side of.

Next Turner explains the experience of ritual—the celebrated feeling of "spontaneous communitas"—as the simultaneous excitation of the two hemispheres of the cerebral cortex. In offering this explanation, he is following Fischer (1971) and d'Aquili, Laughlin, and Lex (1979). "In particular," Turner says speaking of d'Aquili et al.,

> they postulate that the rhythmic activity of ritual, aided by sonic, visual, photic, and other kinds of "driving," may lead in time to simultaneous maximal stimulation of both systems, causing ritual participants to experience what the authors call "positive, ineffable affect." They also use Freud's term "oceanic experience," as well as "yogic ecstacy," also the Christian term *unio mystica*, an experience of the union of those cognitively discriminated opposites typically generated by binary, digital left-hemispherical ratiocination. I suppose one might also use the Zen term *satori* (the integrating flash), and one could add the Quakers' "inner light," Thomas Merton's "transcendental consciousness," and the yogic *samadhi*.

Turner's speculations fit nicely those of C. J. Jung, paralleling as well the most recent work of Jerzy Grotowski. What Jung wrote about Grotowski is trying to do. Namely, identify and perform "archetypes" of human ritual action. Although I do not know the details of Grotowski's "objective drama" project currently underway at the University of California, Irvine, the outline is clear. Working with "masters of ritual" performance from Haiti, India, and other parts of the world, Grotowski, professional performers, and students are trying to find, learn and perform definite rhythms, sounds, and gestures that seem to "work" in a number of the world's rituals. Rather than starting from a basis of meaning, Grotowski and his fellow-researchers begin with strictly "objective" elements: tempo, iconography, movement patterns, sounds. The research is not historical—not how "Om" and "Amen" may both be based on near-Eastern mantras; but that the open "uh" sound followed by a "hummed" closure might not only be an "objective correlative" of Indo-European and Semitic ritual, but also be founded on brain structure and function. If so, this sequence of sounds will be found elsewhere on earth arising not from diffusion or cultural convergence but from archetypes in the brain. Ultimately Grotowski wants to make a new performance bringing together the performative expressions of these archetypes. If the theory of objective drama is correct, this new work should be extremely powerful. And if Turner had lived long enough to go on with his last adventure, I should think he would have been very interested in finding out if a Grotowskian performance made from ritual actions derived from a number of different cultures shared with the source cultures certain attributes at the level of brain activity: autonomic nervous system responses, brain waves, and so on. Furthermore, Turner may have seen

Grotowski's experiment as a paradigm of coadaptation: for Grotowski is working cognitively—that is, theatrically—with brain stem and limbic materials.

I would be foolish to undervalue the work of two such visionary pioneers as Turner and Grotowski. Even more so where their work independently converges. But I note that in the past at least great works of art—and effective ritual performances—have always been very definitely situated in this or that culture, while efforts to transcend or to accumulate cultures fail at precisely the point they want to make: creating actions as powerful, or even more powerful than the sources. Anthologies of cultures—*The Golden Bough* in whatever literary or performative redaction—strike me as either premature or pollyannish efforts at one-worldliness or, worse, expressions of Western hegemony: attempts by Western minds to synthesize—that is, to bring under Western dominance—all of the world's cultures.

Turner was not such a synthesizer. He was always urging people to look for the "minute particular" and to experience the intrinsically unique flavor of this or that culture, subculture, or individual. He delighted in the unique. But "Body, Brain, and Culture" signals his passionately felt need to locate, or relocate, a universal or global basis for the ritual process. I think he believed the future of the world depended on it—as well it might. Near the end of his essay he said:

> I am really speaking of a global population of brains inhabiting an entire world of inanimate and animate entities, a population whose members are incessantly communicating with one another through every physical and mental instrumentality. But if one considers the geology, so to speak, of the human brain and nervous system, we see represented in its strata—each layer still vitally alive—not dead like stone, the numerous pasts and presents of our planet. [. . .] Each of us is a microcosm, related in the deepest ways to the whole life-history of tha lovely deep blue globe swirled over with the white whorls first photographed by Edwin Aldrin and Neil Armstrong from their primitive space chariot, the work nevertheless of many collaborating human brains.

Much as I admire Turner's work—and the adventurer's risks he was always willing to take—I am uncomfortable with his attempt to relocate and thereby resolve the "problems" of ritual action in the workings of evolution or, more specifically, the human brain. Having so said, I say also I am attracted to these very ideas which I expounded in my own way in "Magnitudes of Performance" (1986). Ditto with Grotowski's work. It is thus clear that the problems I'm working on here constitute a bundle of troubles for me as well as for Turner. This writing is a saying-to-myself as much as it is an introduction to Turner's book. I am the poorer because Turner cannot respond, moving the dialogue ahead.

If it is too easy to relocate ancient problems of "free will" versus "fate" either as classical Marxism (all collective free will) or sociobiology (all genetic fate), Turner's coadaptive compromise seems over-generously Christian. Does it solve anything to give Edward O. Wilson what is Wilson's and Marx what is Marx's? However one parcels out responsibility, what, if anything, guides the human future remains obscure in the extreme. The forces within and without human individuals, societies, and environments are more than we understand.

Turner possibly felt this same uneasiness, for he slipped into "Body, Brain, and Culture" a few pages about play. "As I see it," he said, "play does not fit in anywhere; it is a transient and is recalcitrant to localization, to placement, to fixation—a joker in the neuroanthropological act." But play can't be exiled so easily: certainly it is as much "in" the brain as ritual and its ethological-evolutionary roots can be as surely traced. Yet what Turner says about play cannot be understood neurologically or in terms of orthodox evolutionary theory. By "locating" play as that which doesn't fit in, he reverts to his own classical definitions, and these really have little to do with either ethology or neurobiology.

> The neuronic energies of play, as it were, lightly skim over the cerebral cortices, sampling rather than partaking of the capacities and functions of the various areas of the brain. [. . .] Play is, for me, a liminal or liminoid mode, essentially interstitial, betwixt-and-between all standard taxonomic nodes. [. . .] As such play cannot be pinned down by formulations of left-hemisphere thinking—such as we all must use in keeping with the rhetorical conventions of academic discourse. Play is neither ritual action nor meditation, nor is it merely vegetative, nor is it just "having fun"; it also has a good deal of ergotropic and agonistic aggressivity in its odd-jobbing, bricolage style. [. . .] Like many Trickster figures in myths (or should these be "antimyths," if myths are dominantly left-hemisphere speculations about causality?) play can deceive, betray, beguile, delude, and gull.

Which brings Turner back to his own earlier work—the twenty years or more he spent delving into the "ritual process," "liminality," "antistructure," the "subjunctive mood," and the "performative genres." The Trickster hands Turner a ticket out of the brain as a locked-in system. This Trickster is forever shuttling between hemispheres, among the three parts of the triune brain, in between categories. As such play is an activity that has not yet been defined—or, in Turner's terms, play is categorically uncategorizable, the "anti" by means of which all categories are destabilized. This Trickster is the artist, the performer, the playful anthropologist, the adventurer.

[Play] has the power of the weak, an infantile audacity in the face of the strong. To ban play is, in fact, to massacre the innocents. If man is a neotonic species, play is perhaps his most appropriate mode of performance.

In finding a place for it in-and-out of the evolutionary-neurological program, Turner feels that play plays "a similar role in the social construction of reality as mutation and variation in organic evolution." To do this play had to be "detached" from the nervous system's "localizations" enabling "it to perform the liminal functions of ludic recombination of familiar elements in unfamiliar and often quite arbitrary patterns." Some of these patterns might prove adaptive, culturally speaking. Thus play is for Turner a dynamic model of the brain itself: free to move, to find its own ways, to actively contribute to the evolutionary process. Turner's model is actually not structural at all but audaciously processual.

From an orthodox viewpoint the difficulty with all this is that Turner is moving too freely between strict, analogous, and metaphoric thinking. But these contradictions do not disturb me much. What is also happening, and what is strikingly visible in all the essays collected in this book, what makes them so exciting to work from, is Turner's eager searching for appropriate ways to integrate his life's work with new data.

Turner was very much a man of the theatre. He would try, take it again, work out another way, fix a routine and then run it in a new context. He was forever polishing his act, but he was never slick. He enjoyed most the deconstructive-reconstructive processes of workshops and rehearsals. He was not shy about showing work-in-progress. In fact, it was the processual method of working that fascinated him—and it was those areas of human experience that are most processual—pilgrimage, ritual, theatre, and dance: performative genres all—that occupied his imagination.

Still this does not tell what—except for the sheer dazzling restlessness of his spirit—brought Turner to attempt a synthesis between his own brand of speculative humanistic anthropology and sociobiology. Again, I think the answer is religion. Troubled by the state of the world—Turner, who like so many of us, was an optimist in terms of his own life, but much more pessimistic when contemplating the future of the species, even of life on earth—may have been seeking a synthesis not mainly between two scientific viewpoints but between science and faith.

If God (or whatever it is) is the very formulation of the world, then this formulation ought to be most strongly present in the brain, the world's most complicated and sophisticated organ. To put it in Hindu terms, if Atman (innermost, impersonal Self) and Brahman (the absolute) are one, then by examining the brain—the very seat of Atman—humans might learn a great deal about Brahman. They may even find "where" Brahman is. Not where in the sense of

Broca's area or the hippocampus but in the system of relationships and neuro-electronic-chemical exchanges among each individual's several brains. Or humans may discover that Brahman has no individual basis but exists only in the coordinated work of many brains. That there is transcending all individuals the same collectivity—the same "triune" existence—as there is within each brain.

Such contemplation is two steps from the ultimate metatext. The first step is within human grasp: an independent artificial intelligence. The second is contact with superior non-human beings: the extra-terrestrial connection. I am saying what I think Turner might have been coming to. He realized that an organ of contemplation—even the human brain—is not capable of absolute self-examination. The brain will go crazy (or mystically fuzzy) dealing with too many layers of metatextural reflexivity. But the brain might either create an exterior organ of thought or actively seek to come into contact with non-human others with whom it could communicate. Many experiments point in these directions. And it's not only with apes and dolphins that we want to talk. It would seem that if humans are to survive the next step is communication with some genuinely thoughtful other.

Here, popular literature and film—science fiction—is far ahead of science. But not ahead of religion. For has this not been religion's project from the very beginning of human history? To locate, establish, and keep contact with non-human beings? And do not those who believe in gods think of these beings not as "symbols" but as actual existing others? Part of the anthropological romance has been to go to far away places and live with people who daily communicate with and experience divine (or demonic) others. Especially for "positivists," this has been a heady-hearty encounter. And now, as positivism fades, even scientists of the first order want to meet non-human others themselves, first-hand, face-to-face, brain-to-brain. How, or if, this will be accomplished is not yet clear.

From this perspective, Victor Turner's last adventure is a trope modeling his desire to contact those others we humans need to negotiate fate with.

Science fiction? Fiction as science? Or coadaptation in a most definite, concrete way?

New York, February 1985, August 1986.

References

Fischer, Roland. 1971. "A Cartography of the Escatic and Meditative States." *Science*, vol. 174, no. 4012, 26: 897-904.
Myers, Norman. 1985. "The End of the Lines." *Natural History*, vol. 94, no. 2: 1985: 2-12.

Schechner, Richard. 1985. *Between Theatre and Anthropology*. Philadelphia: University of Pennsylvania Press.

— — — — —. 1986. "Magnitudes of Performance" in *The Anthropology of Experience*, ed. Edward Bruner. Champaign, Ill.: University of Illinois Press.

Turner, Victor. 1967. *The Forest of Symbols: Aspects of Ndembu Ritual*. Ithaca: Cornell University Press.

— — — —. 1974. *Dramas, Fields, and Metaphors*. Ithaca: Cornell University Press.

— — — —. 1982. *From Ritual to Theatre*. New York: PAJ Publications.

— — — —. 1985 *On the Edge of the Bush*. Tucson: University of Arizona Press.

Images and Reflections:

Ritual, Drama, Carnival, Film, and Spectacle in Cultural Performance

In anthropology there has been a noticeable shift in theoretical emphasis in recent years from structure to process, from competence to performance, from the logics of cultural and social systems to the dialectics of socio-cultural processes. This has not meant a jettisoning of structuralist discoveries but rather a reintegration of the insights gained from the study of symbol systems such as myth, ritual, and kinship terminology treated as abstract sets of interdependent binary oppositions and mediations into the mainline study of "man and woman alive," the ongoing developing and declining processes of interpersonal and intergroup behavior in communities and networks, and the cultural processes and products involved with these. We are to think of changing sociosymbolic fields rather than static structures.

Anthropology is currently sensitive to the "ethnography of speaking"—a field which lies between what grammars and ethnographies have taken separately—the former treating language essentially as a structure of abstract and self-contained codes, the latter (ethnographies) with the abstract and hence static patterns and structures of sociocultural life. Attention now is on the *use* of language—and other nonverbal types of communication, in the actual conduct of social life.

I want to move directly to the frame of this essay—which includes the ethnography of speaking but extends it to the modes of symbolic action—and that is the peculiar relationship between the mundane, everyday sociocultural processes (domestic, economic, political, legal and the like) found in societies of a given major type, tribal, feudal, capitalist, socialist, or whatever (and each of these has numerous variants) and what may be called using Milton Singer's term—their dominant genres of "cultural performance." My thesis is that this relationship is not unidirectional and "positive"—in the sense that the performative genre merely "reflects" or "expresses" the social system or the cultural configuration, or at any rate their key relationships—but that it is reciprocal and reflexive—in the sense that the performance is often a critique, direct or veiled, of the social life it grows out of, an evaluation (with lively possibilities of rejection) of the way society handles history.

In other words, if the contrivers of cultural performances, whether these are recognized as "individual authors," or whether they as representatives of a collective tradition, genuises or elders, "hold the mirror up to nature," they do this with "magic mirrors" which make ugly or beautiful events or relationships which cannot be recognized as such in the continuous flow of quotidian life in which we are embedded. The mirrors themselves are not mechanical, but consist of reflecting consciousnesses and the products of such consciousnesses formed into vocabularies and rules, into metalinguistic grammars, by means of which new unprecedented performances may be generated. My Africanist colleague Philip Gulliver writes about the "continuum of interaction amongst a given collection of people" (1971:354), as an object of study. I would add here that the "discontinuum" of action among the same collection of people, culturally made possible by setting aside times and places for cultural performances, is equally part of the ongoing social process—the part where those people become conscious, through witnessing and often participating in such performances, of the nature, texture, style, and given meanings of their own lives as members of a sociocultural community.

Anthropologists, as you may have found, are always uneasy when too long separated from what Clifford Geertz calls the "whole vast business of the world," that is, "from what, in this time or that place, specific people say, what they do, what is done to them." It might be useful, then, to break into our major topic by taking a look at what Milton Singer has written on cultural performances, as he came to understand them in the South Indian context, before moving to redefinition of the term in cross-cultural and cross-temporal comparative frames.

Singer, trained in philosophy but enamored later by anthropology, with Robert Redfield as his *guru*, went to India to do fieldwork with a set of hypotheses in mind derived from Redfield's theories about the differences between Great and Little Traditions and the gradations of the urban-rural continuum. He soon found that "the units of cogitation are not the units of observation" (1972:70). All anthropologists discover this and it is the problem produced by this disparity which when met with undeterred zeal distinguished the vocational anthropologist from the mere manipulator of abstract anthropological findings. Singer found himself "confronted with a series of concrete experiences, the observation and recording of which seemed to discourage the mind from entertaining and applying the synthetic and interpretative concepts that I had brought with me. These experiences had an intrinsic fascination, which also tended to discourage the broad reflective view to which I had been accustomed" (p. 70).

Among the most salient "concrete experiences" were what Singer found to be discriminable "units of observation" which he called "cultural performances." These were central and recurrent in the social lives of the Indians he studied in the Madras area. They included what "we in the West usually call by that name—for example, plays, concerts, and lectures. But they include also prayers, ritual readings and recitations, rites and ceremonies, festivals, and all those things which we usually classify under religion and ritual rather than with the cultural and artistic" (p. 71). The performances became for Singer "the elementary constituents of the culture and the ultimate units of observation. Each one had a definitely limited time span, or at least a beginning and an end, an organized program of activity, a set of performers, an audience, and a place and occasion of performance. Whether it was a wedding, an *upanayana* (sacred thread) ceremony, a floating temple festival, a village *Pongal* festival, a ritual recitation of a sacred text, a *bharatanatya* dance, or a devotional movie, these were the kinds of things that an outsider could observe and comprehend within a single direct experience" (p. 71). Singer found that "cultural performances" are composed of what he calls "cultural media"—modes of communication which include not only spoken language, but such nonlinguistic media as "song, dance, acting out, and graphic and plastic arts—combined in many ways to express and communicate the content of Indian culture" (p. 76). He argues that "a study of the different forms of cultural media in their social and cultural contexts would . . . reveal them to be important links in that cultural continuum which includes village and town, Brahman and non-Brahman, north and south, the modern mass media culture and the traditional folk and classic cultures, the Little and Great Traditions" (pp. 76-77).

This is an important point—rituals, dramas, and other performative genres are often orchestrations of media, not expressions in a single medium. Lévi-Strauss and others have used the term "sensory codes" for the enlistment of each of the senses to develop a vocabulary and grammar founded on it to produce "messages"—for instance, different types of incense burned at different times in a performance communicate different meanings, gestures and facial expressions are assigned meanings with reference to emotions and ideas to be communicated, soft and loud sounds have conventional meaning, etc. Thus certain sensory codes are associated with each medium. The master-of-ceremonies, priest, producer, or director creates art from the ensemble of media and codes, just as a conductor in the single genre of classical music blends and opposes the sounds of the different instruments to produce an often unrepeatable effect. It is worth pointing out, too, that it is not, as some structuralists have argued, a matter of emitting the *same* message in different media and codes, the better to underline it by redundancy. The "same" message in different media is really a set of subtly variant messages, each medium contributing its own generic message to the message conveyed through it. The result is something like a hall of mirrors – magic mirrors, each interpreting as well as reflecting the images beamed to it, and flashed from one to the others. The many-leveled or tiered structure of a major ritual or drama, each level having many sectors, makes of these genres flexible and nuanced instruments capable of carrying and communicating many messages at once, even of subverting on one level what it appears to be "saying" on another. Furthermore the genres are instruments whose full reality is in their "playing," in their performance, in their use in social settings – they should not be seen merely as scripts, scenarios, scores, stage directions, or other modes of blueprinting, diagramming, or guiding. Their full meaning emerges from the union of script with actors and audience at a given moment in a group's ongoing social process.

Milton Singer and many other cultural anthropologists see cultural performances and media as casting "much light on the ways in which cultural themes and values are communicated as well as on processes of social and cultural change" (Singer 1972:77). I would agree with this, but only if it is realized that cultural performances are not simple reflectors or expressions of culture or even of changing culture but may themselves be active agencies of change, representing the eye by which culture sees itself and the drawing board on which creative actors sketch out what they believe to be more apt or interesting "designs for living." As Barbara Babcock has written: "many cultural forms are not so much reflective as reflexive." Here the analogy is not with a mirror but rather with a reflexive verb "whose subject and direct object refer to the same person and thing." Performative reflexivity is a condition in which a sociocultural group, or its most perceptive members acting representatively, turn, bend or reflect back upon themselves, upon the relations, actions, symbols, meanings, codes, roles, statuses, social structures, ethical and legal rules, and other sociocultural components which make up their public "selves." Performative reflexivity, too, is not mere *reflex*, a quick, automatic or habitual response to some stimulus. It is highly contrived, artificial, of culture not nature, a deliberate and voluntary work of art. A "reflex" would presuppose "realism," a picturing of people and things as it is thought in that culture they "really" are, without idealization or fantasization. But, of course, in art and literature even realism is a matter of artifice and what is real is ultimately a matter of cultural definition. Nevertheless, cultural realism, however "unreal," is some way from what I consider to be the *dominant* genres of cultural performance.

Since the relationship between quotidian or workaday social process (including economic, political, jural, domestic, etc., interactions) and cultural performance is dialectical and reflexive, the pervasive quality of the latter rests on the principle that mainstream society generates its opposite; that we are, in fact, concerned in cultural performances with a topsy-turvy, inverted, to some extent sacred (in the sense of "set apart," hedged around with taboo and mystery) domain of human action.

For such a domain to be truly reflexive, where the same person(s) are both subject and object, violence has to be done to commonsense ways of classifying the world and society. The "self" is split up the middle—it is something that one both is and that one sees and, furthermore, acts upon as though it were another. It is, again, not a matter of doting upon or pining over the projected self (as Narcissus did over the face in the pool) but of acting upon the self-made-other in such a way as to transform it. I am speaking in the singular; in practice, we are dealing with social and plural phenomena. Ritual and drama involves selves, not self; yet the aggregate of selves in a given community or society is often thought of, metaphorically, as a self. Nevertheless, in practice, the plural reflexivity involved allows freeplay to a greater variability of action: actors can be so subdivided as to allocate to some the roles of agents of transformation and to others those of persons undergoing transformation.

This opposition between social life and dominant genre is also related to what I have called in several publications "liminality." A *limen*, as the great French ethnologist and folklorist Arnold van Gennep has pointed out, is a "threshold," and he uses the term to denote the central of three phases in what he called "rites of passage." He looked at a wide variety of ritual forms, taken from most regions and many periods of history, and found in them a tripartite processual form. Rituals *separated* specified members of a group from everyday life, *placed them in a limbo* that was not any place they were in before and not yet any place they would be in, then *returned* them, changed in some way, to mundane life. The second phase, *marginality* or *liminality*, is what interests us here, though, in a very cogent sense, the whole *ritual process* constitutes a threshold between secular living and sacred living. The dominant genres of performance in societies at all levels of scale and complexity tend to be *liminal phenomena*. They are performed in privileged spaces and times, set off from the periods and areas reserved for work, food and sleep. You can call these "sacred" if you like, provided that you recognize that they are the scenes of play and experimentation, as much as of solemnity and rules. Western views of ritual have been greatly influenced by Puritanism. At any rate both the performances and their settings may be likened to loops in a linear progression, when the social flow bends back on itself, in a way does violence to its own development, meanders, inverts, perhaps lies to itself, and puts everything so to speak into the subjunctive mood as well as the reflexive voice. Just as the subjunctive mood of a verb is used to express supposition, desire, hypothesis, or possibility, rather than stating actual facts, so do liminality and the phenomena of liminality dissolve all factual and commonsense systems into their components and "play" with them in ways never found in nature or in custom, at least at the level of direct perception.

One may perhaps distinguish between secret and public liminality, between performative genres that are secluded from the gaze of the mass and those that involve their participation not only as audience but also as actors—taking place, moreover, in the squares of the city, the heart of the village, not away in the bush, hidden in a cave, or secreted in a catacomb or cellar. I have discussed elsewhere various forms of secluded or isolated liminality—which again withdraw a selected group or category of persons from the wider society—men, women, adolescents, sometimes members of an elite of birth or wealth—in order to raise them to a higher rung of some structural ladder, inwardly transformed to match their outward elevation (most initiations are of this sort) and other rites which are concerned with reclassifying persons who are to pass through the life-crisis of birth, betrothal, puberty, marriage, elderhood, and death—as these are culturally defined. Here, though, the spotlight will be on forms of liminality in theory accessible to all or most members of a given group, where the subject matter of the performative genres involved will be their shared lives as seen from various angles—some of them quite new to audience and actors. The great genres, ritual, carnival, drama, spectacle, possess in common a temporal structure which interdigitates constant with variable features, and allows a place for spontaneous invention and improvisation in the course of any given performance. The prejudice that ritual is always "rigid," "stereotyped," "obsessive" is a peculiarly Western European one, the product of specific conflicts between ritualists and antiritualists, iconophiles and iconoclasts, in the process of Christian infighting. Anyone who has known African ritual knows better—or Balinese or Singhalese or Amerindian.

Let us look at the relationship between social and ritual processes in nonliterate cultures of some complexity—such as the Swazi, Maya, or Pueblo Indians—with particular focus on calendrical or solstitial public ceremonies, such as first fruits, harvest, sowing, etc. I also intend to scan the dynamic relationship between popular festivity, such as the Careme-Carnaval cycle in France and the Mardi Gras masquerades in Brazil and Trinidad and what Geertz has called the "pattern of life" which informs them with meaning—in many cases the superimposition of new on traditional patterns, leading to the analysis of two world views in a single universe of symbolic action—expressed in the performance of popular festivity. We are now out of tribal and into medieval-feudal and early modern society.

In complex societies with some degree of urbanization stage drama emerges in its various subgenres, as a performative mode *sui generis*. Drama is derived from the Greek *dran*, "to do," which itself derives from the Indo-European base **dra-*, "to work." Interestingly, as I have written in various publications, in many societies ritual, too, is described as "work," and the term "liturgy," prescribed forms for public ritual action, also derives from Greek terms meaning "people," *leos*, and "work," *ergon*. Work is indeed performed by these reflexive genres, the work of sustaining cherished social and cultural principles and forms, and also of turning them upside down and examining them by various metalanguages, not all of them verbal. One can work in the subjunctive mood as seriously as in the indicative—making worlds that never were on land or sea but that might be, could be, may be, and bringing in all the tropes, metaphor, metonymy, synecdoche, etc., to endow these alternative worlds with magical, festive, or sacred power, suspending disbelief and remodeling the terms of belief.

Dramas, at their simplest, are "literary compositions that tell a story, usually of human conflict, by means of dialogue and action, and are performed by actors" and presented to an audience, the nature and degree of whose involvement and participation varies from culture to culture. Unlike rituals and carnivals they tend to be assigned to individual authors though there are numerous examples of "folk" dramas and puppet theatre where the playwrights are anonymous. Yet, in performance a drama is a social performance involving many. A drama is never really complete, as its etymology suggests, until it is performed, that is, acted on some kind of a stage before an audience. A theatrical audience sees the material of real life presented in meaningful form. Of course, it is not just a matter of simplifying and ordering emotional and cognitive experiences which in "real life" are chaotic. It is more a matter of raising problems about the ordering principles deemed acceptable in "real life." Various theories exist about the origin of drama. Some see it coming out of religious ritual and myths which are ritual's charter. Others see it originating in choral hymns of praise sung at the tomb of a dead hero. At some point, a speaker was distinguished from the chorus singing the paean. The speaker acted out in dramatic mimetic gestures the key deeds in the hero's life. The acted part, it is held, became more elaborate and the chorus's role attenuated. Ultimately, the stories were performed as plays, their origins forgotten.

More secular theories exist. Some see drama coming out of story-telling round the old camp fire where hunting or raiding achievements were vividly and dramatically retold with miming of the events and roles. Whatever its origins, which probably vary from society to society, drama tends to become a way of scrutinizing the quotidian world—seeing it as tragedy, comedy, melodrama, etc., in the West, according to Aristotelian categories and their subsequent development in different cultures of that tradition (plot, character, thought, diction, music, and spectacle, and their subdivisions); and in other traditions, such as the Japanese Noh and Kabuki, as concerned with the aesthetics of salvation and honor as well.

I hope to scrutinize some isolable dramatic forms or movements; in England, for example, medieval morality plays, Elizabethan drama (Marlowe, Lyly, Shakespeare, Jonson), Stuart drama (Jonson, Webster, Beaumont and Fletcher, the later Shakespeare, etc.), Restoration drama (from the reopening of the theatres after the Puritan ban which lasted from 1642-1660) which included the works of Etherege, Congreve, Otway and Dryden—not to mention Wycherly, Colley Cibber and Sir John Vanbrugh, eighteenth-century drama (especially Steele, Gay, Goldsmith, and Sheridan), and the rise of Realism in the late nineteenth century (Shaw and Wilde). In France, of course, there is the neoclassical drama of Corneille and Racine in the tragic, and Molière in the comedic modes, the Enlightenment "tragedy" of Voltaire and Diderot and the comedy of Marivaux and Beaumarchais, to be followed by the Romanticist drama of Victor Hugo and Alfred de Musset. In Italy in the 1500s there was the folk drama of the Commedia dell'Arte which followed a scenario rather than a written dialogue and became one of the most potent influences in shaping comedy throughout Europe in the seventeenth and eighteenth centuries—and still reverberates in modern theatre. Masks, roles, and troupes remained remarkably constant in this tradition. Molière and Shakespeare were influenced by the genre. Spain had its Golden Age of theatre in the sixteenth century with Lope de Vega and in the seventeenth century with Calderón, though decline set in on Calderón's death in 1681. One of my own favorites is the Japanese Noh theatre which originated in the 1300s, achieved its present form in the 1600s, and still continues. The Japanese Bunraku Doll theatre and Kabuki theatre developed in the 1600s, especially that of Chikamatsu Monzaemon in the Genroku period between 1688-1703, equivalent to the Elizabethan theatre. And, of course, there is Greek Tragedy, Old Comedy and New Comedy, Roman Tragedy and Comedy, the Indian Theatre whose great figure is Kalidasa (373-415) author of *Shakuntala* (and of Ujjain in Central India), the great Russian Theatre of Gogol, Turgeniev and Chekhov, and the Scandinavian Theatre of Ibsen and Strindberg. In the twentieth century Western Europe and America lost many of its national, localized characteristics and became identified with transnational literary, political, and philosophical movements, so that we have Symbolist theatre, represented, for example, by Maurice Maeterlinck of Belgium; Expressionism, by Georg Kaiser of Germany (1878-1945) who rejected Stefan George's "art for art's sake," was author of *From Morn to Midnight*, and who defined the new man as "of infinite potential and inherent potentiality"; Strindberg of Sweden and Eugene O'Neill and Elmer Rice of the U.S.A.; Brecht and the German Epic Theatre; the Realistic Tradition of Sean O'Casey in Ireland; Arthur Miller in the U.S.A. and John Osborne in England; and the fascinating Theatre of the Absurd of Sartre and Genet in France, Ionesco, a Rumanian settled in France, Pinter in England, and the Irish exile in France, Samuel Beckett.

In all these cases—and of course there are many more—take Chinese drama, for example—the aesthetic drama of the age can be only partially understood and hence appreciated if the social, political, and economic factors are overlooked. What we are looking for here is not so much the traditional preoccupation with text alone but text in context, and not in a static structuralist context but in the living context of dialectic between aesthetic dramatic processes and sociocultural processes in a given place and time. In other words, it would be necessary to do some homework on the history, social history, and cultural history of the "worlds" which encompass the dramatic traditions we are considering. And also on the history and sociology of the "ideas" which impregnate these dramas. This does not mean any rejection of the pleasures of the text, but rather a refinement of those pleasures through the increased intelligibility gained by study of the cultures in which dramas arose, through what Geertz would call an "unpacking" of the meaning of "key" terms, and through an understanding of the social and political processes to which the dramas bear direct or oblique witness.

For example, Edie and I are working on a paper[1] which discusses the Noh play, *Aoi No Uye*, presented in the fifteenth century, but based on a celebrated incident in the novel by Lady Murasaki, *The Tale of Genji*, from which materials for many Noh dramas were drawn. This will involve a look at several literary genres, (novel, poem, play), at two periods of Japanese history (the Heian, in which Murasaki wrote, and the Muromachi, "The Dual Dynasties" period, in which the Noh drama first appears, and receives not only its dramatic ally but also theoretically finest expression in the work of Zeami, who was an actor, composer, playwright, and critic—he created a theatre of suggestion in which meaning was implied rather than stated, and in which various types and levels of framing and discipline brought to an intense emotional focus basic human problems). Not only will this study involve the delineation of sociocultural and political contexts but it will also necessitate some study of the Shugendo cult of mountain ascetics, for one of these helps to save the soul of the ghost of one of the protagonists. This shifting of genres from novel to drama gives the playwright an additional opportunity to be "reflexive" about the values of Muromachi society—it was also the age of Zen and the preponderance of Samurai values.

The general study of dramatic forms might include other performative traditions—for examples, as I mentioned earlier, the Commedia dell'Arte, the Italian comedy, which already in the sixteenth century existed alongside the regular or legitimate theatre, and which, migrating to France, influenced not only the farces and high comedy of Molière (1622-1673) but also migrating across the Atlantic penetrated folk celebrations like the Trinidadian and other Caribbean carnivals, to which it gave such traditional masks as Pierrot Grenade. In Commedia dell'Arte—at the opposite pole to that other masked tradition, the Noh Drama—all is improvisation, spontaneity, the scripts are scanty. Enormous scope is allowed for social and cultural satire and critique.

It would be important to examine that archtheatre of what I call the liminoid (successor of the liminal in complex large-scale societies, where individuality and optation in art have in theory supplanted collective and obligatory ritual performances), Antonin Artaud's spiritual progeny, the Theatre of Cruelty and the Theatre of the Absurd. Let me quote briefly from his *The Theater and Its Double* (1958 [1938]:90-91).

> The question, then, for the theater, is to create a metaphysics of speech, gesture, and expression, in order to rescue it from its servitude to psychology, and "human interest." But all this can be of no use

---

[1]Included in this volume as "Rokujo's Jealousy: Liminality and the Performative Genres" (pp. 99-122)

unless behind this effort there is some kind of real metaphysical in-clination, an appeal to certain unhabitual ideas, which by their very nature cannot be limited or even formally depicted. These ideas, which touch on Creation, Becoming, and Chaos, are all of a cosmic order and furnish a primary notion of a domain from which the theater is now entirely alien. They are able to create a kind of pas-sionate equation between Man, Society, Nature, and Objects.

It is not, moreover, a question of bringing metaphysical ideas direct-ly on to the stage, but of creating what you might call temptations, in-draughts of air around these ideas. And humor with its anarchy, poetry with its symbolism and its images, furnish a basic notion of ways to channel the temptation of these ideas . . . by positive means (means of spellbinding music, dance, pantomime, mimicry, turning words into incantations, etc.), the sensitivity is put in a state of deepened and keener perception, and this is the very object of the magic and the rites of which the theater is only a reflection.

The group of European and American dramatists, mainly of the 1950s and 60s, who held in common a sense of metaphysical anguish at what they regard-ed as the absurdity of the human condition, and who esteemed Artaud as their voice, were represented by Eugene Ionesco, Samuel Beckett, Jean Genet, Fer-nando Arrabal, N.F. Simpson, and Harold Pinter. Although the theatre of the absurd seems to have died a quiet death, it appears, rather like one of the witchfinding movements which periodically swept Central African village society, as a liberating force on conventional drama.

Some of the problems that beset the study of the Commedia dell'Arte reap-pear when we take a look at the screenplay, the written version of a motion pic-ture—for the Renaissance Italian and modern panindustrial genres exist truly not as literature but in performance. A screenplay, formally, is a generic term for any transcription of a complete film, short or long, story, document, or car-toon. No fixed form is considered mandatory. But a screenplay must be detail-ed enough to encompass whatever dialogue is used, with a description of ac-tion, movement, settings, backgrounds, transitions, and sounds. If one looks at published screenplays—for example, by Bergman, Antonioni, Fellini, Kubrick, etc., one sees at once the difficulty of translating sights and sounds into language—this difficulty, by the way, also haunts the anthropologist of ritual. In fact, the only element in a motion picture directly translatable or reproduci-ble is the dialogue: the other elements require interpretation. The screenwriter may stress what he calls "the color" or "texture," the vivid quality or structural quality, of the cinematic events, or he may emphasize technical factors, such as camera angles, lighting and lenses, contrasting images and transitions, and the use of sounds and music. Behind all of this, of course, is the screenwriter's estimate of the relationship of cinema to other art forms—the novel, stage drama, epic, painting, etc. The very term "screenplay" suggests that an analogy is being drawn between stage play and film performance. But this is a comparison, I think, that is hard to sustain. Cinema comes back again to ritual almost, in the great length of time and elaborate organization needed. Stage plays are relatively simple by comparison. The starting point of a movie may be a written text of some kind, but this is rarely what we eventually buy as a screenplay. The beginning text may be just somebody's good idea, or it may be based on a novel, a play, a biography, or a historical incident—even a contemporary incident like the Entebbe Raid. But when a screenwriter is assigned the task of developing this material, he is by no means free to indulge his personal Muse. He has been hired to do a job. The job entails discussing what he writes at every stage with the producer, the director, and other persons involved in the business or technical side of the film. His first task is to "get out" a brief synopsis, followed by a longer outline called a "treatment." Indeed, several drafts may be called for, requiring the services not of one but several writers. Economic and technical considerations—characteristic of this technological, postindustrial epoch—impose constraints on this draftwriting process, such as cost of production, availability of performers, shooting schedules, suitable locations, etc. When the director gets into the act, he must remain within the limits of his budget and try to meet each day's projected quota of scenes. Despite these constraints the director, as against the screenplay writer, has a great deal of control over what happens and he can improvise and modify in living response to the conditions of production, camera setups, actors' temperaments, unexpected lighting effects, and other contingencies and vicissitudes. Then there is the editing process, exercised literally on the strips of celluloid which distill the activities mentioned. A musical score is introduced; there must be a creative matching of images and sounds. What has happened after all this to the original screenplay? It seems to have faded like "an insubstantial pageant." But, indeed, it has been absorbed into a multigenred and multicoded and collectively orchestrated finished product, the concentrated essence of all the processes that have acted upon the original unidimensional script. Perhaps we can now speak of it as having a creative life of its own. Certainly the *Three Screenplays* of Fellini (1970: *I Vitelloni, Il Bidone,* and *The Temptations of Doctor Antonio*) have this quality—something more than a stenographic record of the producer's manipulation of the camera—something, rather, available for interpretation, just as a play's scenario is to be interpreted.

It must be remembered that in terms of storage systems film outlasts drama. Stage rehearsals lead to a creative event that is ephemeral in the sense that it can be repeated N times, each time being unique and different from the others, while a film is a permanent record on a perforated ribbon of celluloid. The director imposes his stamp much more finally on film than play, where writers and actors may counterpoise a producer's efforts. Nevertheless, for the purpose of this discussion we have to admit that both drama and film are collaborative, social performative systems. Dudley Nicols, in his part of the Introduction (with John Gassner) of *Twenty Best Film Plays* (1943), wrote that the making of a film is "a series of creations . . . a vast collaboration in which, if you have ever achieved a satisfactory film, you must accept a humble part." Even although "the collaboration must always have a dominant will and personality," i.e., the director, there has to be a "sympathy and shared attitude" among all concerned in this work of public liminality and social creativeness.

I have often tried to analyze the effect which the script of Fellini's *Il Bidone* — of which he was both writer and director — had and has on me — especially the last two scenes (the final act of conmanship of the old disreputable swindler Augusto dressed as a Monsignor extracting a peasant's savings for his own daughter and suddenly moved by his conversation with the peasant's own paralytic daughter to renounce not the 350,000 lire but his general life of hypocrisy; followed by the savage beating up of Augusto left for dead by his accomplices when they find the money he claims to have given back to the old man in the sole of his shoe; and completed by what Fellini calls "the attainment of Augusto's salvation" when having dragged himself up a rocky slope in a sort of parody of the paradigm of the *via crucis* he sees a little group of children pass by him without seeing him. His last words are: "Wait for me . . . I'm coming . . . I'm coming with you.") It struck me that whereas the stage dramatist often has his creative "flash" or *satori* before the production process, a filmmaker like Fellini has his in the actual plural reflexivity of the film-making process itself — and it is the trace of this flash which is inscribed in the script. The one precedes, the other follows the rehearsals. And, of course, the movie reaches thousands of viewers, and they interpret it in thousands of ways.

I mention these cases merely to give an impression of the range of topics available when we scrutinize the ongoing reciprocal relationships between the sociocultural process and major genres of ritual and dramatic performance from the standpoint of public liminality and the development of reflexive metalanguages.

References

Artaud, Antonin. 1958 [1938]. *The Theater and Its Double*. New York: Grove Press.
Fellini, Federico. 1970. *Three Screenplays*. New York: Orion.
Gulliver, Philip. 1971. *Neighbors and Networks*. Berkeley: University of California Press.
Nicols, Dudley, and Gassner, John. 1943. Introduction, *Twenty Best Film Plays*.
Singer, Milton. 1972. *When a Great Tradition Modernizes*. New York: Praeger.

Social Dramas in Brazilian Umbanda:

The Dialectics of Meaning

Anthropologists' notebooks are charged with accounts of discriminable sequences of events for which their spontaneous temporal ordering is crucial for analysis. It is only in relatively stable societies, occupying a single region for many generations, that such sequences may for some purposes be regarded as variant expressions of an invariant cultural grammar and lexicon of customary elements. In periods of major sociocultural change the grammar and lexicon themselves may be irreversibly altered by potent processes of social action. I mention this "generative" capacity of certain spontaneous series of vivid interactional events because fieldwork experience has shown me that "meaning" is not mere cognitive hindsight but something existentially emergent from the entanglement of persons wholly engaged in issues of basic concern to the central or representative actors, the formulators of "positions" or life-stances. True, narratives abound after the event, they explain that event, extol it, ethicize it, excuse it, deprecate it, repudiate it, name it as a significant marker of collective life-experience, as a model for future behavior. Indeed, such narratives become scripts or arguments to be used by the instigators of new sequences, and equally by those who aim to rebut them. One "social drama," as I have called an objectively isolable sequence of social interactions of a conflictive, competitive or agonistic type, may provide materials for many stories, depending upon the social-structural, political, psychological, philosophical, and, sometimes, theological perspectives of the narrators. It must also be remembered that stories are told at least as much to entertain as to instruct or interpret, and that some sequences of events are intrinsically more diverting or interesting than others. The problem, of course, remains of how to account for the fact that the social drama is processually "structured" before any story about it has been told.

When I say that a social drama is "processually structured," I mean that it exhibits a regular course of events which can be grouped in successive phases of public action. These are: (1) *breach* of regular norm-governed social relations made publicly visible by the infraction of a rule ordinarily held to be binding, and which is itself a symbol of the maintenance of some major relationship between persons, statuses, or subgroups held to be a key link in the integrality of the widest community recognized to be a cultural envelope of solidary sentiments; this course of events moves on to the second phase (2) of *crisis*, when people take sides, or rather, are in the process of being induced, seduced, cajoled, nudged, or threatened to take sides by those who confront one another across the revealed breach as prime antagonists. As Durkheim and René Girard have argued and my observations confirm: crisis is contagious. When antagonisms become overt ancient rancours, rivalries, and unresolved vendettas are revived. Nonrational considerations prevail: temperamental dislikes, unconscious desires and aggressions, reanimated infantile anxieties, as well as the conscious envies and jealousies which break loose when a major normative knot is cut. Crisis may or may not involve physical violence. It frequently involves the threat of such violence. In preliterate communities (bands, hordes, villages) it may involve supernatural dangers: threats of witchcraft, fear of ancestral spirits or deities who are believed to punish disputes between kith and kin with illness or other misfortune. Most public crises have what I call "liminal" characteristics, since each is a "threshold" (*limen*) between more or less stable or harmonic phases of the social process, but it is not usually a "sacred" or ritualized *limen*, hedged about by taboos and thrust from the centers of public life. Rather does it take up its menacing stance in the forum or agora itself, and, as it were, challenges the representatives of order to grapple with it. Their response inaugurates the third phase, (3) the application of *redressive or remedial procedures*. These range from personal advice and informal mediation or arbitration to formal jural and legal machinery and, to resolve certain kinds of crises or legitimate other modes of conflict-resolution, to the performance of public ritual. This phase is perhaps the most reflexive of the social drama. The community, acting through its representatives, bends, even throws itself back upon itself, to measure what some of its members have done, and how they have conducted themselves with reference to its own standards. Sometimes this phase, too, is initially violent; alleged law-breakers or witches are arrested, factions fight, indeed, revolutions may be part of the redressive phase of an extended social drama on the scale of a nation. But the violence is here conceptualized as being an instrument of a value-bearing group's solidarity and continuity, not as serving sectional or personal ends. In phase (3), however, there is usually a process of stock-taking, of plural self-scrutiny. A liminal space, religious or legal, is often created, in which is presented a distanced replication and then critique of the events leading up to and composing phase (2), the "crisis." This replication may be in the rational idiom of the judicial process, where antecedent events are scanned and assessed by the yardstick of the "reasonable man or woman." It may also or additionally be in the metaphorical or symbolic idiom of the ritual process, and not infrequently involve an act of sacrifice, in which the tensions and animosities of the disturbed community are discharged by the immolation (real or in token form) of living subjects or valued objects. Much could be said on these matters, but they must be laid aside to focus on the social drama and how it comes to be reconstructed as a narrative. The *fourth phase* (4) of the social drama consists either of the *reintegration* of the disturbed social group, or of the *recognition and legitimation of irreparable schism* between the contending parties. If the social drama runs its full course, is *satiated*, so to speak, the final phase consists of actions restorative of peace, often of a practical sort, as in the case where African villages split like cells, with one party abandoning its huts and moving out to found a new village, a process I described in some detail in *Schism and Continuity in an African Society*.

But social dramas, especially under conditions of major social change, may not complete the course indicated here. Where consensus over key values no longer exists, the redressive machinery premised on such a consensus loses its legitimacy, with the result that there is a reversion to crisis, with less likelihood of crisis #2 being resolved by redressive machinery #1. In some cases much ingenuity may go into the creation of better jural or ritual procedures, more in tune with contemporary interests and issues. However, in large-scale, complex communities, continuous failure of redressive institutions may develop into a revolutionary situation, in which one of the contending parties generates a program of societal change. In many societies, social dramas may escalate from limited or local crises to a general national crisis, as the redressive machinery available at each hierarchical level of social control fails to function. Under colonial conditions, the vertical momentum of crisis may be blocked by the superior force of the foreign rulers. In this case, as in British India or among the Pueblo villages of the American southwest, one may find what Siegel and Beals (1960) have called "pervasive factionalism," a state of endemic, low-key conflict between cliques of adversaries who oppose one another on almost every issue. Here there is no clearcut, overt resolution of crisis that may, at least temporarily, free the social atmosphere of suspicion. Instead social life is constantly clogged by clandestine animosities and disturbed by cabalistic intrigues.

Nevertheless, when one examines both cross-cultural and historical evidence, it cannot be denied that chronicles of completed social dramas are of global distribution. Like Hayden White I distinguish between chronicle and story. A chronicle deals with events in the temporal order of their occurrence, while a story arranges the events into a process which more clearly than the chronicle structures the events as completed diachronic processes by the use of "inaugural motifs," "transitional motifs," and "terminating motifs." But I would like to make the point that even before they are chronicled the sequences I have called social dramas have a developmental order. This order is not that of a story or narrative, the result of post-hoc emplotment; nor is it equivalent to "the parallelogram of forces" posited by Friedrich Engels to be the social structural resultant of a multitude of contending wills and interests. Rather is it the consequence of shared understandings and experiences in the lives of members of the same changing sociocultural field. I am not, of course, arguing that personalities are the puppets of culture. Rather do I support Theodore Schwartz's view that each human being is an "idioverse" with his/her "individual cognitive, evaluative, and affective mappings of the structure of events and classes of events" (1978:410) in his/her sociocultural field. Schwartz postulates that "a culture has its distributive existence as the set of personalities of the members of a population" (pp. 423, 424), thus allowing for negotiation and dispute over what should be authoritative or legitimate in that culture, in other words, for social dramatic action. As Schwartz writes (p. 432): "the model of culture as a set of personalities does not preclude conflict; rather the inclusion of the differences as well as the similarities among personalities in the culture makes social coordination a central research problem implied by this model. Differences may lead to conflict or complementarity. The perception of commonality or difference are themselves constructs which, at times, may mask their opposite." Schwartz further stresses that "Although individual personalities and their cognitive-evaluative-affective constructs of experience are the constituents of culture, they may be discrepant and conflicted among (and within) themselves or with central tendencies or configurations in the overall population of personalities comprising a culture or subculture" (p. 432).

This "distributive" model of culture, as opposed to the earlier integral or gestalt model, however, does not posit the complete autonomy of each idioverse. They communicate by means of verbal and nonverbal symbols, they share values, they are interlinked in economic and social structures, often they share a religious root paradigm. By this I mean not only a set of rules from which many kinds of social actions can be generated, but also a consciously recognized cultural model of an allusive metaphorical kind, cognitively delineated, emotionally charged, and with moral force, so impelling to action. In societies of the Christian tradition, for example, Christ's *via crucis* and resurrection has sometimes constituted a paradigmatic process for martyrs and heroes, though only insofar as the social dramas in which they took part have been transformed into narratives; for it may well be that the paradigmatic character of their actions owes a good deal to pious or partisan embellishment. Yet I am not suggesting that order and sequence in social dramas are solely the effect of cultural models in the actors' heads. Rather, it would seem that there is an inherent sequential momentum in human agonistic behavior which moves from unruly contestation through ritualized procedures to the restoration of order expressed in purified and recharged symbols of unity and continuity. As I have said, the process may be aborted or turned back upon itself, but in general there is a strain towards fulfillment. I have observed dozens of such social dramas, not only in African villages and chiefdoms but also in western families and university departments; and of course, the causes célèbres of our culture, such as the Dreyfus case and the Watergate affair which unfold in the social drama form.

It may perhaps be argued against me that I have imposed a Western, even an Aristotelian, form on my field data after having made a structural-functional analysis, using both statistical methods and the elicitation of ideal norms to construct a model, for example, of the Ndembu social system. In other words, I have transformed a chronicle into a narrative. Indeed, in my book *Schism and Continuity* I introduced the concept of the social drama as late as page 91 only after having made a careful analysis of Ndembu village structure. I presented a systematic outline of the principles on which Ndembu villages are constructed and used the social dramas to show how certain principles of organization and certain dominant values operated through both schisms and reconciliations and how the individuals and groups concerned tried to exploit the varied, and often situationally conflicting, principles and values to their own ends. In other words, I was operating with a vocabulary and rhetoric derived in the main from the positivist tradition of British functionalist rationalism. Hence, it may be legitimately argued that my social dramas are, indeed, "narratives" shaped by a specific Western world view, not chronicles in any sense. And yet, when I relive in memory the experiences behind the narratives, and reread the field notes made just after the events, I have to say, with Galileo, "*e pur se muove*," "and yet it moves." The drama *is* rooted in social reality, not imposed upon it. Other scholars deny this rootedness, insist that I have lopped my data to fit into a Procrustean bed of form. I have been sternly rebuked by some of those in the functionalist tradition, including Raymond Firth, Max Gluckman, and Lucy Mair, for imposing the metaphor of drama on sequences of social relations where in their view it is quite inappropriate. Firth, for example, taxes me for "adopting as a model a stylized aesthetic construct, the drama," and worries that the anthropologist *qua* dramatist may "deliberately shape, distort, and contrive his data for didactic purposes, and desert the facts it is his duty to study" (*Times Literary Supplement*, 13th Sept., 1974). I repeat: "*E pur se muove*"! Human sociocultural life certainly has long stretches of non-dramatic activity, even to the point of tedium. By temperament and training many social scientists prefer these "harmonic" periods, for the social interactions they contain misleadingly resemble natural phenomena which can be measured and quantified. But perhaps it is no less "distorting" to metaphorize human social processes as physical or biological rhythms and regularities than it is to recognize an affinity between spontaneous human disturbances, group life, and that genre of cultural performance which we call "drama." The Greek term "drama" means a "deed" or "act" and was only later applied to an action represented on the stage. Though Liddell and Scott in their Greek lexicon insist that "drama" means especially to "do some great thing good or bad," a sense that fortifies my use in "social drama."

But you will have noticed that the phase structure of social drama itself contains narrative, for the redressive phase, when its dominant vehicle is a ritual process—may in many preliterate societies, be subdivided into (1) *sickness* or misfortune afflicting a member or members of contending parties in social drama phase 2, *crisis*; (2) recourse to divinatory or oracular procedures whose verdicts bear directly on or relate obliquely to phases 1 and 2; (3) remedial ritual action ostensibly directed to the cure of the afflicted person, but usually involving confessional and homiletic statements which refer to the antecedent crisis—sometimes such statements may represent an almost complete inventory of the disputes, open or suspected, between the principal actors in the social drama; (4) the ritual cooperation enjoined upon participants and celebrants, and the religious theory that the invisible causes of affliction will not be removed unless there is unanimity of heart among all parties may itself be a potent means of redress. However, there is usually recourse to some mode of rational scanning before ritual means are employed. Nevertheless, as one follows the steps of ritual redress, one becomes aware that a narrative is being slowly constructed from the pieces of behavior scrutinized by diviners and other ritual specialists. Meaning and sense are being given to the words and deeds of the protagonists. Diviners probe into the doings of those intimately connected with the patients or dead people whose fate they are evaluating. Such doings may have occurred well before phase 1 of a social drama, and, indeed, may well explain why one of the actors transgressed a rule and set the whole dramatic process in train. Since the evaluative frame is here a ritual one, the deeds examined are assessed in terms of ethical standards held to be binding on all persons of good will who subscribe to the culture's moral order. Witchcraft puts one beyond the pale of this order, and if it can be established by a diviner that one of the main figures in a social drama is a witch that person is stigmatized so deeply that it must seriously impair his chances of success in any competition for political office. So one of the manipulative gambits of village politics in preliterate societies is to work for the ritual stigmatization of a feared rival.

The judicial process itself is, of course, a dialectic between prosecutors and defendants from which, it is expected, a narrative will emerge sufficiently self-consistent as to provide the material for a rational decision as to culpability by a person or persons (judge and/or jury) defined as situationally impartial. The cross-examination of witnesses, the application of the standard of "the reasonable man/woman" when conflicting evidence is presented, the introjection of legal maxims and proverbial wisdom by elders—all these tend to result in a narrative which frames the antecedent phases of the social drama in terms meaningful to all interested parties.

Thus, in the "natural unit" of the social drama we have already more than the germ of narrative. We have sophisticated instruments of social reflexivity which aim at reproducing as exactly as possible chains of social events leading to consequences disruptive of social harmony and, in many cases, individual peace of mind. But this recapitulation of events, forensically established as authentic, is still no more than the wrinkled surface of the process to be examined. In many societies, motivation is not an important concern of the judicial process. The character of the act is what interests the court. A tariff or scale is set up which assesses compensation in terms of the importance, for example, of the person or object destroyed or damaged. For example, in descending order of importance one might find the slaying of a free man, of a free woman, a slave, an ox, a dog, and a sheep requited by diminishing penalties. Why the defendant killed one of these might be of little significance to the judicial authorities. Hence, motivation might play little part in the narrative construed by them from the evidence. But in ritual processes within the same society, particularly when a person is accused of killing another by witchcraft/sorcery, a diviner will find the accused's motives most pertinent in establishing his culpability. We need not be surprised by this: anthropology has taught us that the components of any investigation into the human condition are distributed variously among the institutions of society, some allocating to religion, others to law, others again to aesthetic processes the dominant role in probing for motivation in situations of human delict.

Jural and divinatory "narratives" are therefore attempts at "establishing the facts" significantly contextualizing the events leading up to and constituting the crisis, and eliciting in certain cultures the hidden motives impelling the actors. Such narratives are frequently saturated with moral implications, and in both legal and religious procedures of redress, the deeds of participants are assessed by the ethical yardsticks of the group.

However, in all cultures that have been adequately studied, it is clear that narrative exists independently as a genre of cultural performance and is not necessarily linked functionally with the social drama. Indeed, it is usually not long before the entire social drama, including its third phase, becomes itself the subject of a tale. In preindustrial societies, such tales may be told by skilled, even by professional storytellers, often in liminal times and places, usually accompanied by a good deal of miming dramatis personae. Audiences are never passive and criticism of the storyteller may induce him to make repeated revisions of his account until whatever had been left of chronicle is swallowed up by narrative. As often happens, storytellers borrow from one another, add artistic embellishments and draw morals of their own, until what began as an empirical social drama may continue both as an entertainment and a metasocial commentary on the lives and times of the given community. I have myself observed how these metamorphoses occur among the Ndembu of Zambia. The first two social dramas I analyzed in *Schism and Continuity* (1957:95-98, 116-120) took place several years before my fieldwork. My reconstruction, my "narrative," if you like, was based on data collected from a large number of interviews and conversations with living persons, who actively participated in them. Already there seemed to be in the most widely accepted accounts, certain mythical elements. The dramas had concerned a struggle for the village head-manship and the majority of the received accounts had acquired the character of a "mythological charter," to use Malinowski's expressive phrase, that is, a social justification for the exclusion of one of the main candidates from the succession. His own account, and those of the minority still loyal to him, differed in certain significant details from that given wide currency in the area. These details concerned the disappointed candidate's stigmatization as a sorcerer: the dominant narrative contained accounts of incidents and dialogue which pointed to his being a practitioner of the evil arts, and hence an unworthy candidate. Later I was able to see this process of "mythologization" or "fabulization" at work, beginning from my own observations of social dramas and continuing into the collection of narratives about those social dramas. Even participants produced different accounts. Interestingly enough, these accounts were often perspectival views, and much light was shed on their variation by simply scanning genealogies, examining hut ownership diagrams (noting whose hut was near to or far from whose), comparing biographical materials, and studying the pattern of garden ownership. Political position, incumbency of ritual office, wealth obtained by petty trade, former slave status and other social structural characteristics also supplied clues as to what aspects of the social drama would be accentuated, suppressed, distorted or "invented" by informants. Finally, once the narrative had been taken over by a gifted storyteller, usually a person uninvolved in the social drama itself and perhaps only remotely connected by kinship or affinity to any of its enactors, aesthetic considerations, the urge to entertain, attempts to relate the humdrum village events to some pantribal cultural root paradigm or heroic legend, would so transmogrify the actual deeds, would so drench them with "meaning" (as the culture defined this telic realm) that I for one would rub my eyes and wonder whether the dry record of my field notes was the true illusion, not the "marvellous tale" it had become. When I wrote *Schism and Continuity*, I tried to exclude these "narratives" from my analysis, and instead made my own narrative of the events I saw or had almost immediate feedback about if I did not see them from the standpoint of the main enactors. I did not understand, then, that my narrative was just as tendentious, that is, "stretching" things (from the Latin, *tendere*), as those of local storytellers. I did veritably believe, as a structuralist-functionalist, that my "formal" analysis of the social structure of the community concerned in the social drama "explained" how individuals acted: parallel segments of a village matrilineage descended from a common founding ancestress competed with one another behind male candidates contending for high office; sorcery accusations lay between matrilineal kin of adjacent genealogical generations, commonly classificatory not primary kin, those with most numerical support from close matrilineal kin would win the prize, and so on and so on. I even compared, in my book, the situation in an Ndembu village with that found in Greek tragedy where one witnesses the helplessness of the human individual before the Fates: but in the African case, analysed in the structuralist-functionalist mode, the Fates turn out to be the necessities of the social process. In all this I acted as though I were a true great-grandchild of Emile Durkheim, whose sociologism was mediated to me through Radcliffe-Brown and Max Gluckman.

It was only later, after long study of various genres of cultural performance, in many cultures, eastern, western, northern, and southern, that I came to appreciate the fact that culture, like verbs in many if not all languages, has at least two "moods," indicative and subjunctive, and that these, in any particular situation, are almost hopelessly intermingled. A social drama is mostly, at least on the surface, under the sign of indicativity. That is, it presents itself as consisting of acts, states, occurrences that are factual, in terms of the cultural definition of factuality. Every culture has a theory that certain "things" actually happen, are "really true," that "have been" or "are"—though, of course, the frames within which these assertions are made may vary from culture to culture. One culture's truth may be another culture's fantasy. Thus, medieval Icelanders, on the evidence of the saga literature, apparently placed much credence in dreams as portents of actual happenings; our Western urban culture sees them as messages from the occulted portion of the Self to the conscious part. Icelandic dreams would, therefore, be in the "indicative mood," ours in the "subjunctive"; the former are engrossed in actuality, the latter in potentiality, in Western terms. I do not want to enter, even briefly, the vicissitudes of the tradition devolving, in shorthand, from Jerusalem-Athens-Rome, in conflict or cahoots, which produces this particular "cut" between the world of "is" and the worlds of "may be," "might be," even "should be"—though I suspect there is in many cultures an itch for the indicative to conform to the conditional (the "should" or "ought to be") at least in its paradigmatic narratives. Heroes and saints are always our best possibility. But narrative which admits the possibility of heroes also expresses the frailty of heroes, the Lancelots and Rustums, and thus inserts entertainment, dubiety, choice, into its plots. For the "subjunctive" (so legislates Webster), "expresses supposition, desire, hypothesis, possibility," rather than "states an actual fact, as the mood of were in 'if I were you.'" The subjunctive indeed, contains the dialectical, that is, the notion that an idea or event generates its opposite, it is not merely a matter of making the indicative unquestionably exemplify the ideal; heroes must go through hell to attain paradise—their own natures oppose the ethical schema—hence the entertainment they provoke—the very word "entertainment" means the liminal in English, for it means literally, from the Latin, "to hold between," to be neither this nor that, but the problem in the middle—a problem which staged in liminal surrounds "entertains" rather than threatens. Universal indicativity is boredom, "ennui," "spleen." We escape from it into liminal narrative, which makes meaningful our events. Perhaps, due to en-culturation, our events have an initial encrustation of meaningfulness before they have been definitively "narrated" that is, after a series of tales, the last of which gains widespread acceptance in a given sociocultural field, due either to its aesthetic or ethical fittingness in the terms of the given culture.

I am arguing that in all cultures social dramas provide the "raw stuff," both in the indicative and subjunctive moods, from which less existentially embedded cultural genres escape, the better to make generalized interpretations of events which are always, inescapably, connected with the intertwined destinies of par-ticular persons, even if these "idioverses" are forced into almost lifelong prox-imity by certain axiomatic rules of the culture, notably those controlling the behavior of kin. The liberated, generalized forms, the narratives' *pur sang*, ac-quire an almost paradigmatic character in certain cases, and can be reapplied, like prolonged proverbs, to the particularity of subsequent social dramas. Geertz has spoken of myths and rites as "imaginative works built out of social materials." This is also applicable to other genres of cultural performance such as folk-epics, ballads, dramas, and *märchen*. All these genres interact with one another and with social reality in a process that manifests the cross-fertilization of the "natural languages" of the forum and agora with the "meta-languages" of cultural performances. Social dramas may draw their rhetoric from cultural per-formances; cultural performances may draw on social dramas for their plots and problems. Genres of cultural performance are not simple mirrors but magical mirrors of social reality: they exaggerate, invert, re-form, magnify, minimize, dis-color, re-color, even deliberately falsify, chronicled events. They resemble Rilke's "hall of mirrors," rather than represent a simple mirror-image of society. But, as Barbara Myerhoff has written (1980), they nevertheless together constitute the plural "self-knowledge" of a group. As she writes (p. 7): "Cultural performances are reflective in the sense of showing ourselves to ourselves. They are also capable of being *reflexive* (my emphasis), arousing con-sciousness of ourselves as we see ourselves. As heroes in our own dramas, we are made self-aware, conscious of our consciousness. At once actor and au-dience, we may then come into the fullness of our human capability – and perhaps human desire – to watch ourselves and enjoy knowing that we know. All this requires skill, craft, a coherent, consensually validated set of symbols and social arenas for appearing. It also requires an audience in addition to per-formers." Each genre carries its own mode of reflexivity: my "Rokujo's Jealousy" chapter in this book (p. 99) examines how in Japanese culture an event which may have had its prototype in a social drama of the Japanese Heian court in the eleventh century A.D., was passed through the novelistic imagination of Lady Murasaki in the *Tale of Genji*, where it was coolly and psychologically scruti-nized, and later passed into the Noh drama, where it was revised in terms of the Buddhist theologies, combining aristocratic Zen and populist Pure Land beliefs, dominant some centuries later. The same event, involving belief in the lethal possession of a living woman by the sexually jealous spirit of another living woman—a belief still extant in rural Japanese areas, and an ingredient in Phase Three of many rural social dramas—is handled in a singularly "secular" fashion by Murasaki, and later as a theological ingredient in the salvation of the jealous woman's soul through release from the "earth-binding" of her passion after death in the Noh play. The multiplication of "mirrorings," preserved in written texts, cumulate towards what Myerhoff would call "collective self-definitions" in Japanese culture.

This problem of the interplay between social drama and narrative—or other genres of cultural performance—is very much in my mind at the moment for my colleague Ann Mabe and I are presently engaged in a technical, anthropological analysis of the rich materials of the Icelandic *Sturlunga Saga*, in its literary and sociological context. Our problem is that underlined by Julia H. McGrew in her Introduction to *The Sturlunga Saga* (1974:10) of "why the development of historical writing in Iceland was not . . . the familiar European development from annals to chronicles to the writing of history, but was . . . far more completely interwoven with the development of fictional writing." One could, I suppose, postulate that the thirteenth century Icelanders were still innocent of the later attempts to conform historiography to positivistic notions of "objectivity," "evidence," and "documentation," and that their "narratives" are value-laden. One of the most conspicuous features of Icelandic saga-writing, however, is its famed stylistic "objectivity"—its sober, matter-of-fact epic authority. Yet since the "objectivity" is stylistic, made up of carefully calculated artistic effects, and not of substance, one cannot regard sagas relating even contemporary or near-contemporary events as straightforward records, but rather as aesthetic restraint the better to stress the violent passions described so soberly. But to display the contexts or co-texts adequately which give sense and point to the *Sturlunga Saga*, the genealogies, maps, historical records, literary traditions, church policy documents, and so forth which would of necessity be involved in an adequate social drama analysis is beyond the scope of this paper and beyond the stage of research Ann Mabe and I have attained. I therefore propose to document my argument about the relationship between social dramas and narrative with information gleaned partly from my recent visit to Brazil and partly from the extant literature on Afro-Brazilian folk ritual which my wife and I have been studying for several years.

The basic document I shall use is an excellent study of the genesis, decline and fall of one *terreiro*, or cult center of the Umbanda religion in a suburb of Rio de Janeiro by the anthropologist Yvonne Maggie Alves Velho, who teaches at the Federal University of Rio de Janeiro. The book is entitled *Guerro de Orixá: Um Estudo de Ritual e Conflito*, "War of Gods: A Study of Ritual and Conflict," and describes the vicissitudes of a newly created local congregation of adherents to the Umbanda religion over the three months of its existence. In effect it is a study of consecutive social dramas, and indeed Velho tried to apply my methodology and analysis from the outset of her fieldwork to data obtained from her participation in the life of the *terreiro*. Her study is remarkable in that it is based on the diary she kept of detailed observations of successive events in the life of the congregation. What we must look out for is the how and why of the intrusion of mythological and other narrational structures into the descriptions and interpretations of persons immediately implicated in the events. Even as events happen they are invaded by interpretations derived from the religious culture, and these interpretations partially shape subsequent events. Yet, as we shall see, these interpretations are not completely "culture-bound," but admit of a certain "lee-way," a certain scope for individual reformulation of cultural rules.

Yvonne Velho found a major problem when she attempted to employ my social drama concept to make sociological sense of the observational facts of the birth, life, and death of the cult-center named *Tenda Espiritu Caboclo Serra Negra*, from its ritual inauguration on Sunday, June 24th, 1972 until its schism on September 13th of that year. Whereas I had studied an Ndembu village in a small-scale society where the kinship system provided a model for analyzing the principal regularities of social relationships, and where the structural limits and boundaries were quite well-defined, Velho had to reckon with the embedment of the cult-center in a complex, urban social field, whose limits and boundaries were by no means easy to establish. The members of the *terreiro* did not live their whole lives in it, as villagers often did. They were not a homogeneous group; differences of social class, education, occupation, geographical origin, earlier *terreiro* affiliation, and many other factors made them a heterogeneous group. Formally, in Tonnies's classic terms, the Ndembu village was a *Gemeinschaft*, the *terreiro* a *Gesellschaft*. I would like to suggest here that wherever individuals have multiple memberships in groups or association, one group, perhaps two or three, becomes the focus of a special concentration of psychic energy, of sociocultural cathexis, to borrow Freud's term. Relationships in such a "star" group or "marked" group are of a generally higher level of intensity than those entered into by membership of other groups. The star group need not be a *primary* group, designating by this term a group in which the activities are unspecialized. But it does possess some of the characteristics of what W. G. Sumner (*Folkways*, 1906:12) was the first to call an *in-group*, which is typified by "we"—feelings, loyalty to the group, sacrifice for it, and comradeship among its members. The nature of its mode of social interrelatedness, I have elsewhere called "normative communitas," distinguishing it thus from "existential communitas," a direct unmediated, and total confrontation of human identities, often ephemeral in duration, akin to Buber's *I-Thou* or "Essential We" relation. But an "in-group" is not precisely what I mean by a "marked" group or "star group." The star group emerges from the social experience and choice of individuals and only becomes an in-group when those individuals come together and devise rules for themselves. I am stressing the subjective and orectic aspects here, for the star group is the group one most desires to belong to and enjoys belonging to. It is not a "reference group," in standard sociological parlance, for *reference group* is often distinguished from *membership group*, while the star group is definitely a group in which one is a member. Reference groups, to the contrary, are usually defined as "groups in which [the individual] aspires to attain or maintain membership . . . membership groups and reference groups may or may not be identical" (A. E. and S. Siegel, 1957:360). In so far as reference groups set and enforce standards for the person against which s/he can evaluate him/herself, reference groups fall more fully within the dimension of social (normative) structure than "star" groups, which, whatever their degree of internal structuring, are seen by the individual as potential loci for the experience of spontaneous communitas, an experience denied or attenuated in other groups. In the case of the Central African village, membership options are minimal as compared with large-scale industrial societies with an advanced development of the social division of labor and many modes of voluntary association. Nevertheless, I have observed that friendship groups, as distinct from kinship groups, quite often associated with membership in ritual curative cults, tend to arise in Ndembu village society, and that these sometimes influence the outcome of major social dramas, for friends of contenders may act as mediators, and kin who, additionally, are friends may elect to leave a village together after a dispute and build a new one together. Thus, the beginnings of star-group choice can be detected in preindustrial types of society. When a clear-cut cleavage between working time and leisure time developed in industrial societies, possibilities multiplied of forming groups in the leisure domain on the basis of shared interests and predilections. In proportion as productive processes became boring and alienative, and family life diminished by urbanization, wage-labor, bureaucratization of social control and education, and so forth, so did star-groups ramify beyond the pale of domestic and economic relations. Recreational and sports clubs, religious and political associations, musical ensembles, philatelic and folklore societies, amateur dramatic groups, innumerable candidates for the position of star-group competing for the attention of individuals have arisen, particularly in post-Renaissance Western society. Utopian communities have even attempted to restore the multiplex relationships and multifunctional role-sets of preindustrial villages under the aegis of cultural values derived from a variety of literate religious and ethical systems, and to substitute themselves for the productive and domiciliary groups of capitalistic society. I do not want to pursue this line of argument beyond the point of noting that one's personal star-group may take a wide variety of forms: a counter-cultural commune, the Elks, a morning Bridge Club, the Quadrangle Club, a Trade Union Local, the Carmelite Tertiaries, an informal group of friends at the Explorers' Club, the county Democratic or Republican Party Branch, a boys' peer group street gang, the town's Charles Dickens Society, its Chess Club.

Social dramas, in my view, take place among those members of a given group for whom it is a "star-group." Only those who feel strongly about their membership in such a group are impelled to enter into relationships with others which become fully "meaningful," in the sense that the beliefs, values, norms, and symbols "carried" in the group's culture become so internalized in a member that they constitute a major part of what s/he might regard as his/her identity, what makes that member a specific person. A further distinction must, I think, be made. Subjectively, even, quite often objectively, a star-group appears under two aspects. The first is the ideal model or paradigm, the pure and perfect image of its harmonious operation. The second is the concrete manifestation of that ideal in the experience of the member. Social dramas almost always contain episodes which manifest discrepancies between components of the actual and ideal group models. To "star" a group in one's subjectivity is already, even before joining it, to idealize it, and contrast that ideal with one's experience of the "muddled" and "dirty" conduct of members of groups to which one has already belonged. And often to disprize one's own *persona* as it has been constructed in the social processes of previous memberships. Both individual religious and political conversion and the genesis of reformative religious movements clearly emerge from this clash of ideal and real in consciences and consciousnesses. Social dramas nearly always involve passionate reflexivity, and Phase Three, *redress*, may often contain episodes of purification and sacrifice, both of which aim to remove the pollution of self-serving or factional conduct and restore, sometimes in the image of an ideal or mythical past, a pure state of relations among the members. Social dramas contain, therefore, processes of definition and redefinition (where the ideal has become blurred by pollution), where crises of belief rather than social relations are involved. Barbara Myerhoff has written of these "definitional dramas" (her term in *Number Our Days*, 1978:32): "no social rearrangements are accomplished, but rather unquestionable truths, made unquestionable by being performed." In my own experience both social relations and belief are modified, sometimes even transformed or reformulated, in almost all social dramas, whether only minimally or extensively.

So far, then, as the social drama is concerned, Yvonne Velho's problem about the difference between social dramas in a village and in a modern urban setting is secondary to the fact that for the main participants their actions take place within their star groups. Both sets of actors, African villagers and Brazilian Umbandistas, are passionately engaged in crises and attempted redressive actions, in groups about which they care intensely, and whose ideals and essential ideas are upheld in the face of conduct which they assert is liable to pollute and even destroy the lifeways they cherish. No matter that the villagers spend most of their days and nights in the same dwelling and agricultural spaces, while the Umbandistas meet regularly only once a week, on Sundays, though their religion also provides them with numerous other occasions for meeting. No matter that the villagers interact in almost every social and economic activity, while the Umbandistas are divided by occupation, class, ethnicity, kinship and many other criteria. The Umbandistas are devoted to their *terreiros* and see them as the central arenas of their lives, where meaning is injected into the chaotic impersonality of modern city existence. What Barbara Myerhoff wrote (1978:32) about the senior citizens of the Jewish Community Center she studied in Los Angeles could be applied just as fittingly to the Umbandistas: "The Center people are agreeing upon and making authoritative the essential ideas that define them. In these dramas they develop their collective identity, their interpretation of their world, themselves, and their values. As well as being social dramas, the events are definitional-ceremonies, performances of identity, sanctified to the level of myth."

Before and other than Velho, anthropologists have stressed, in Durkheimian fashion, the integrative function of *Umbandà*, and its kindred "cults," *Candomblé, Batuque, Candomblé de Caboclo, Kardecismo* and the like. Many have paid attention to the complex cosmologies associated with their religious activities. Others have traced items and complexes of beliefs and practices found in them to West and Central African, Portuguese Catholic, Amerindian, and European Spiritist sources. Latterly, investigators have turned their attention to the physiology and psychology of trance and other hyper-aroused states associated with cultural beliefs in spirit—and deity—possession which form a prominent part of cult performances. But Yvonne Velho was interested in the problem of how the relatively small cult-centers, the *terreiros*, managed their internal affairs, particularly how they resolved their quarrels and disputes. For inasmuch as religious groups are star-groups, one would expect them to generate social dramas which manifest struggles for power and authority among their members and are simultaneously definitional dramas, attempts to develop "collective identity." It would be possible to regard the nightlong sessions or "turns" (*giras*) of *Umbanda* as being themselves redressive performances in the sense that they restore order and redress violations of integrity in the lives of the urban individuals who convene every Sunday for corporate rituals. Indeed, healing and advice on personal problems make up a good deal of what goes on in a session. Moreover, scholars have argued that many features of *Umbanda* reveal that symbols of a sylvan African or Amerindian past, and of anti-urban habitats form significant framing devices in such sessions, signs of a pure "Nature."

which acts as a salve against an impure urbanized "Culture," full of inter- and intra-class conflict, and police brutality. But this very remedial and salvific role, paradoxically, gives the *terreiro* group its "star" quality, and makes its relationships so significant that they can arouse the powerful sentiments of loyalty to the cult if not to the cult-center among Umbanda adherents. It becomes most important to them how the *terreiro* is run, and who is pure and wise enough to run it. In this way, the *terreiro* is para-politicized and para-legalized, that is, it comes to contain its own modes of leadership and social control, which imply its own sets of sanctions and rewards for conformity or nonconformity to its own rules. The Brazilian state, of course, insists that every *terreiro* should be registered with the local police headquarters. There are also nationally based coalitions of *Umbanda terreiros*. But neither State nor coalition has much effective day-to-day control over *terreiro* life. Such control is mostly couched in the idiom of religious belief. It has always been my contention that belief, myth, evaluative frames, moral norms, and the like, only emerge in their plenitude in processes of social action, and that these should be minutely observed. No abstract listings of rules, creeds, tenets, doctrines, or myths, the Holy Word or the Holy Writ, can capture the full life of religious culture viewed as a vital set of "structures of experience," to use the term which Wilhelm Dilthey applied to the inwoven trinity of cognitive, affective, and volitional responses human beings give to natural and sociocultural challenges. Such structures of experience thread critical events, such as social dramas, and give them purport and tensional continuity.

It has been against my lifelong habit, since I am a kind of natural historian of human socioculture, to refrain from bombarding my audience with microdescriptive and microanalytical data. Hence I shall be shameless about giving you a strip or two from Velho's detailed documentary. What you will see is the investigator's narrative of social conduct governed by Umbanda beliefs and norms, with the constant introjection of personal narrative fragments by participants to make sense of their experience of the events. There is a clear chronological sequence and an equally clear evaluative frame by which individuals seek to validate their actions and motivations.

Religion, like art, *lives* in so far as it is performed, that is, in so far as its rituals are "going concerns." If you wish to spay or geld religion first remove its rituals, its generative and regenerative processes. For religion is not a cognitive system, a set of dogmas, alone, it is meaningful experience and experienced meaning. In ritual one *lives* through events, or through the alchemy of its framings and symbolings relives semiogenetic events, the deeds and words of prophets and saints, or if these are absent, myths and sacred epics. Anyone who has visited Brazil must have been impressed not only by the mushrooming urbanization of that nation, but also by the great popularity of its performative genres. It is hard to know how to classify these. For operational purposes I use "celebration" as the generic term and "ritual" and "ceremony" to denote respectively transformative processes (with religious flavor) and processes of confirmation or ratification. While it is clear that Catholic Masses and Corpus Christi processions are rituals, and that performances of Umbanda, Candomblé, or Batuque are also rituals, what is one to make of *Carnaval*, which the distinguished Brazilian anthropologist Roberto Da Matta in his *Ensaios de Antropologia Estructural* (1973) called *"um Rito de Passagem,"* contrasting it with the military parade on Brazilian Independence Day? Whereas Carnival creates *communitas* (thereby making it a ritual in my sense), the military parade celebrates *structure* since it is a symbolic representation of hierarchical distinctions. It would, therefore, be a ceremony. Having experienced the full four days of *Carnaval* this Spring (1979), I felt its transformative power and sensed that its place in the Catholic calendar just before Lent was no accident. Its ludic character was still tinctured with genuine ritual liminality. A soccer game in the huge Maracaná Stadium between the great Rio rivals Flamenco and Fluminense has something of a ritual quality too, with its "*baterias*" of drummers, banners borne aloft when a team scores, fireworks, clouds of powder ejected upwards, club colors, praise songs, corporate groups of supporters each based on a traditional *bairro* of the city: in all this one can detect a transcendence of mundane reality and a sense of civic and national history made present.

But to call *Carnaval* and *Futebol* "ritual" is perhaps to strain unduly the sense of this term. The true thrust of ritual proper in Brazil seems to be moving away from Catholic liturgical performance and settling on such religions as Kardecist Spiritism and the so-called Afro-Brazilian religious groups. Brazil is indeed what S. N. Eisenstadt has called a "post-traditional" society, that is, a society in which strong traditions persist through processes of modernization. But traditional forces or groups tend to reorganize themselves, in new modern settings, in effective ways. In shaping the responses to the initial "Western" model of modernization many forces that develop from within a society's traditions may indeed by of crucial importance. Brazil, almost from the beginning, has shown a cultural capacity for synthesis and, in the religious domain, of syncretism, which can correlate the inputs from diverse ritual systems in new formations. For example, Roger Bastide, in his book *African Civilizations in the New World* (1971:87), after scanning the data on the meeting of African and Amerindian religious cultures, writes:

> The impression one gets is that Negro syncretism, at least in the major urban centers, has moved on from the old spontaneous syncretism of African and Indian practices [found in the early days of the Portuguese settlement]; the syncretism we now find has been oriented, controlled, turned into a Brazilian religious ideology, parallel to the development of political nationalism in the proletarian class. In this connection we may note what the priests of *Umbanda* assert—namely, that the "spiritualism" which joins Catholic saints, Indian spirits, and the *orisha* (Yoruba deities) of one-time African slaves in a single act of adoration, also, on the mystical plane, offers a precise translation of the meeting and fusion (on the human plane) of the three major races that constitute the country's population. In contrast to such myths as those of white supremacy or negritude, this encounter between Indian and Negro allowed the development of a quite different myth, that of intermarriage and racial fusion.

I am not sure that I would call this process syncretization or fusion. Rather, are the African cosmologies, deities, and rituals "masked" in Catholic ritual culture: the "accidents" are Catholic, the "substance" West and Central African traditional religion. Professor Velho managed to get us an invitation to attend a "session" (sessão) of Umbanda in a terreiro in Novo Iguacu, a large working class district some fifteen miles north of Rio de Janeiro. A session (sessão) or gira, meaning "movement in a circle," is a ritual dedicated to all the Orixás, those divinities of Yoruba origin who enter into contact with human beings through possession. The term terreiro means literally, a "courtyard," but refers in practice to an entire sacred complex, including: a building with a shrine where the Umbanda rites take place; several dwelling houses for officiants and their families; and some outdoor shrines, all contained in a courtyard. The terreiro we visited was a terreiro tracado, literally a "cut up terreiro," since it could be used for Candomblé as well as Umbanda rites. In Candomblé the African influence is more pronounced than in Umbanda. Candomblé came to Rio from the state of Bahia where it is estimated that more than seventy percent of the population are of direct African descent. Umbanda grew up in Rio and is more eclectic and syncretic, drawing upon many extrasacramental Catholic practices flourishing in Brazil a century ago, as well as upon the Kardecist doctrines of "Spirit evolution" and "reincarnation," first formulated by Leon Rivail (who took the name of his "spirit guide," a Breton called Allan Kardec) in the 1850s.

I have no time to produce here a detailed disquisition on the scholarly literature on Afro-Brazilian sects and cults (Batuque, Macumba, Xangô, Candomblé, Umbanda and others) to which such authorities as Melville Herskovits, Roger Bastide, Edison Carneiro, Arthur Ramos, Gilberto Freyre, and, more recently, Seth and Ruth Leacock and Esther Pressel, have notably contributed. Although I do not stress here the taxonomy and cultural history of ritual types, I have taken the works of the above authors fully into account. My emphasis is on the performing of ritual, how we experienced a particular performance and how ritual relates to social drama.

My wife and I were immediately struck, on entering the terreiro, by what Jacques Macquet might have called the "Africanity" of the scene. We had lived in Central and East African villages and studied their rituals as participant-observers for about three years in all, in the 50s and 60s. We saw, in the main room devoted to ritual, fourteen women and two men, all wearing something white, dancing slowly in a circle counter-clockwise to the beat of three drums played by men, while ten women and two men, in ordinary clothes, sat on benches along the side walls; at the back right was an altar with several tiers crowded with images of santos which under the similitude of Christian saints represented the Orixás. Yvonne Velho told us that in the terreiro studied, the terms Orixás, Guias ("guides"), Santos ("saints"), and Entidades ("entities") are used almost interchangeably—though in other terreiros, and in parts of the literature, Pretos-Velhos (the spirits of old black slaves), Exus (named after Eshu-

Elegba, the Trickster Diety of the Yoruba and Fon of West Africa), *Pombas-Giras* (the "wives of *Exu*," represented as women of easy virtue) and *Caboclos* (entities representing Indians or "rural" types, such as *boiadeiros* or "cowboys") are classified as "guides," not as *Orixás*. The people themselves rarely use the term Umbanda, except as a general description of what goes on in the many localized *terreiros*: they speak of "working in *Macumba*" and say that *Macumba* is the drum (*tambor*) which is the "instrument of the *Santos*," while a person who "works in the *Santo* (*no Santo*)," they call a *Macumbeiro* or "drum-player," whether he or she plays an instrument or not. All this reminded us of our two-and-a-half year's fieldwork among the Ndembu of Northwestern Zambia, where the term for a ritual performance is *ng'oma*, which literally means "drum," and where three drums, as in Umbanda, are considered indispensable components of all ritual. Indeed, among the Ndembu the very term Umbanda means "curing" and the senior officiant at what I have called a ritual of affliction is known as a *chimbanda*. We were to find that healing is an important part of a *sessão*, and that, as with the Ndembu again, white and red clay are used for anointing the body. Even the term for "white clay" is the same: *mpemba* for the Ndembu, *pemba* for the Umbandistas or Macumbeiros.

The African influence is indeed wide and deep. As in many liminal situations generated by poor or structurally "low"-positioned people, fictitious hierarchies abound in Umbanda. The main hierarchy is structured by African, mainly Yoruba, deities. The major *Orixá* is called *Oxalá* or *Zambi*; *Nzambi* is, of course, the name for the otiose High God among many Central Bantu-speaking peoples. *Oxalá* has no "horse"—as the human "medium" (feminine media) of an *Orixá* is called. He only rules over the other *Orixás* who are classified into seven "lines" (*linhas*). These lines are broad categories which define how each *Orixá* should "work" (*trabalhar*), i.e., what his or her behavioral characteristics are when he or she "rides a horse," i.e., possesses a medium—the type of dance peculiar to that *Orixá*, his or her bodily manifestations (dress, gestures, intonation, vocabulary, and so on), what colors are appropriate to him or her, what day of the week is dedicated to him or her, and so forth. The seven lines of Umbanda are as follows: (1) *the line of Iemanjá*, a female *Orixá* who represents the sea and rivers; this line is also called "the line of the water-people." She is spoken of as the Mermaid of the Sea (*a Sereia do Mar*), and her image on the altar may be one of the "advocacies" of the Virgin Mary; (2) *the line of Xangó*, a male *Orixá*, whose cult throve originally among blacks of Yoruba origin in the regions of Pernambuco, Alagoas, and Sergipe, representing thunder, tempests, and lightning, and the fire latent in stone—*Oxalá* is "the fire of heaven"—*Xangó* is ceramically represented by an image of the crusty Catholic saint Jerome; (3) *the line of Oxósse* or of *Caboclos-Oxósse* is often spoken of as a "guide" (*guia*) (a sort of guide-line perhaps) and represents indigenous or rural symbolic types, otherwise referred to as *Caboclos*, a term of Amerindian origin. The Brazilian writer Dilson Bento (in *Malungo: Decodificação da Umbanda*) speaks of this line in Eliadian terms as the "heirophany of ecology." It is the primordial *land*, as yet unravished by history. *Oxósse* is a conserver, related to vegetation and the healing properties of herbs. His own "phalanx" is known as *Jurema*. (4) *the line of Ogum*, a male *Orixá* representing war and portrayed by an image of the now "demoted" Catholic saint George. His physical manifestation is that of a strong man with a sword in his hand. He dances as if he were riding on horseback. (5) *the line of the Pretos-Velhos*, literally "old or ancient Blacks," individually these have names preceded by "Grand-Dad" or "Grandma" (*Vovós e Vovás*) or "uncle" or "aunt" (*tios e tias*). A person possessed by a *Preto-Velho* walks with a stooping gait and sometimes supported by a cane and speaks in a rambling fashion. These ex-slaves have been aged medicine men or aged warriors. Their ceramic images represent them as elderly blacks with white hair and country-style white clothes. Invariably they smoke pipes. In Central African curative cults ancestral spirits act as agents of affliction; when propitiated, they become a source of blessing. In Africa ancestral spirits are associated with particular families, lineages, and clans. But under New World conditions, these specific linkages were liquidated when slaves were separated from their kinfolk and fellow tribesmen, and what was left of the lineage ancestors was a "symbolic type," to use Don Handelman's terms, representing "ancestorhood." The *Pretos-Velhos* are generalized ancestors in Umbanda and, indeed, can possess whites as well as blacks; (6) *the line of the Child (Criança)*, the Child is an *Orixá* which stands for archetypal Childhood. Members of this line are also called "children of *Ibeji*," African twin deities associated with the Catholic saints Cosman and Damian, whose ceramic images represent them. As individual "entities" they take names in the diminutive, such as *Pedrinho* ("little Peter"), *Joãozinho* ("little John"), etc.; (7) *the line of Exu, Exu or Leba* is an entity who represents both good and evil. I had discussed *Eshu* in an article I wrote on "Myth and Symbol" for the *International Encyclopedia of the Social Sciences* some years ago. Little did I think then that I would meet *Exu* face to face one night and be told that I had him "on my shoulder!" And, later still, that I was a "*Son of Exu*," a dubious distinction, as we shall see! In Brazil, Catholic priests sometimes identify *Exu* with the Devil, while dismissing Umbanda itself as "devil-worship." His ceramic image certainly represents him as a man with goat's feet, pointed ears, sometimes clutching a trident, often clad in a red and black cape, and wearing a silk top-hat—a diabolic dandy in short! But he is also portrayed as a man with a bare chest. One just cannot pin *Exu* down! I speak of *Exu*, but *Exus* are usually thought of in the plural. Their "name is legion." When they enter the *terreiro*, they talk and gesticulate obscenely, utter piercing cries and strident peals of laughter. The symbolic type *Exu* is ambiguous, being at once good and evil, his manifestations and refractions may unexpectedly become dangerous and powerful. The relationship of men and women to the *Exus* is always a risky one for these tricksters can dupe their "children" (as the mediums of *Orixás* are called), telling them one thing but doing another. The *Exus* (as in West Africa)

are the lords of the crossroads and of the graveyard, where offerings are made
to them. One of the types of refractions of *Exu* is *Exu* of the Two Heads. His image was prominent among the images on the altar of the *terreiro* we visited. He
wears a red cape and carries a trident. One of his heads is that of Jesus, the
other of Satan. As a Catholic saint he is sometimes represented as Saint Peter,
in the double sense of Gate-keeper and denier of his Lord.

Each of the seven "lines" has its chief and his or her subordinate entities.
Each "line" is subdivided into seven "phalanxes," each with its own chief and
subordinates, the whole group being under the hegemony of the line chief. For
example, in the Line of *Iemanjá*, the water goddess, one phalanx is commanded
by *Iansã*, a female *Orixá* who dances balancing a cup or wineglass in her hand.
She wears a gilded crown ringed with pearls. Her Catholic form is the image of
Santa Barbara. Another phalanx in *Iemanjá's* "Line" is *Mamãe Oxum's*; *Mamma
Oxum* is a female *Orixá*, represented as a weeping woman, often as the Catholic
Mater Dolorosa.

Each "line" is associated with a locality (sea, forest, crossroads, and so forth),
a color, a day of the week, and stipulated kind of food. There is also the
category of "*Orixá cruzado*," "intersected *Orixá*," which defines an *Orixá* who
belongs to two lines at the same time. For example, a *Caboclo* may be "crossed"
with *Exu*; he may be half *Caboclo* and half *Exu*. This gives great flexibility to the
system.

Umbandistas also speak of "nations of Candomblé" among the invisible entities. These include *Queto, Jeje, Nagô* (or Yoruba), *Angola, Omoloco, Cambinda,*
and *Quiné*. Such names—there are supposed to be seven in all—refer to real or
imaginary regions of Africa from which the slaves came in the colonial period.

There is a hierarchy of human roles as well—or rather two hierarchies in each
terreiro. These are known as the *Hierarchia Espiritual* and *Hierarchia Material*
respectively. The spiritual hierarchy consists of either a *Pai* ("Father") or *Mãe*
("Mother") *de Santo* (literally "of Saint or *Orixá*"); a *Mãe-Pequena* (a "little
mother"), the second-in-command; a *Samba*, the helper of the *Mãe-Pequena*; the
Filhos or *Fihas de Santo*, the Sons or Daughters of Saint, who are also called
Médiums or *Médias*. A *Médium* is a person who "works in the saint": who enters
into trance and controls the idiom of possession. For there is nothing wild
about Umbanda trance, except perhaps its first moments when the entranced
one jerks and jack-knifes galvanically, though never actually falling on the
ground. Those who do occasionally fall on the ground are onlookers, and this
behavior marks them out as candidates for mediumship. They become
mediums by undergoing the initiatory ritual known as *Fazer Cabeça*, literally
"to make (perhaps 'inspire') head." Mediums are admired for the degree to
which they control their trances. Since the "entities" who "incorporate" with
them have many human traits, it is fitting that the mediums in trance act more
or less like normal human beings, although prominently displaying the distinctive behavorial features of the *Orixá* or *Guia* riding them. Some mediums "see"

Orixás (*Médiuns videntes*), others "hear" their commands (*Médiuns ouvintes*). Possession is at once a collective and an individual phenomenon, Velho writes (p. 95), for the "entities" "received" belong to a mythological system, yet each medium gives the entity s/he personifies an idiosyncratic elaboration. Each medium has a *Preto-Velho*, but the medium Mario has his own *Preto-Velho*, "Pai Benedito." There is therefore what Raymond Firth calls (writing of Tikopian mediumship) a "subtle blend of personal and social characteristics."

The Material Hierarchy organizes the internal affairs of the *terreiro* and deals with its finances. At the head is the President, but there may also be a Secretary, a Treasurer, and a Councillor of the *Socio(a)s*, those who contribute monthly dues for the general maintenance of the *terreiro*. Yvonne Velho's book contains case-histories of the conflict between officers of the Spiritual and Material Hierarchy in a single *terreiro*, the former rupturing ties with the mundane life outside, the latter injecting its criteria of prestige into the *terreiro's* organization of authority.

I mention all these classifications and organizational formats in order to give some idea of how a *terreiro* is *framed* both culturally and organizationally. Recently I published a paper whose title, "Frame, Flow, and Reflection" indicates some of the main factors that I think important in analyzing most kinds of performance, whether these belong to the worlds of ritual or of entertainment. By "frame" I refer to that often invisible boundary—though here visibly bounded by the *terreiro's* limits—around activity which defines participants, their roles, the "sense" or "meaning" ascribed to those things included within the boundary, and the elements within the environment of the activity, in this case the Umbandista "session," which are declared to be "outside" (*fora*) and irrelevant to it. I am indebted to such scholars as Gregory Bateson and Erving Goffman for this usage. The framing process continues throughout the whole time of the activity—indeed what Goffman calls "frame slippage" is an ever-present danger. The occasional, unsolicited intrusions of *Exu* probably manifest this danger. But in Umbanda, as we shall see, there is a culturally programmed ritual process, an invariant sequence of episodes which keeps the frame intact until the end of the session. The order in which the entities of the lines appear varies in different regions of Brazil, but in each *terreiro* the series is fixed. "Flow" is a term for which I am indebted to my former colleagues at the University of Chicago, John MacAloon and Mihaly Czikszentmihalyi (see Czikszentmihalyi, 1975). Flow for them is an interior state which can be described as the merging of action and awareness, the holistic sensation present when we act with total involvement, a state in which action follows action according to an internal logic, with no apparent need for conscious intervention on our part. Flow may be experienced, say these scholars, in play and sport, in artistic performance and religious ritual. Flow is made possible by a centering of attention on a limited stimulus field, by means of framing, bracketing, and usually a set of rules. In flow, there is a loss of ego, the "self" that normally acts as broker between ego and alter becomes irrelevant. One might argue that the grammar and lexicon constituted by the rules and symbols of Umbanda can generate "frames," within which "flow" might emerge. But flow dispenses with duality and contrariety, it is nondualistic, non-dialectical. And Umbanda sessions, like many ritual performances, are impregnated with problems, and problems always involve contradictions to be resolved. Mediums, especially the *Mãe de Santo*, are regarded as seers who can give spiritually guided advice about problems and contradictions in people's lives. The members of a *terreiro* are also members of an urban society, subject to the stresses and alienating influences of a rapidly industrializing nation. Part of the reason they come regularly to the *terreiro* with its dominating mother and father figures as leaders is to get some authoritative advice about how to live their lives, at all levels, marriage, family, neighborhood, work, surrounded by urban crime and often assaulted by police. The *terreiro* "session" is a liminal, space-time "pod" in which they can distance themselves from immersion in the status-role structures of the present by iden-tification with the gods, ancestors, and traditions of African roots organized in terms of "lines" that bring the gods of sea, rivers, waterfalls, forests, mountains, and other "natural" habitats into healing contact with the impurities of modern urban "culture." This figure/ground relationship between a "pure" Africanity and pure "nature" on the one hand, and an impure post-slavery world in cities dominated by powerful whites on the other, surely induces "reflexivity." Reflexivity must be an arrest of the flow process, a throwing of it back against itself; framing procedures make this possible. The rejected ego is suddenly remanifested. In reflexivity one is at once one's subject and direct object, not only in a cognitive way, but also existentially. Or one might say, ransacking the terminology of depth-psychology, that the deepest reflexivity is to confront one's conscious with one's unconscious self. Flow perhaps elicits or "seduces out" the unconscious levels of the self. Umbandist trance being perhaps a sort of "hyper-flow," but these unconscious manifestations are then scrutinized by the conscious self. Maybe not in "scientific" terms, in the case of Umbanda, for example. But certainly in terms of values preserved and elaborated in the innumerable performances of Umbanda that go on every night in the vast territory of Brazil, *terreiro* (or *terra* as the *Orixá* call their "places") by *terreiro*. A ritual performance is a flow/reflexivity dialectic. One can only "know" this in performance itself. For knowledge, as Dilthey divined, is based on "structures of experience" that are at once cognitive, affective and voli-tional—*all* of which contribute to the "form" of the actual performance itself. The protocols, scenarios, and scripts may be given sharp coherent "shape" by cognitive schemata. These guidelines would correspond, for example, to the transecting taxonomies of Umbanda. But into the final "form" must go the unique, once-only emotional experiences of the particular performance which are not only articulated by the formal grammar of Umbanda but which also suc-ceed in "blurring" and "melting" its ideal outlines. In other words the experience of the conjoined performers is a *primary* component in the specific performance. Similarly it is not only the *generic* teleology or goal-structure of Umbandist religion that is important, but the *specific* goals, the multiple entelechies of the mediums and spectators actually present, their problems, dilemmas, sufferings, successes, that must be taken into account if we are to characterize a performance, rather than spell out a cognitive paradigm. Ritual is multidimensional; any given performance is shaped by the experiences poured into it as much as by its conventional framing structures. Experiences make the structures "glow," the structures focus and channel the experiences.

Perhaps I can convey something of the atmosphere of the performance we attended in Novo Iguáçu by quoting some notes from Edie Turner's journal of March 10th, 1979, written just afterwards:

> Barn-like hall, mud-and-wattle construction, corrugated iron roof, mud floor. Three drums on stand at left end. Cozy atmosphere, drumming, singing, and dancing (casual step) in circle. *Mãe de Santo* introduced to us by Yvonne. Big, stout woman, with great presence and ease, in lacy white blouse and long wide skirt, old-fashioned, perhaps Bahian style, all white. Hair put up, tucked neatly in. Habitual expression of knowledge and authority—air of listening carefully to everything going on. When *Exu* takes her over she has deep, listening, pouting expression, closes eyes like Vic dancing to Brazilian music. Way of singing like Ndembu: a soloist leads, others reply in chorus. Melodies slightly more sophisticated than Ndembu, harmony missing, drums just the same. Mediums, just like Ndembu *ayimbuki* or "adepts," all in white blouses. An older lady came into the *terreiro*. She was related to *Mãe de Santo*, one of the two men and one woman with a small girl were her children. She became possessed by *Exu*—all sessions begin with *despacho*, literally "dismissal" or "putting out of the way," an offering made to the *Exus* to prevent them from troubling the rest of the ritual. But the *Exus* are also the "openers" of the rites, who mediate between the humans and the *Orixás*. She went into a crouching posture as if struck, then writhed backwards and forwards—she acted as if some entity were flinging her about. Later she rejoined the circle with open eyes. Another woman became possessed, staggered around, then was gathered into what was called a "net" of four women, two of them holding a wide cotton band between them, against which she fell. They took off her beads—in Umbanda "sons and daughters of a *Santo* or *Orixá*" wear a kind of collar of rosary-like beads of the colors appropriate to their "Guide's" *Linha*—and bound her bosom around tight with the cotton binder "to keep the *Orixá* in." Then, they said, she could dance well under the control of the *Orixá*. In this case, since the songs and dances were dedicated to the *Exus* it was appropriate

that the "rider" was a *Pomba-Gira*, the prostitute-cum-gypsy wife of an *Exu*. Indeed, the woman's beads and gypsy-like dress were signs that she was a "daughter of *Pomba-Gira*," *Pomba* literally means "a dove or pigeon," but here it seems to have some indecent overtone. Yvonne told us that this woman was the *Mãe de Santo's* younger sister and that her husband had recently been sentenced to six year's jail for homicide—he had been cheated out of his wages by the man he killed after a brawl. But the defense attorney was the woman's employer—she worked for him as an *empregada* or housemaid, and due to his personal interest in the case he had used his influence with the judge to procure a light sentence for the accused. Yvonne spoke of the strangely intimate relationship that often existed in Brazil, still in many ways what Max Weber would have called a "patrimonial" society. For example, many employers, knowing their servants "trabalha," "work" in Umbanda, in Candomblé, or in Santo, treat them well for fear of offending them and thus causing them to use injurious magic (known as *Quimbanda*) against them. An example of what Vic calls "the power of the weak"! Also if an employer wishes to be associated with a *Samba* School, one of those prestigious groups that organize Carnival, he or she has to be introduced to the black elders who run it by the domestic servant. Yvonne also admitted that the queenly *Mãe de Santo* of this *terreiro* was formerly her own maid. Their roles were now reversed, since Yvonne was regarded there as a kind of *Filha-de-Fé*, "daugher of faith," an apprentice medium. Yvonne, however, after years of studying *terreiros*, had never succeeded in going into trance, though she had "tried." Indeed, as Vic says, anthropologists tend to be voyeurs rather than exhibitionists!

Back to the session . . . The possessed woman, we learned, had the rank of *Mãe Pequena*. Her rather pretty daughter was there too, also dressed in *Pomba-Gira* style. A man in early middle age came in, dressed completely in white. He was reverently greeted by all the mediums, who went down on the ground before him. We learned that he had until recently been the *Pai de Santo* of another *terreiro* in the vicinity. The police had closed it down because there had been a murder "in the *terreiro*" recently. Novo Iguáçu is obviously a rough area, rather like much of Chicago. The *Pai de Santo* danced *Exu*-style, swaggering and lurching, and seemed to make some attempt to take over, but the resident *Mãe de Santo* soon asserted her dominance and he went off to sit on the bench to the left. I took his photo—he seemed camera-shy yet pleased in a way.

Yvonne said that he was a rather tragic figure. His wife had left him, he had no work other than his ritual activities which he could no longer practice. He had been drinking heavily and was said to be a homosexual. Soon *Mãe de Santo* became possessed by *Leba*—another name for *Exu*. She told people she had seen skeletons. This suggested the presence of *Exu Caveira*, chief of "the phalanx of the cemetery," whose image is represented by a skeleton or just by a skull (*caveira*). The *Mãe* had shoved the skeletons out of the door, she said. Later, she set up a little shrine, and sat on the platform before the altar in majesty. She took up a pipe, lit it, and blew smoke over the little shrine, took a bottle of cheap wine and drank some out of a cup. She seemed to be a cross between *Exu* and a *Preto-Velho*. The shrine, consisting of a candle and a container with water, seemed to make up some kind of divinatory apparatus. People came to consult her about their troubles and ailments. She gave "treatment" by "laying on of hands," though it was more a matter of touching and squeezing. She took a candle and passed it over the body of a sick person. Then she danced, possessed, holding the lit candle directly under her chin, with the wine bottle under her other arm. These and similar ordeals demonstrate the truth and depth of possession. She then made a round of visits to those sitting on the benches. First she embraced each person twice with an explosive roar. One woman with a modern hair-do, fashionable blouse and slacks embraced her violently, then staggered forward, twisted dizzily and fell flat on her face. This behavior is said to indicate that a person is ripe for initiation as a medium. She too was taken into protection by the four women and danced possessed, the four very kindly concerned over her. The whole atmosphere bears no comparison with a hospital's impersonal coldness. It might occur to one, why *should* a hospital be so cold, what's the idea? Kindness heals. In her role as an old wise Black doctor, *Mãe* drew Vic's arthritis down from his hip, took it out of his foot and threw it out of the door. She then gave Yvonne a herbal prescription for Vic. He was to wash with the herbs all over, but not on his head. These may be obtained in any of the Umbanda shops that one finds all over Rio, often next to fashionable boutiques in Copacabana, where one can buy every kind of ritual object, from candles to statues, as well as herbal medicines. When a medium is possessed by a spirit, people should greet that entity with an *abraço*, two hugs and kisses on each cheek. Yvonne, for all that she is a distinguished professor, looks so much less sophisticated and mature than her former maid, the *Mãe de Santo*—though the latter sometimes forgets her ritual role and calls Yvonne "Dona" or "Senhora." *Mãe* told Vic that he was a "son of *Ogum*" but also a "son of *Exu*" and a "son of *Xangô*." She said that he was "good, but not as good as he could be" offering to perform a purification ritual for him. Probably the initiation rite, *Fazer Cabeça*, which initiates into *médiunidade*, mediumship. Vic replied, "Perhaps next time I come to Brazil." She told me, "You are a daughter of *Iemanjá*, truly." It seems to be assumed that anyone who attends a session has mediumship potential.

After the *Exus* had gone, *Ogum*'s songs and drums took over. Then the *Caboclos* arrived, the Indians and the country types. It was remarkable to see the *Mãe Pequena*, who had recently been possessed by the wanton *Pomba-Gira* "with seven husbands," throw off her head scarf, comb her hair straight, stick a cigar between her teeth, don a cowboy hat, utter gruff cries, and strut about scowling like the most *macho* of *gauchos*. She was now possessed by a *Boiadero*, or cowboy "guide." This was the woman whose husband was doing time for murder. After the *Caboclos* had gone, the "Line" of the *Pretos-Velhos* took over. We could not stay after 4 A.M.—another busy day tomorrow—but were told that all seven "Lines" would appear before the session was over. The lines appear in a set "canonical" order, though *Exu* may break in at any stage unless firmly restrained.

Clearly, the *terreiro* is characterized by something akin to a "familial" atmosphere, containing as it does several family groups and members of the same neighborhood. In this way it partly acts to counter the impersonal world of urban work and state bureaucracy. However the lines of *Orixás* and Guides bring aspects of nature into the *Terreiro* (a name derived from *terra*=earth). Natural forces, sea deities, cowboys, hunter gods, forest Indians, are involved in the healing of urban afflictions. The Old Blacks represent the ethnic roots of most of the participants. Indeed, the television series *Roots* has some of the characteristics of Umbanda particularly the *Pretos-Velhos* aspect. Again, the mediums can play out, though within certain framed limits, fantasies of being other than their circumscribed lives in urban slums and factories allow them to be. The urban poor have only a restricted set of status-roles open to them. In Umbanda they can enjoy a multiplicity of roles, some of them rural and romantic, and be a multitude of "selves." *Carnaval* is, of course, another way of doing the same thing. In Portuguese, the term *fantasia* denotes a carnival disguise, and one is supposed to don one's most cherished "fantasy" openly. Both are in the subjunctive mood of culture, as are the "fictitious or pseudo-hierarchies" that emerge at their organizational level. My wife's account did not mention that the *Mãe de Santo* of the *terreiro* visited was, in Yvonne's words, a very "moralistic lady." Indeed, according to Yvonne, she gave the visiting *Pai de Santo* a "piece of her mind" rebuking him for his habitual drunkenness which the *Orixás* did not like. Actually, in her roles as a *Preta-Velha*, and as *Exu*, she had herself drunk some rum and wine, but had sobered up completely when she came out of trance. None of the other mediums were allowed to drink alcohol. Umbandistas consider themselves to be disciplined and "pure," as against the unruliness of urban society in general. Their devotion to their "riders" imposes on them restrictions: interdictions on eating certain foods, abstinence from sexual activities on certain days and at certain seasons, and so forth—by no means does the Umbanda display the farrago of deviltry ascribed to the cult by some Christian priests and ministers. In their view, the whiteness of their garb proclaims their purity. *Exu*, though, is not pure or simple, as his dual colors, black and red, proclaim. He is the lord of the *limen* and of *chaos*; the full ambiguity of the subjunctive mood of culture, representing the fundamental indeterminacy that lurks in the cracks and crevices of all our sociocultural "constructions of reality," the one who must be kept at bay if the framed order of the ritual proceedings is to be maintained. He is the abyss of possibility; hence his *two* heads, Jesus and Satan, for his potential as both Savior and Tempter. He is also Destroyer, for he is in one aspect, Lord of the Cemetery. He reminds me too, having just come from India, of some aspects of Shiva in Hindu myth and ritual, even, to the detail that both wield a trident.

In her book Velho presents her Umbanda data as a sequence of episodes, leading from the formation of a new *terreiro*, or cult-center, to its schism. She gives biographical data on four participants for whom the *terreiro* congregation was clearly a "star group." She reveals how a "plot" is inherent in the fissioning process; not a plot retrospectively imposed by story-tellers but one embodied as surely in the conduct of the Umbandistas as the deities and other entities they "receive." Her book's title, *War of Orixás*, gives a clue to the cultural plot, the concept of "*Demanda*" elaborates that clue. *Demanda* means, literally, "a contest, dispute, combat." In Umbanda it refers to the invocation by someone, usually out of malice, of certain of his/her *Orixás* and their dependent entities, in order to send them into battle against the *Orixás*, guides or entities or another cult-member. There ensues a "war of the *Orixás*," the aim of which is to capture one or more of the guides of the victim, who tries in his/her turn to reinforce magically the powers of his own *Orixás* and their "phalanxes." *Demanda* is a concept often employed to account for misfortunes collective or individual which befall members of a *terreiro* ridden by conflict over its leadership.

The formal processual structure of the episodic sequence in Yvonne Velho's book could be represented as: 1). *Demanda* between the priestess of the new *terreiro* and her former leader, the priestess of her previous *terreiro*; 2). *Demanda* between the new priestess and her mediums; 3). *Demanda* between the new priestess and her successor, the new priest (*Pai-de-Santo*) brought in when she was committed to the hospital; 4). *Demanda* between the new priest and the new *Presidente*, leaders respectively of the Spiritual, and Material Hierarchies of the new *terreiro*. Yvonne Velho points out that the inception of a new *terreiro* itself can be viewed as an attempt to redress a crisis in an established *terreiro* by schism in which a number of dissident members split off and found their own unit. In a sense it is a split between spiritual genealogical generations, for the priest/priestess founder of the new *terreiro* was formerly a "child" (*filho/filha*) of the *Pai/Mãe-de-Santo*, "Father/Mother-in-holiness" of the old *terreiro*. It is argued that the schism is the result of a *Demanda* begun by the original priest/priestess. The new leader, it is alleged, is forced to flee, along with his/her basic clientele, in order to avoid the madness which goes with having one's "guide" captured by the Priest/Priestess of record. In terms of the Social Drama model, the breach had occurred during the life of the old *terreiro*. The *crisis* phase and the attempted redressive phase took place in the earlier *terreiro*. But the new *terreiro*—and, according to Velho, every *terreiro*—is generated out of a conflict situation. Contradictory norms are involved: on the one hand, there is the rule that a medium must obey his/her *Pai/Mãe-de-Santo* implicitly. On the other hand, there is the belief that such a priest or priestess can obtain power over an initiand or neophyte in the initiation ritual known as *fazer cabeça*, can, it is said, get to "know their strengths and weaknesses," and thus control their thoughts, words, and deeds. Some priests may act unethically and use supernatural powers against their "children" in Umbanda. Yvonne Velho sees the fissive or schismatic process as continuous: *terreiros*, which are usually small groups, continually split, some members constituting the core of a new group, others going as individuals to already established groups. She does not take the traditional view of many Brazilian ethnographers that such groups represent havens of *Gemeinschaft*, communitarian spirit, in the midst of the *anomie*, alienation, and atomization of modern urban, industrial life. Rather does she regard Umbanda culture and social conflict as constituting what Geertz, no doubt, would call a "metasocial commentary" on Brazilian urban life, as a school for understanding its competitiveness, mobility, divisions of labor, class antagonisms, and the transience of its loves and friendships. Umbanda, part of the subjunctive domain of Brazilian culture—an extensive domain, as in many cultures of the politically circumscribed, may be seen as a complex rehearsal system for the problems of "real," "indicative" social life in the work and domestic situations. But since subjunctivity—including such institutionalized modes as carnival, soccer, and the electronic media, plays a major role in Brazilian culture, due to political oppression, its performative genres acquire, paradoxically, an indicative character. It is in such modes as Umbanda, the Samba School system, Soccer, Kardecism, and so on that individuals of the poorer classes can acquire a measure of prestige, fame, and even some secular power. Hence, there is a certain edge in the competitions for positions of authority or other prizes, in such groups. In a hypertrophied "play" world, play becomes, to an extent, "indicativized," "for real." Conflict for Umbanda office is, as our psychologistic jargon has it, "overdetermined." Yet it retains a certain ludic character, and is liminal between the indicative and subjunctive modes of being human, for real socioeconomic distinctions and conflicts are brought into the (god-dominated) "sessions," minimally as the solicitation of advice about how to act in the everyday world and, more importantly, as the implicit assertion of external status and connections in struggles for power in the Umbanda arena.

But this formal presentation fails to convey the cultural richness of Umbanda, indeed, that which frames and formulates its appropriate behavior and seeks to define deviant behavior. I shall, therefore, present several of the episodes Yvonne Velho has recorded in her book, with some amplifying commentary.

How did the whole affair, the sequence she describes and analyzes, begin? Let me try to convey it mostly in her own words, literally translated from the Portuguese:

Sunday, 25th June 1972

Today the *terreiro* was inaugurated. The house was full of spectators. The *Mãe-de-Santo*, Maria Aparecida, a huge black lady, presided over the "works" (the ritual actions), cigar in mouth, and with enormous eyes. She commanded ritual songs to be sung, and "received" various *Orixás*. The Inauguration Ritual had the same sequence of events as the (regular) Sunday sessions, but omitted the Consultation phase (when people consult the "incorporated" guides). That Sunday was the first time I met the group, and the first occasion that I decided to observe the social life of a new *terreiro*. My first impressions were confused and ambiguous. Sometimes I thought I was in a theatre; the events resembled a dramatic spectacle, cathartic, aggressive too, for the possessed mediums cursed and swore at one another. Yet I also felt that it was not men and women who were there but gods on earth, so distinctive were the bodily gestures of the actors. My confusion increased when I saw a student of mine, a budding sociologist, named Mario, "fall in the saint," i.e., enter into a trance state. It was a disorderly trance and the mediums immediately came to his aid. Had this ever happened to him before? I have to confess that I was frightened, yet this very event provoked me to continue with the research. Would I perhaps enter trance and be the gods' horse?

The *Mãe-de-Santo*, Maria Aparecida, I soon learned, was responsible for the *terreiro*. She named it after one of her guides, *Caboclo Serra Negra*. The *Exu* image in the corner near the entrance to the *terreiro* yard was also her own *Exu*—the *Exu Mangueira* (lit. Mango Tree). It was her clientele that composed the original group of mediums in this *terreiro*. According to the group, she was "excellent, knew the 'law' very well," and was very good in "saintcraft," i.e., she knew the rituals well, how to dance, see the future and understand the past of the consultants, and could cure their ailments, etc. She had considerable authority over the members, partly because her link with them was of long standing, had helped all the mediums in the group in the course of consultations on their problems.

Friday, June 30th

(The following episode was not directly observed by Velho but reported to her by group members.)

The *Mãe-de-Santo* appointed this Friday for a "work of the cemetery." This is an "obligation" or, in other words, a ritual in which offerings are made to the *Orixás* of food and drink consecrated to each divinity at the places where they are regnant (for instance, the seashore for *Iemanjá*, waterfalls for *Mamãe Oxum*, the woods for *Oxósse*, and so on). The cemetery is the place of the "cemetery people" whose chief is *Obaluae*, an *Orixá* associated with the Catholic saint Lazarus. When they reached the cemetery they found another *terreiro*, whose members were unknown to them, making an obligation there. Both *terreiros* tried to place their offerings at the same site, and a struggle began between them. All the mediums were "incorporated," that is, possessed, and the *Mãe Pequena* ("little mother," or *Mãe-de-Santo*'s lieutenant), Marina by name, incorporated with her *Exu*, began the struggle with a medium from the other *terreiro*. This medium accused Marina of doublecrossing her own *Mãe-de-Santo*. He accused her of being in a state of *Demanda* with her so that she would quit the *terreiro*. Soon the group left the cemetery and headed for the *terreiro*. When they arrived, the *Mãe-de-Santo*, Aparecida, seized Marina by the arms and threw her out of the house. She then grasped hold of another medium and began to kick her, then drove out almost all the mediums, leaving only the President and two or three other mediums in the *terreiro*.

Monday, July 3, 1972

The *Mãe-de-Santo* summoned the mediums to meet in the *terreiro*. When they arrived they found money scattered everywhere, in the house of *Exu*, in the room of the *gongá* (the altar room), and the main room for Umbanda sessions, together with the insignia of many *Orixás*. The *Mãe-de-Santo* asserted that the coins and insignia were part of a "work" that Marina was making against her. Since this was a day for consultation, the mediums began to clean up the *terreiro*. This was the day that the process began which the group defined as the "madness" (*loucura*) of the *Mãe-de-Santo*. She started to say "strange things"; for example, "Ah, the dead one, he went away already." The mediums became terrified and several left. When the *Mãe-de-Santo* left the *terreiro*, one of the mediums decided to accompany her. When she reached the street, however, Aparecida sent her away and went on alone. From afar the mediums saw her cross the road apparently oblivious of the traffic. They said, "She's crazy, completely nuts!"

Aparecida then went to Marina's house and proceeded to smash up everything she could find inside it. Then she entered her *madrinha's* house and started to beat her up, hurling her to the ground. [*Madrinha* literally means "godmother," but in Umbanda stands for a female ritual sponsor in the initiation rites, known as *fazer cabeça*, "making a head."] After some time the mediums who remained in the *terreiro* saw her come in, accompanied by her *madrinha's* daughter. She was "completely beside herself," they said. They made her lie on the floor and gave her sedatives, but nothing was of any use. Mario, the president, decided to remove her to his own home. He told me [that is, Velho] that she spent three sleepless nights there. He could not calm her down, and finally called in a doctor, who, after examining her, recommended her committal to an institution. Mario took her to the Pinel Hospital, whence she was quickly transferred to the Psychiatric Hospital of Engenho de Dentro. The *terreiro* then remained closed for some time.

[So far we have had a bare chronicle of events as reconstructed by Velho from eye-witnesses' accounts. Narrative structuring soon begins when the mediums try to make sense of what happened in terms of Umbanda concepts. Velho relied particularly on the accounts of Marina, Sonia, and Mario, the President—who, incidentally, was lessee of the property on which the *terreiro* stood. These informants agreed that] from the Friday until the Monday, the *Mãe-de-Santo* had performed some acts which the whole group classified as part of her "madness." They were "very dangerous acts" for the mediums, and, in their view, could have brought about their death or made them mad. She had made "works" against Marina, and succeeded in "capturing her Guides," since she (Aparecida) "threw seven *Exus* on Marina's head." These *Exus* were the only "entities" Marina was able to "receive." She told me that she went "nearly crazy." She saw enormous beasts before her eyes, and could not get to sleep. Sonia, the second *Mãe-Pequena*, told Velho that Aparecida had put her head down below the altar, seeking in this way to deprive her of her Guides. Sonia only obeyed her because she did not know of the danger involved, since she was only "new in sainthood." It was only later that she was told that such an act could have made her mad.

There was, then, at this period a "war of *Exus*" in the *terreiro*. One night, the President woke up to find himself in the house of *Exu*. He had broken all the images there. "I was asleep," he said, "and when I awoke I had broken up all the images; I was in *Exu's* house, with my clothes all torn."

At first, the group interpreted what had been going on as a direct consequence of the *Demanda* made in the *Terreiro da Rua do Bispo*, from which Aparecida, Mario, and a number of other mediums had just split off. But after the *Mãe-de-Santo* had begun to say those "strange things" and to beat people up, the mediums agreed that many of these events were the result of her "madness" or "illness."

Now why had she become "crazy?" Various causes were advanced. She might have been exhausted by the "works" involved in opening up the new *terreiro*. Such works draw on the psychical force of a medium. Everyone in the group was surprised to hear from Aparecida's "*madrinha*" that she had twice previously been interned in psychiatric hospitals. At that time she had had another *terreiro*, which had been closed down for the same reason. The doctor told them that her madness was caused by "traumas" which she had experienced in infancy. But the group asked the question – familiar to anthropologists who have studied witchcraft beliefs cross-culturally – "why had she become crazy just at that precise moment and no other?"

One answer – also familiar to anthropologists from their informants' accounts and conduct – was that she had committed "errors" in her ritual handling of the *terreiro's* opening. But it was also argued that she had made those mistakes because she was already "mad" from some other cause. Whatever may have been the case, her initial errors were the immediate cause of the untoward events that had occurred in the *terreiro*. Her first error had been "to work with *Exu*," the Lord of Ambiguity, during the inauguration rites. This should have been done seven days afterwards, though some said seven months should first elapse. There is great danger in "working with the *Exus*" thus prematurely. For it is an inducement to a category of *Exus* known as "*Quiumbas*," or "*Exus* without Light" to intervene, and these "do not want to cause love and usually cause disorder (chaos)." Some informants told me (Dr. Velho) that it was these *Exus* who were responsible for Aparecida's madness, and hence for the whole crisis in the *terreiro*. Later there would be what they were to call "war between brother and brother, and *Pai-de-Santo* and his 'children,'" all attributable to the "*Exus* without Light." However, other "errors" were added. Aparecida was said not to have had "the agreement of the appropriate *terreiro*," in other words she had broken with the *Terreiro da Rua Bispo* without the permission of that group. Furthermore, she had not "baptized the *atabaque* drums." She had, they alleged, failed to perform an important ceremony which marks the passage of the *atabaques* – percussion instruments used in all rituals – from simple musical instruments to sacred instruments. In this ceremony the *atabaques* are washed with water mixed with special herbs. All these mistakes, it was said, came about because "she did not have the guidance of her *Mãe-de-Santo*." One medium said: "No *Filha-de-Santo* (Daughter-in-sainthood) can open a *terra* ("land") without the guidance (*orientação*) of his/her *Mãe-de-Santo*." It was that "absence of firm guidance" which had brought her to madness and caused the crisis in the *terreiro*. She did not have that guidance because she had a "War of *Orixás*" with her *Mãe-de-Santo*. The President was inclined to stress the ritual errors as the cause of the crisis and underemphasized the *Demanda*. But the whole group agreed that an important factor was the *Demanda* that Aparecida had with her own *Mãe-de-Santo*.

Because she was "mad," a "crazy crackpot," Aparecida was unable to take responsibility for the *terreiro*, since, according to the group, it involved "too much work," "work of great responsibility." However, if she so desired she could visit the *terreiro* and attend its sessions, but not in the capacity of its *Mãe-de-Santo*.

The President, Mario, resolved to reopen the *terreiro* after the *Mãe-de-Santo* was hospitalized. He explained to me that the *terreiro* could not be closed, because, according to a rule of the Congregação Espirita Umbandista—of national scope—the organization to which most *terreiros* are affiliated, a *terreiro* may not be closed until it has functioned for a full year. "It may change its site, but may never be closed." And so, some fifteen days after the Inauguration, the *terreiro* was opened again, with, this time, a new *Pai-de-Santo* (Velho, 1975:1-99 passim).

The story goes on . . . the new *Pai-de-Santo* acquires influence over the mediums by insisting that he can defend the *terreiro* against the continuing *Demanda* instigated by Aparecida. Eventually, he conflicts with Mario, the President, and there is a new crisis, a new state of *Demanda* between the two men and their *Orixás* and Guides. There was a physical schism of the group, the *Pai-de-Santo* and his followers being expelled by the President Mario from the *terreiro*. In another paper I discuss this material in terms of the interpenetration of personal and group crises, the group's own cultural metalanguage of interpretation, and the Western observer's attempts to encompass these events and indigenous hermeneutics within his own "culture of science," *our* own "rational and collective effort to systematize a world of unique situations, incidents, and phenomena" (Roy Wagner, 1979:20). In this essay I think that we have enough data to reconsider my original argument about the relationship between social dramas and cultural performances. One problem is: where to locate the beginning of the social drama in Velho's chronicle. For one might argue that the very foundation of the new *terreiro* (*Tenda Espiritu Caboclo Serra Negra*) represented a *breach* of crucial relations in its parent *terreiro* (*Da Rua Bispo*). Or it could be regarded as a social drama's second phase, *crisis*, following the breach between the *Mãe-de-Santo* and her (then) "daughter," Aparecida. As Velho writes (p. 87): ". . . whenever a new *terreiro* is created, there always exists the danger of *Demanda*, whether from neighboring *terreiros*, from *terreiros* of origin, or from mediums who have newly joined it . . . according to their own exegesis the members of the *terreiro* studied had foreseen a crisis after the inauguration. But that crisis could have been obviated or had a different type of development from the actual course of events." Again, the decision to make a new *terreiro* might be seen as the fourth phase of a social drama, *social recognition of irreparable breach*—were it not for the fact that Aparecida founded the new group without the blessing of her own *Mãe-de-Santo*, thus denying the group legitimacy in terms of the ethics of Umbanda.

What the establishment of the new *terreiro* clearly was *not* was an exemplification of the third phase of a social drama, *redress*. Rather was it a response to the failure of redressive machinery. This very failure, however, sheds light on the sociocultural dynamics of urban life in an industrial economy. In a rural African village, a high value is usually attached to the unity and continuity of the residential group, the village, which is the principal arena of social dramas. Since villages are dominantly bonded by kinship and the ascribed statuses kinship and affinity generate, the redressive institutions, legal and ritual, which aim at perpetuating their structures, are powerful and comprehensive. But *terreiros* are essentially matrices of voluntary association, where mobile transients of urban modernity come together because they have chosen to share certain beliefs and agree to perform certain rituals in common. But no one is obliged to remain in a *terreiro* by any theory that to be kinsfolk means to share common substance (D. Schneider), to be primordially bonded, though it is true that most *terreiros* contain small clusters of mediums who are also kin. The rhetoric of Umbanda also abounds in kin or quasi-kin terms: "father," "mother," "son," "daughter," "godfather," "godmother," while Guides can be "grandparents." But this rhetoric is part of the "framing" of what I called a "subjunctive" cultural mood. It is an "as-if" world that emerges in the long, nocturnal sessions of Umbanda, a world in which "one man (or woman) plays many parts," and ever lets his/her fancy/fantasy roam. In this world kinship is equally subjunctive, and is "played with." If an Umbanda session has a redressive function this is directed to crises in individual lives rather than to the ongoing life of the group to which the members belong. Thus redress has a multiple referent to individuals voluntarily assembling; breach, crisis, and unitive or schismatic outcome a single referent—the relatively transient group envelope wherein they assemble. The ethical and ontological units involved in urban Umbanda are primarily individuals, not collectivities, as in rural communities of the "tribal" or "feudal" types.

You would, then, be entitled to argue that I have turned a chronicle into a narrative by imposing on the former, as Procrustes imposed his torturous bed, a supposedly general processual logic inappropriate to the nature of *terreiro* formation, deformation, and schism. But I would be entitled, I think, to reply that Velho's data do not rebut my formulation, rather they compel its amplification in terms of a laminated and ever-shifting modern industrial context. For example, I think that Velho today would not seal her sample at the level of a single *terreiro*. Rather would she see the relevant social process as passing through a temporal succession of opening and closing *terreiros* whose sociospatial context would include an inner ring of territorially contiguous *terreiros*, with outer rings of socioeconomic fields in which *terreiro* members, indeed all Umbandistas, held multiple memberships; memberships, however, which often gave them little psychological satisfaction. For the majority of Umbandistas fall within the middle and lower strata of industrial society, in need of rich subjunctive compensation for the limited scope of their indicative lives. Umbanda, with its mythical Africanity and Amerindian root images, presents a world of culturally defined "primordial nature" (lorded over by gods of the sea, forests, rivers, and mountains) to offset the "tentacled cities" that have become a stultifying "second nature" to the workers and petty bourgeois from whose ranks mediums are drawn.

Umbanda sessions, as we have seen, have their own deviousness, their own "*courbes, Méandre*," to invoke Paul Valéry as *Guia!* Nevertheless, there is a sense in which being "incorporated" with a supernatural, "invisible" potency enables one to be boldly frank, to say with full legitimacy what one means to a superior or even an equal, at least in the subjunctive domain of a *sessão*. Social stratification, in that curious combination of post-feudal and industrial capitalist social fields that constitutes modern Brazil, sets distances between classes and individuals that make for hypocrisy, mendacity, and other kinds of deviousness in interpersonal relations both in private and public life. But when one is incorporated with or even "irradiated by" (to use an Umbanda idiom for incomplete possession) a god, in a situation where all share a belief in the lively possibility of such possession occurring, then one can say what one likes with full confidence. In other circumstances, "props" or "media" such as masks, ventriloquial puppets, automatic writing, might be used. In Umbanda—and related forms such as Candomblé and Batuque—the physical being of the medium is itself the mask or glove—at least the "horse"—of a prescient, potent entity, who can see into the secrets of the human heart and disclose what is hidden in the past, clouded in the present, and barely discernible in the future.

Velho, since her theme is conflict for prestige and office within a single *terreiro*—but hypothecating that similar conflicts, hinged on the *Demanda* theme account for the fact that in Rio *terreiros* are opened and closed in large numbers—deliberately excludes considering the integrative function of Umbandist rituals. In her book there are many scattered references to "consultations," in which a prestigious medium, usually a *Pai-de-Santo* or *Mãe-de-Santo*, incorporated with a Guide, gives advice to a succession of individual clients on their personal problems and predicaments. One might argue that in terms of the sociocultural dynamics of Brazilian society at large, Umbandist sessions, together with other genres and subgenres of cultural performance, like Kardecist services, Candomblé sessions, Samba School rehearsals, Catholic and Protestant liturgies and church-related activities, have a redressive function with regard to the biographical processes of individuals. Hence, formally, at the level of macro-cultural action, the whole Umbanda complex is a standardized mode of redress for interpersonal and intrapersonal conflicts. But viewed as a "star group" its sessions have become arenas of parapolitical struggle. Since each *terreiro* is conceived as the sacred arena wherein are performed innumerable sessions of redressive action oriented to heterogeneous individuals who bring in problems from their disparate secular experiences, it is not seen primarily as a collective redressive instrument for mending its own corporate fissions. It cannot, so to speak, lift itself by its own bootstraps. Of course, there are many examples in the literature, of *terreiros* that have persisted for many years. In the Candomblé cults of Bahia, for example, Edison Carneiro mentions *terreiros* which have endured for more than a century, even though they hive off new *terreiros* of dissidents fairly frequently (*Journal of American Folklore*, Vol. LIII, pp. 272-273, 1960). Here a core membership persists. The many Kardecist (Spiritist) temples in Rio which draw large congregations also resist major fission. I suspect that it is the greater Africanity of the Candomblé membership contextualized in more stable neighborhood relationships, on the one hand, and, on the other, the greater "bureaucratization" of Kardecism—approaching that of universalistic religions such as Christianity, which account for the temporal persistence and durability of their local units. Rio Umbandistas, by and large, are drawn from a floating, atomized urban population, many of whom are immigrants from rural areas and other Brazilian cities. What they seek is "incorporation" with a source of life and power—as individuals, not as a corporate group, as in the case of the African village. Only by melding with a god or guide can they achieve identity, wholeness. Indeed, Velho's informants say (p. 50) that "the moment a medium loses contact with one of his guides, or several of them, he loses his identity as a human being, as a person." This, in fact, is the great danger that threatens the human target of a *Demanda*. An Umbandista is incomplete without his "guide," his divine rider. He can go crazy, like Aparecida or Marina, the *Mãe Pequena*, who, in addition to having "seven *Exus* in her head," temporarily lost her own *Preto Velho*, through capture in a "War of the *Orixás*." When he returned to her in a dream, she knew she was safe and sane again. "Finally I met myself." It becomes part of the "self" for a medium that s/he is able to "incorporate" with a number of "Guides" and play their roles in sessions. All these "possibilities of being," as Rilke wrote in his poem on the Unicorn, become manifest in the subjunctive world of the Umbandista session, and their manifestation in this permissive milieu becomes the essential stuff of self. Deprived of it, the medium goes mad or loses a central motive for living. In Umbanda the principles of continuity, stability, unity seem to be lodged in the cosmology of the belief system, in the symbolic types manifested as the *Orixás* and other entities, rather than in the social dimension. From this perspective, the specific *terreiro* is reduced in importance. Its sessions are conceived as providing occasions for the incorporation of individuals with gods and guides, who may then converse with one another. They are not seen as occasions for simple, mundane human interaction, or even as occasions for celebrating the power and glory of a transcendental deity. In Umbanda the gods come down and when they do so, they give identity and significance to the human "horses" they ride. When incorporated, the human steeds, like Balaam's ass, speak ultimate truths and prophesy. The downtrodden and oppressed are ennobled by the greater "Self" that inhabits them, and whose loss is indeed "Self"-loss.

Yet since each *terreiro* provides the Umbandistas with a stage for manifesting the normally constrained selves of their wish-world, the group of mediums is, at least temporarily, a "star-group." Thus there are many crises and schisms in the *terreiros*, for each would have it the perfect stage for his/her performances. Each "demands" of his god that the gods and guides of the others shall not prevail.

All the *Orixás* and *Guides*, and the ways they possess and enter into relations with the living, day by day, week by week, season by season, in the immensely popular Afro-Brazilian cults, represent ways of portraying, talking about (that is, using a metalanguage), and coming to an understanding of life in a rapidly changing, urbanizing, industrializing, ethnically, culturally and religiously "plural" society, where feudal and patrimonial institutions and attitudes are being increasingly penetrated by bureaucratic, capitalistic, and socialistic processes, models, and ideologies. Yet the "session" or "gira" of any *terreiro* is clearly a "ritual" as I have earlier defined it, not a "ceremony," or a "secular ritual," or "formal" or "conventional" patterned behavior. It is a transformative performance, "a symphony in more than music," operating through a multiplicity of expressive genres and symbols in the full range of sensory codes, with the goal of relating chaos and cosmos, byss and abyss, flow and reflexivity, to one another in the heightened and deepened consciousness of participants. And its not unworthy purpose is to impart a life-saving meaning to the welter of events in the world outside the humble *terreiro* where the Gods of Africa and the Saints of Portugal still care for their exiled children.

References

Bastide, Roger. 1971. *African Civilizations in the New World*. London: Hurst.

Czikszentmihalyi, Mihaly. 1974. *Beyond Boredom and Anxiety*. San Francisco: Jossey-Bass.

Da Matta, Roberto. 1973. *Ensaios de Anthropologia Estructural*, Petropolis: Editora Vozes.

Firth, Raymond. 1974. "Society and its Symbols," Review of Victor Turner, *Dramas, Fields, and Metaphors. Times Literary Supplement*, no. 3784, September 13.

McGrew, Julia H. 1974. Introduction to vol. 2, *The Sturlunga Saga*, tr. Julia H. McGrew and R. George Thomas, New York: Twayne.

Myerhoff, Barbara. 1978. *Number Our Days*, New York: Dutton.

————1980. "Life History among the Elderly: Performance, Visibility, and Remembering," in Kurt Beck, ed., *Studies of the Human Life Course*, American Association for the Advancement of Science.

Siegel, A. E. and Seigel, S. 1957. "Reference Groups, Membership Groups, and Attitude Change," *Journal of Abnormal and Social Psychology*, vol. 55.

Siegel, Bernard J., and Alan R. Beals. 1960. "Conflict and Factional Dispute." *Journal of the Royal Anthropological Institute*, 90. Pp. 107-17.

Summer, W. G. 1906. *Folkways*, Boston: Ginn.

Schwartz, Theodore. 1978. "Where is the Culture? Personality as the Distributive Locus of Culture," in George Spindler, ed., *The Making of Psychological Anthropology*, Berkeley: University of California Press.

Turner, Victor. 1957. *Schism and Continuity in an African Society: A Study of Ndembu Village Life*, Manchester: Manchester University Press.

Velho, Yvonne Maggie Alves. 1975. *Guerra de Orixa: Um Estudo de Ritual e Conflito*, "War of Gods: A Study of Ritual and Conflict," Rio de Janeiro: Zahar Editores.

Wagner, Roy. 1979. *Lethal Speech*, Ithaca: Cornell University Press.

The Anthropology of Performance

For years, I have dreamed of a liberated anthropology. By "liberated" I mean free from certain prejudices that have become distinctive features of the literary genre known as "anthropological works," whether these are field monographs, comparative studies, or textbooks. Such features have included: a systematic dehumanizing of the human subjects of study, regarding them as the bearers of an impersonal "culture," or wax to be imprinted with "cultural patterns," or as determined by social, cultural or social psychological "forces," "variables," or "pressures" of various kinds, the primacy of which is still contested by different schools or coteries of anthropologists. Briefly, the genre apes natural scientific treatises in style and intention—treatises which reflect the thinking of that period of five centuries which in the West is known as the "modern era." The modern is now becoming part of the past. Arnold Toynbee coined the term "postmodern," Ihab Hassan has given it wide prominence, and *Performance in Postmodern Culture*, edited by the late Michel Benamou and Charles Caramello, attempts to give it greater specificity. I don't like these labels, but it is clear to me that there has been what Richard Palmer, in an article in the Benamou volume, called a "postmodern turn" taken in recent thinking which is having a liberating effect on anthropology, as on many other disciplines. Premodern, modern, postmodern—these are crude and inelegant terms for the naming of cultural eras of disparate duration. But they may give us a preliminary purchase on the data on performance.

"Premodern" represents a distillation or encapsulation of many world-views and cosmologies before and, later, outside the specific emergence in Western consciousness, about five centuries ago, of the modern perspective. Indeed, the Swiss cultural historian Jean Gebser holds that it was, quite literally, the rise of perspective which, as Palmer writes, is "the key to modernity." He summarizes Gebser's argument as follows: "Perspective spatializes the world; it orients the eye in relation to space in a new way . . . it represents a rationalization of sight (William M. Ivins) . . . . Perspective leads to the founding of mathematical geometry, which is the prerequisite for modern engineering and modern machinery . . . for steadily increasing naturalism in European pictorial representation (but also for its purely schematic and logical extensions) . . . both are due to the growth and spread of methods which have provided symbols, repeatable in invariant form, for representation of visual awareness, and a grammar of perspective which made it possible to establish logical relations not only within the system of symbols but between that system and the forms and locations of the objects that it symbolizes . . . the combination of the abstractedness of numbers as symbols that measure, with perspective, a way of relating those numbers as symbols to the visual world, leads to a sense of space as measured, as extending outward from a given point; ultimately the world is measurable—epitomized in Galileo's maxim, 'to measure everything measurable and to make what is not measurable capable of being measured' [this attitude is still common among anthropologists—thus George Spindler remarks in the book he edited, *The Making of Psychological Anthropology*, 1978: 197-198, "if it happens you can count it"]. The spatialization of vision has metaphysical and epistemological implications . . . the overemphasis on space and extension divides the world into observing subject and alien material objects . . . words are seen as mere signs for the material objects in the world . . . time itself is perceived in spatialized terms . . . it is regarded as measurable, as a linear succession of present moments . . . the perspectival model makes man the measure and measurer of all things . . . technologized rationality harmonizes with the protestant ethic—God places his blessing on the individualistic, competitive person (implicitly male) who exercises restraint and represses desires in the interest of more 'rational' goals: power and control . . . History, perceived as a straight line that never circles back on itself, becomes the story of man's gradual self-improvement through the exercise of reason" (pp. 22-25).

This, at any rate, was the "modern" climate of thought in which my anthropological training took place. It was a climate in which academic disciplines had clearly defined boundaries which one transgressed at one's peril—boundary ambiguity was, in Mary Douglas's words, a form of pollution, much interdisciplinary work was regarded as an abomination. Within anthropology there was a tendency to represent social reality as stable and immutable, a harmonious configuration governed by mutually compatible and logically interrelated principles. There was a general preoccupation with consistency and congruence. And even though most anthropologists were aware that there generally are differences between ideal norms and real behavior, most of their models of society and culture tended to be based upon ideology rather than upon social reality, or to take into account the dialectical relationship between these. All this follows from the perception of reality in spatialized terms. So, too, did the study of statistical correlations between social and cultural variables such as we find in G. P. Murdock's *Social Structure*. In all this work, as Sally F. Moore has pointed out in her book *Law as Process* (p. 36): "Whether ideology is seen as an expression of social cohesion, or as a symbolic expression of structure, whether it is seen as a design for a new structure or as a rationalization for control of power and property, the analysis is made in terms of *fit*" (my italics).

During my field work I became disillusioned with the fashionable stress on fit and congruence, shared by both functionalism and different types of structuralism. I came to see a social system or "field" rather as a set of loosely integrated processes, with some patterned aspects, some persistences of form, but controlled by discrepant principles of action expressed in rules of custom that are often situationally incompatible with one another. This view derived from the method of description and analysis which I came to call "social drama analysis." In fact this was thrust upon me by my experience as a field worker in a central African society, the Ndembu of Northwest Zambia. In various writings I have given examples of social dramas and their analysis. More to the point, since we will be dealing with the anthropology of performance, I would like to bring to your attention a man of the theatre's discussion of my schema. He is Richard Schechner, Professor of Performance Studies at New York University's Tisch School of the Arts, and former Director of The Performance Group, an avant-garde theater company. As he sees it (in the Group, an avant-garde theatre company. As he sees it (in the chapter "Towards a Poetics of Performance," *Essays on Performance Theory, 1970-1976*, 1977:120-123): "Victor Turner analyzes 'social dramas' using theatrical terminology to describe disharmonic or crisis situations. These situations—arguments, combats, rites of passage—are inherently dramatic because participants not only do things, they try *to show others what they are doing or have done*; actions take on a 'performed-for-an-audience' aspect. Erving Goffman takes a more directly scenographic approach in using the theatrical paradigm. He believes that all social interaction is staged—people prepare backstage, confront others while wearing masks and playing roles, use the main stage area for the performance of routines, and so on. For both Turner and Goffman, the basic human plot is the same: someone begins to move to a new place in the social order; this move is accomplished through ritual, or blocked; in either case a crisis arises because any change in status involves a readjustment of the entire scheme; this readjustment is effected ceremonially—that is, by means of theater." In my book, *Drama, Fields, and Metaphors* (pp. 37-41) I define social dramas as units of aharmonic or disharmonic social process, arising in conflict situations. Typically, they have four main phases of public action. These are: (1) *Breach* of regular norm-governed social relations; (2) *Crisis*, during which there is a tendency for the breach to widen. Each public crisis has what I now call liminal characteristics, since it is a threshold (*limen*) between more or less stable phases of the social process, but it is not usually a sacred limen, hedged around by taboos and thrust away from the centers of public life. On the contrary, it takes up its menacing stance in the forum itself, and, as it were, dares the representatives of order to grapple with it; (3) *Redressive action* ranging from personal advice and informal mediation or arbitration to formal juridical and legal machinery, and, to resolve certain kinds of crisis or legitimate other modes of resolution, to the performance of public ritual. Redress, too, has its liminal features, for it is "betwixt and between," and, as such, furnishes a distanced replication and critique of the events leading up to and composing the "crisis." This replication may be in the rational idiom of the judicial process, or in the metaphorical and symbolic idiom of a ritual process; (4) The final phase consists either of the *reintegration* of the disturbed social group, or of the social recognition and legitimation of irreparable schism between the contesting parties.

First let me comment on the difference between my use of the term "ritual" and the definitions of Schechner and Goffman. By and large they seem to mean by ritual a standardized unit act, which may be secular as well as sacred, while I mean the performance of a complex sequence of symbolic acts. Ritual for me, [as Ronald Grimes puts it], is a "transformative performance revealing major classifications, categories, and contradictions of cultural processes." For Schechner, what I call "breach," the inaugurating event in a social drama, is always effected by a ritual or ritualized act or "move." There is some truth in this. I will use as an example here the first social drama in my book on Ndembu social process, *Schism and Continuity*. The book contains a series of social dramas focused on one individual ambitious for the power and influence that goes with the office of village headman. In the first episode this protagonist, Sandombu, "dramatizes" to others in his effective sociocultural field that he is weary of waiting for the old headman, his mother's brother Kahali, to die, by ostentatiously refraining from giving him the portions of an antelope he has killed that would be appropriate to Kahali's status, age, and relationship. This refusal to follow custom might be regarded as a ritualized act as well as a transgression of a custom with ritual implications—since the dividing of a slain animal implies the sharing of sacred substance held to constitute matrilineal kinship. Here is shown the symbolism of blood in matrilineal kinship, and there are many rituals connected both with matriliny and the hunting cults which contain symbols for these "types of blood" (*nyichidi yamashi*). But I would prefer the terms "symbolic transgression"—which may also coincide with an actual transgression of custom, even of a legal prescription—to "ritual" in the frame of phase 1 (*breach*) of a social drama.

What is more interesting to me in this context than the definition of ritual is the connection established by Schechner between social drama and theatre, and the use made of "the theatrical paradigm" by Goffman and myself. For Goffman, "all the world's a stage," the world of social interaction anyway, and is full of ritual acts. For me the dramaturgical phase begins when *crises* arise in the daily flow of social interaction. Thus if daily living is a kind of theatre, social drama is a kind of metatheatre, that is, a dramaturgical language about the language of ordinary role-playing and status-maintenance which constitutes communication in the quotidian social process. In other words, when actors in a social drama, in Schechner's words, "try to show others what they are doing or have done," they are acting consciously, exercising what Charles Hockett has found to be a feature peculiar to human speech, reflectiveness or reflexiveness, the ability to communicate about the communication system itself (1960:392-430). This reflexivity is found not only in the eruptive phase of *crisis*, when persons exert their wills and unleash their emotions to achieve goals which until that time have remained hidden or may even have been unconscious—here reflexivity follows manifestation—but also in the cognitively dominant phase of redress, when the actions of the previous two phases become the subject matter for scrutiny within the frame provided by institutional forms and procedures—here reflexivity is present from the outset, whether the redressive machinery be characterized as legal, law-like, or ritual.

It is obvious that Goffman, Schechner, and I constantly stress process and processual qualities: performance, move, staging, plot, redressive action, crisis, schism, reintegration, and the like. To my mind, this stress is the "postmodern turn" in anthropology, a turn foreshadowed in anthropological modernity perhaps, but never in its central thrust. This turn involves the processualization of space, its temporalization, as against the spatialization of process or time, which we found to be of the essence of the modern.

Although there is a major difference between linguistic and anthropological definitions of performance, something of the change from modern to postmodern ways of thinking about sociocultural problems can be aptly illustrated by considering Edmund Leach's recent attempt to apply the linguist's vocabulary to matters anthropological in his article, "The Influence of Cultural Context on Non-Verbal Communication in Man" in *Non-Verbal Communication*, Robert A. Hinde, ed. (1972:321-322). Leach writes that "the anthropologist's concern is to delineate a framework of cultural *competence* in terms of which the individual's symbolic actions can be seen to make sense. We can only interpret individual *performance* in the light of what we have already inferred about competence, but in order to make our original inferences about competence we have to abstract a standardized pattern which is not necessarily immediately apparent in the data which are directly accessible to observation." It was Chomsky who introduced this competence/performance dichotomy, competence being mastery of a system of rules or regularities underlying that kind of language behavior which, for example, we call "speaking English." It was Dell Hymes who pointed out the hidden Neo-Platonism or Gnosticism in Chomsky's approach, which seems to regard performance as generally "a fallen state," a lapse from the ideal purity of systematic grammatical competence. This is clearly exemplified in J. Lyons' article "Human Language" in the same volume as Leach's essay just quoted. He is writing (p. 58) of three stages of "idealization" in "our identification of the raw data" of language-behavior. "First of all," he says, "we discount all 'slips of the tongue,' mispronunciations, hesitation pauses, stammering, stuttering, and so forth; in short, everything that can be described as a 'performance phenomenon.'" He then goes on to "discount" (p. 59) a certain amount of the "systematic variation between utterances that can be attributed to personal and sociocultural factors."

The "postmodern turn" would reverse this "cleansing" process of thought which moves from "performance errors and hesitation phenomena" through "personal and sociocultural factors" to the segregation of "sentences" from "utterances" by dubbing the latter "context dependent" (hence "impure") with respect both to their meaning and their grammatical structure. Performance, whether as speech behavior, the presentation of self in everyday life, stage drama or social drama, would now move to the center of observation and hermeneutical attention. Postmodern theory would see in the very flaws, hesitations, personal factors, incomplete, elliptical, context-dependent, situational components of performance, clues to the very nature of human process itself, and would also perceive genuine novelty, creativeness, as able to emerge from the freedom of the performance situation, from what Durkheim (in his best moment) called social "effervescence," exemplified for him in the generation of new symbols and meanings by the public actions, the "performances," of the French Revolution. What was once considered "contaminated," "promiscuous," "impure" is becoming the focus of postmodern analytical attention.

With regard to the structure/process dichotomy mentioned earlier, which is similar, if not identical, to other oppositions made by anthropologists: ideal norms/real behavior; mechanical models/statistical models; structure/organization; ideology/action, and so on, Sally Moore has many pertinent things to say in *Law as Process*.

She is aware that, as Murphy has argued, "it is the very incongruence of our conscious models and guides for conduct to the phenomena of social life that makes life possible" (1971:240), but also insists that "order and repetition are not all illusion, nor all 'mere' ideology, nor all fictive scholarly models, but are observable [and I would add often measurable] on a behavioral level, as well as in fixed ideas" (p. 38). She proposes that social processes should be examined in terms of the inter-relationship of three components: "the processes of *regularization* [SFM's italics], the processes of *situational adjustment*, and the factor of *indeterminacy*" (p. 39). This is really a revolutionary move on Sally Moore's part for she is challenging the Idealist formulations of her prestigious contemporaries. Like Heraclitus she is insisting that the elements (in her case, the sociocultural elements) are in continual flux and transformation, and so also are people. Like Heraclitus, too, she is aware that there is also a strain towards order and harmony, a *logos*, within the variability, an intent, as James

Olney puts it (1972:5) to transform "human variability from mere chaos and disconnection into significant process." This is, in effect, what the redressive phase in a social drama (the processual microcosm) attempts to do, and what in complex cultures the liminoid performative genres are designed for.

Moore's experience as a practising lawyer underlies her view that (p. 39) "social life presents an almost endless variety of finely distinguishable situations and quite an array of grossly different ones. It contains arenas of continuous competition. It proceeds in a context of an ever-shifting set of persons, changing moments in time, altering situations and partially improvised interactions. Established rules, customs, and symbolic frameworks exist, but they operate in the presence of areas of indeterminacy, of ambiguity, of uncertainty and manipulability. Order never fully takes over, nor could it. The cultural, contractual, and technical imperatives always leave gaps, require adjustments and interpretations to be applicable to particular situations, and are themselves full of ambiguities, inconsistencies, and often contradictions." But Moore does not see everything social as amorphous or as unbounded innovation or limitless reinterpretation. She sees that common symbols, customary behaviors, role expectations, rules, categories, ideas and ideologies, rituals and formalities shared by actors do exist and frame mutual communication and action. But she is claiming that the fixing and framing of social reality is itself a process or a set of processes. Whereas anthropologists like Firth and Barth have contrasted structure and process (Barth sees process as a means of understanding social change), Moore sees structure as the ever-to-be-repeated achievement of processes of regularization. As she writes:

> The whole matter contains a paradox. Every explicit attempt to fix social relationships or social symbols is by implication a recognition that they are mutable. Yet at the same time such an attempt directly struggles against mutability, attempts to fix the moving thing, to make it hold. Part of the process of trying to fix social reality involves representing it as stable or immutable or at least controllable to this end, at least for a time. Rituals, rigid procedures, regular formalities, symbolic repetitions of all kinds, as well as explicit laws, principles, rules, symbols, and categories are cultural representations of fixed social reality, or continuity. They present stability and continuity acted out and re-enacted; visible continuity. By dint of repetition they deny the passage of time, the nature of change, and the implicit extent of potential indeterminacy in social relations. Whether these processes of regularization are sustained by tradition or legitimated by revolutionary edict and force, they act to provide daily regenerated frames, social constructions of reality, within which the attempt is made to fix social life, to keep it from slipping into the sea of indeterminacy (p. 41).

But as Moore points out, however tight the rules, in their application there is always "a certain range of maneuver, of openness, of choice, of interpretation, of alteration, of tampering, of reversing, of transforming" (p. 41). In brief, "within the cultural and social order there is a pervasive quality of partial indeterminacy" (p. 49). Processes of situational adjustment involve both the exploitation of indeterminacies in sociocultural situations and the actual generation of such indeterminacies. Or they may be concerned with the reinterpretation or redefinition of rules and relationships. By regarding a field of sociocultural relations, which may include networks and arenas as well as relatively persisting corporate groups and institutions, as a plurality of processes, some of regularization (or *reglementation* as Moore now prefers to call them: see pp. 2-3, 18, 21, 29), others of situational adjustment, Moore proposes a model of social reality as basically fluid and indeterminate, though transformable for a time into something more fixed through regularizing processes. "This is a framework," she holds, "usable in the analysis of (particular situations and their detailed denouement, and equally usable in the analysis of) larger-scale phenomena such as institutional systems" (p. 52). She warns that "whether the processes are unchanging or changing is not the dichotomy proposed. Processes of regularization and processes of situational adjustment may *each* [my italics] have the effect of stabilizing or changing an existing social situation and order. What is being proposed is that the complex relationship between social life and its cultural representation may be easier to handle analytically if the interlocking of processes of regularization, processes of situational adjustment, and the factor of indeterminacy are taken into account" (pp. 52-53).

My own work for many years had inclined me in a similar theoretical direction. This direction is towards postmodern ways of thinking. Clearly the factor of indeterminacy has assumed greater importance in today's world. Historical events have played their part: wars, revolutions, the holocaust, the fall and fragmentation of colonial empires. But scientific developments in many fields have helped to undermine the modern views of time, space, matter, language, person, and truth. Processes of regularization are still potent in politics and economics; capitalistic and socialistic bureaucracies and legislatures still attempt to fix social reality. In the sciences and humanities work is still done within the constraints of prestigious "paradigms" (in Thomas Kuhn's sense). In the political macrocosm sharp divisions continue to exist fostered by the regulatory processes of nationalism and ideology. Nevertheless, there is detectible an extensive breakdown of boundaries between various conventionally defined sciences and arts, and between these and modes of social reality. In sociocultural studies the spatiality of modern thought, dependent on what Richard Palmer calls "one-point perspective," shows signs of giving way to multiperspectival consciousness, a field with several variables. The notion of society as an endless crisscrossing of processes of various kinds and intensities is congruent with this view. Time is coming to be seen as an essential dimension of being as well as multiperspectival, no longer merely as a linear continuum conceived in spatial terms.

With the postmodern dislodgement of spatialized thinking and ideal models of cognitive and social structures from their position of exegetical preeminence, there is occurring a major move towards the study of processes, not as exemplifying compliance with or deviation from normative models both etic and emic, but as performances. Performances are never amorphous or openended, they have diachronic structure, a beginning, a sequence of overlapping but isolable phases, and an end. But their structure is not that of an abstract system; it is generated out of the dialectical oppositions of processes and of levels of process. In the modern consciousness, cognition, idea, rationality, were paramount. In the postmodern turn, cognition is not dethroned but rather takes its place on an equal footing with volition and affect. The revival of what has been termed "psychological anthropology," exemplified by the publication of *The Making of Psychological Anthropology* (George Spindler, ed., 1978) is, in my view, not unconnected with this view of process and performance, of which the units are total human beings in full psychological concreteness, not abstract, generalized sociocultural entities, but each, in Theodore Schwartz's term, an "idioverse" with his/her "individual cognitive, evaluative, and affective mappings of the structure of events and classes of events" (1978:410) in his/her sociocultural field. If Schwartz's formulation seems to be derived from the products of processes of reglementation, and hence to be somewhat abstract, the notion of idioverse is a valuable one, for it postulates that "a culture has its distributive existence as the set of personalities of the members of a population" (pp. 423-424), thus allowing for negotiation and dispute over what should be authoritative or legitimate in that culture, in other words, for social dramatic action. As Schwartz writes (p. 432): "The model of culture as a set of personalities does not preclude conflict; rather the inclusion of the differences as well as the similarities among personalities in the culture makes social coordination a central research problem implied by this model. Differences may lead to conflict or complementarity. The perception of commonality or difference are themselves construals which, at times, may mask their opposite. This view of Schwartz's of a culture as consisting of "all the personalities of the individuals constituting a society or subsociety, however bounded" (p. 432), is entirely consistent with Sally Moore's processual position, since it allows scope for the coexistence of processes of regularization (overall "social coordination") and situational adjustment ("conflict," "masking of commonality or difference," and *situational* modes of social coordination). Schwartz is also aware of "indeterminacy" as the following quotation indicates (p. 432):

A given personality (the individual's version and portion of his culture) is not necessarily representative in a statistical sense, nor is the approximation to some central tendency the aspect of culture stressed by a distributive model. Rather, this model emphasizes the whole array of personalities, the constructs they bring to and derive from events, and their structuring of events in construct-oriented behavior. Centrality (or typicality) would not necessarily be predictive or (it may even be negatively correlated with) the contribution of a given personality to the structuring of events. *It is essential, then, to emphasize that although individual personalities and their cognitive-evaluative-affective constructs of experience are the constituents of culture, they may be discrepant and conflicted among (and within) themselves or with central tendencies or configurations in the overall population of personalities comprising a culture or subculture* [my italics]. Similarly the constructs of the individual will vary in the adequacy with which individuals anticipate and conduct the course of events.

If performance seems then to be a legitimate object of study for postmodern anthropology, it seems appropriate that we should examine the literature on types of performance. We need not confine ourselves to the ethnographic literature. If man is a sapient animal, a toolmaking animal, a self-making animal, a symbol-using animal, he is, no less, a performing animal, *Homo performans*, not in the sense, perhaps, that a circus animal may be a performing animal, but in the sense that man is a self-performing animal—his performances are, in a way, *reflexive*, in performing he reveals himself to himself. This can be in two ways: the actor may come to know himself better through acting or enactment; or one set of human beings may come to know themselves better through observing and/or participating in performances generated and presented by another set of human beings. In the first instance, reflexivity is singular though enactment may be in a social context; in the second case, reflexivity is plural and is based on the assumption that though, for most purposes, we humans may divide ourselves between Us and Them, or Ego and Alter, We and They share substance, and Ego and Alter mirror each other pretty well—Alter alters Ego not too much but tells Ego what both are!

When we scan the rich data put forth by the social sciences and the humanities on performances, we can class them into "social" performances (including social dramas) and "cultural" performances (including aesthetic or stage dramas). As I said earlier, the basic stuff of social life is performance, "the presentation of self in everyday life" (as Goffman entitled one of his books). Self is presented through the performance of roles, through performance that breaks roles, and through declaring to a given public that one has undergone a transformation of state and status, been saved or damned, elevated or released.

Human beings belong to a species well endowed with means of communication, both verbal and non-verbal, and, in addition, given to dramatic modes of communication, to performance of different kinds. There are various *types* of social performance and *genres* of cultural performance, and each has its own style, goals, entelechy, rhetoric, developmental pattern, and characteristic roles. These types and genres differ in different cultures, and in terms of the scale and complexity of the sociocultural fields in which they are generated and sustained. But let us take a look for a while at some theories of communication, particularly nonverbal communication, because the genres we shall study in this essay, ritual, carnival, theatre, spectacle, film, and so on, contain a high proportion of nonverbal symbols. Nonverbal communication is a topic which forces us to give heed to what ethologists, primate sociologists, and other scientists of animal behavior have to say. I have myself always argued for the importance of biological components in symbolism, since I see the planet Terra as essentially a single developing system, based, in its vital aspect, on cellular structures which display a remarkable uniformity in different genera and species of living things. I am sure that a biologist from outer space would find the various Terran life-forms to be made of similar stuff, a planetary kinship group, from biological amoeba to high-cultural products like the works of Homer, Dante and Shakespeare, Leonardo and Beethoven. Mankind differs from most other "kinds" in the degree of its self-consciousness, its evolving reflexivity, made possible by language and the dialectic then made mandatory between linguistic and biological modes of responding to environments of varying kinds.

In an article entitled "Formal Analysis of Communicative Processes" (in the Hinde volume, *op. cit.*, pp. 3-35), D. M. MacKay uses the "information-system approach" in order to understand what is going on in non-verbal communication. His detailed argument results in a simple model:

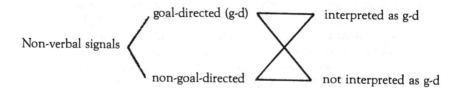

MacKay argues that "communication" in the strict sense only occurs when the originator of a non-verbal signal A's action is goal-directed to a recipient B. One must use a more neutral expression, he argues, when there is no goal-directedness or "intention" (from *intendere arcum in*, Latin for "to draw a bow at," implying A's selection of B as a "target"). For example, we may simply say that B perceives whatever he does about A, or that information flows from A to B. He gives several examples of how to distinguish communication proper from mere perception or information flow. "Suppose," he says (p. 20), "that in the Boy Scout tent, A, poor fellow, turns out to have sweaty feet, B's internal state of readiness is likely to be very different according to whether he perceives A as an unsuspecting sufferer or as one who knows his olfactory armament and has the *aim* of stimulating B with it." Only the second case would constitute *communication*. MacKay distinguishes between *in such a way as* and *in order to*. For example, "a new-born baby cries *in such a way as* to get attention. Later on, it may learn to cry *in order to* get attention" (p. 24). MacKay claims that his model raises a series of scientific questions for further research. In this case, the question is posed as to what are the stages by which the baby's crying "in such a way as" develops into crying "in order to" get attention. "What kinds of behavioral situation might be diagnostic of the presence and nature of evaluative feedback upon the action concerned? . . . and so on" (p. 24).

Robert Hinde has criticized MacKay's model, though mainly from the viewpoint of an evolutionary biologist. These scientists have (p. 88) tended to focus on the distinction between behavior which appears to have become adapted in evolution for a signal function, and that which does not. But behavior adapted for a signalling function may or may not be "goal-directed" to that end. Indeed, some such behavior may be goal-directed in a sense, but towards broadcasting signals rather than towards affecting the behavior of a particular individual. Furthermore, behavior which is goal-directed towards affecting the behavior of others may be idiosyncratic and not adapted through processes of natural selection to that end. Nevertheless, MacKay is saying some useful things about *human* communication which may be applied to performance theory.

If we take into account the Freudian model according to which human personality consists of several differentiated, but interrelated structures (for example, id, superego, ego), involving unconscious, preconscious, and conscious levels of awareness, we may conjecture that non-verbal signals may be goal-directed by unconscious *id* wishes and desires of the sender and interpreted either consciously or unconsciously by the receiver in terms of some internal goal criterion of his/hers. Similarly signals may be emitted from the *superego*, or normative-prescriptive system of the sender to a receiver who may interpret them at the cognitive-perceptual or *ego* level—or at the unconscious level by *id* or *superego* structures. There may also be conflict within the personality of the receiver over the interpretation of the nonverbal signal on both levels and in and between the structures. A woman's smile might be interpreted, for example, by a male receiver as at once politeness, invitation, and temptation, with the consequent problem as to which was really intended, and if so what signal to emit in response. How nonsensical, even arch, the "communication engineering" type jargon sounds!

Social and cultural performance is infinitely more complex and subtle than the non-verbal communication of animals. Its messages are through both verbal and non-verbal media, and its verbal media are varied and capable of communicating rich and subtle ideas and images. This may be a good opportunity to discuss some of the approaches which I have found useful as conceptual underpinning for the analysis of types and genres of performance.

In the first place, the Western anthropological tradition has moved well away from the study of what D. H. Lawrence called "man alive," or, better, "man and woman alive." It shared the Western passion from Plato on, (even some aspects of Heraclitus, his backing of the Logos, for example) for explanation via models, frames, paradigms, competence, plans, blueprints, preliminary representations, hypothetical or stylized representations. In practice, this way of thinking rests on the real political power of effecting what one proposes, making one's archetypes work by the effective application of force. The Western philosophical tradition—Plato, Aristotle, Descartes, Hegel, Kant, to name but a few, and all the anthropological structuralisms, are hooked on this belief in predetermined orderings. In my view there is such a thing as "natural" or "social" law; communitas rests on Buber's I-Thou and "essential We." Extreme individualism only understands a part of man. Extreme collectivism only understands man as a part. Communitas is the implicit law of wholeness arising out of relations between totalities. But communitas is intrinsically dynamic, never quite being realized. It is not being realized precisely because individuals and collectivities try to impose their cognitive schemata on one another. The process of striving towards and resistance against the fulfilment of the natural law of communitas necessitates that the unit of history and of anthropology (which takes into account the sociocultural schemata) and also the unit of their analysis is drama, not culture or archive. And certainly not structural relationship. Structure is always ancillary to, dependent on, secreted from process. And performances, particularly dramatic performances, are the manifestations par excellence of human social process.

In saying these things I reveal myself an adherent of that epistemological tradition which stresses what Wilhelm Dilthey calls "lived experience." For Dilthey experience is a many-faceted yet coherent system dependent on the interaction and interpenetration of cognition, affect, and volition. It is made up of not only our observations and reactions, but also the cumulative wisdom (not knowledge, which is cognitive in essence) of humankind, expressed not only in custom and tradition but also in great works of art. There is a living and growing body of experience, a tradition of communitas, so to speak, which embodies the response of our whole collective mind to our entire collective experience. We acquire this wisdom not by abstract solitary thought, but by participation immediately or vicariously through the performance genres in sociocultural dramas.

I will now call your attention to the distinction between such static models for thought and action as cosmologies, theologies, philosophical systems, ethical systems, and ideologies, and what Dilthey calls a *Weltanschauung*. The former are static, the latter is dynamic. And since Dilthey insists that experience is equally woven from the three strands of thought, feeling, and will, a *Weltanschauung* has, like a prism, a three-sided structure. Thus it consists of: (1) a *Weltbild*, that is, a body of knowledge and belief about what is cognitively taken to be the "real world"; on this (2) is raised a set of value judgments expressing the relation of the adherents to their world and the meaning (*Bedeutung*) which they find in it—Dilthey sees value as dominantly formed by affect; (3) this set in turn supports a more or less coherent system of ends, ideals, and principles of conduct, which are the point of contact between the *Weltanschauung* and praxis, the sociocultural interaction, making it a force in the development of the individual, and, through him, of society at large. This last component represents the action of the will, the connative aspect of systematized experience. The point is that for Dilthey the *Weltanschauung* is not a permanent, fixed structure of eternal ideas but itself represents at any given moment a dispensable stage in mankind's unending struggle to find a convincing solution to what Dilthey calls "the riddle of life." He seems to mean by this the mysteries and paradoxes that surround the great crises of birth, mating, and death, the seasonal round, and its perils of drought, flood, famine, and disease, the endless battles of man's rational activity against the forces and necessities of nonhuman nature, the never ending task of satisfying with limited means his unlimited appetites, the paradoxes of social control in which a person's or group's loyalty to one legitimate cause, or moral principle, automatically renders them disloyal to others equally valid—in summary, the whole mystery of humanity in the world. *Weltanschuungen*, then, are built up as much on tropes as on reasons, as much on metaphors and synecdoches as on concepts. What is unknown is guessed at on the analogy of the known, what is unintelligible is explained on the analogy of the intelligible. But *Weltanschuungen* are continually subject to revision, their personifications and metaphors are much more mutable than cognitive constructs. Their forms differ as the collective experiences underlying them differ, in ways conditioned by climate, topography, history, technological invention, and by the genius of rare individuals. I am sufficient of a cultural Darwinist to suppose that there is a kind of competition among *Weltanschuungen*, whereby the fittest survive and are selected to receive detailed development at the hands of successive generations. Particular periods of history and particular clusters of societies and nations become dominated and characterized by a particular *Weltanschauung*.

But *Weltanschuungen*, like all else that motivates humankind, must be performed. Dilthey saw this clearly and argued that every type of *Weltanschuungen* expresses itself in at least three modes. These are what he calls "religious, esthetic, and philosophical forms." An anthropologist might find this distinction to be itself the mark of a specific cultural type, "Western Civilization," for these three categories have arisen in that cultural tradition.

Nevertheless, let us bear with him a while, for his discriminations proceed from one of the most creative minds in social science.

The ground of *religion*, according to Dilthey, rests on two opposite types of reflection—mankind is a reflexive species, as I have so often insisted. The first is those regular but mostly uncontrollable processes of nature, both meteorological and biological, with which we all have to come to terms. The second is represented by those mysterious accidents by which our lives are sometimes so powerfully affected, even when our circumstances seem to be most fortunate. Religion posits that both regular processes and unexpected accidents are due to the agency of invisible, transhuman powers or beings, and in each *Weltanschauung* the idea of such powers is gradually elaborated by mythological fantasy and theological speculation. Since, so Dilthey argues, a *Weltanschauung* must give meaning to practical life, the question arises how we are to order and systematize our relations with these unseen powers. In Sally Moore's terms means must be found to reduce the indeterminacy of their action and to regularize their relations with us. Therefore, says Dilthey, primitive societies generate over time a system of symbolic ideas and practices, a ritual system, which eventually gives rise to and comes under the control of a group or class of priestly regulators. Dilthey further supposes that as societies increase in scale and complexity something like the notion of an "inner life" develops and individuals of genius, shamans, prophets, and mystics emerge who begin to develop a reflexive system of doctrine which reinterprets traditional ritual and mythology in terms of inner experience. Today anthropologists would demur. They believe that shamans, and other types of inspirational religious specialists, are more prominent in hunting and gathering societies, considered simpler, than in societies with well developed agricultural systems, in which calendrical cults, supervised by priests, and with cognitively well developed cosmologies are dominant. However, Dilthey is correct in supposing that prophets, shamans raised to a higher power, tend to emerge when relatively stabilized agricultural societies are seriously threatened by political and cultural change. Mystics, on the other hand, may emerge in response to the growing banality of ritualistic action in well bonded societies characterized by the absence of variety, let alone change, over many generations. Viewed from the religious standpoint, a *Weltanschauung* sees the meaning of visible social life to be determined by its relation to an unseen world from which the known experienced world has proceeded. For social peace and development it is held to be necessary that individuals and groups, through cultic observances and solitary prayer and meditation, should find meaning and value to be derived from messages credibly transmitted from the unseen world through various media: prophecy, visions, apparitions, miracles, heroic acts of faith such as martyrdoms, divination, augury, and other extraordinary processes and phenomena. Ethical standards are believed to be promulgated by invisible powers; they are put beyond the range of human wisdom and creativity.

Dilthey considers that the aesthetic or artistic viewpoint, which can be detected in many *Weltanschauungen*, is not only different from, but also antithetical to the religious. The artist tries "to understand life in terms of itself," rather than in terms of the supernatural. The thoughts and passions and purposes of human beings, and the relationships into which they enter with one another and with the natural world provide for the artist a sufficient basis from which to derive the meaning of life. He is alert to all the senses, not merely sight, and it is in intense and complex sensory codes that he attempts to give performative reality to that meaning. He is often a fierce opponent of theory, particularly cognitive theory. He scorns to contribute to philosophy. Yet, for an anthropologist, given to inference, a *Weltanschauung* is fairly easily inferrable from aesthetic production. Aesthetics, in complex cultures, are pervaded by reflexivity. The style and content of novels, plays, and poems reveal what Geertz has called metasocial commentary. In literature of all types writers directly or through their characters proliferate in reflexive generalizations, which nevertheless stop short of cognitively elaborated theories. The strain towards system, paradoxically, seems to be strongest in preliterate or barely literate agricultural cultures, and in the heads of sophisticated literate urbanized individuals of Western high cultures. Artists tease their readers or viewers with works which the latter treat as a type or "re-presentation" of reality, which they compare with the rest of their experience, and are compelled to reflect upon their meaning. The aesthetic form of *Weltanschauung*, one might say, cleaves closest to the experiential ground of all valid knowledge.

According to Dilthey the philosopher differs from both the man of religion and the artist. His great aim is to elicit from experience a system of concepts and universal truths bound together by a chain of mutual logical implication. Although most philosophers have been, as anthropologists would assert, "culture-bound," their goal is to know, if possible, all that is to be known, and to find for that knowledge a logically exact and valid foundation. To this end, particularly since Kant, they engage in endless criticism, whose goal is to reduce every experience to constituent factors and to trace every proposition to its ultimate ground, never resting till they have related all facts to an ultimate reality, all knowledge to a highest truth, and all value to a supreme good. Their ideas are derived from every possible source, including religion and art, as well as empirical science, but the intelligible whole in which these data are evaluated has a distinctive character. The world is represented as a rational system whose structure and properties can be made the object of a demonstrable science. For Dilthey, this science is "metaphysics." Religion, aesthetics, and philosophy are what he regards as the three media of expression of every *Weltanschauung*. As an anthropologist I propose to translate these epistemological media into cultural media, that is, such institutions as ritual, carnival, theatre, literature, film, spectacle, and television.

But Dilthey, with his German passion for classification, and his scientist's drive to comparative study, proceeds to classify *Weltanschauungen* into three types. Personally, I regard this taxonomic frenzy of Dilthey's as a culture-bound denial of his own true position, as we shall see. For what he sees as separate types are often processes which have different characteristics at different times. Nevertheless, his types are useful heuristic devices, helping us to find our way into a new sociocultural "field." For Dilthey, *Weltanschauungen* may be classified into three broad types: (1) *naturalism*; (2) *the idealism of freedom*; and (3) *objective idealism*. *Naturalism* sees the criterion of the good life either in *pleasure* or *power*, both regarded by Dilthey as representing the animal side of human nature. In religion this represents an assertion of the claims of the world and the flesh and proclaims a revolt against otherworldliness, even, in some instances, against religion itself as the epitome of other-worldliness. In art, naturalism takes the form of "realism," the picturing of people and things as it is thought they really are without idealizing. Its use in literature must, however, be distinguished from philosophical Realism, which is, of course, the doctrine that universals or abstract terms are objectively actual (here the opposed term would be Nominalism which asserts that universals and abstract terms are mere necessities of thought or conveniences of language and therefore exist as names only and have no general realities corresponding to them). For Dilthey, though, realism in art tends to manifest the dark forces of passion, thereby exposing higher ideals and principles as illusory or even hypocritical. At the philosophical level Dilthey regards Naturalism as a view of the world as a mechanical system composed of elements all of which are clear and distinct, that is, mathematically determinable. The natural world, known and experienced scientifically, is all that exists—there is no supernatural or spiritual creation, control or significance. This view, says Dilthey, may be held as a doctrine of the nature of reality—in which case it is better termed materialism—which explains thought, will, and feeling only in terms of matter, that is, whatever occupies space and is perceptible of the senses in some way, either directly or by means of instruments. It may also be held, more cautiously, as a methodological principle—as in the case of Positivism, established by Auguste Comte, and still deeply influential in the thinking of the social sciences. Here philosophical thought is held to be based solely on observable, scientific facts and their relations to one another; speculation about or search for ultimate origins is firmly rejected. *Naturalism*, in Dilthey's sense, is associated with *sensationalism* in philosophy, the belief that all knowledge is acquired through the senses, the ability of the brain and nerves to receive and react to stimuli. In *ethics* Naturalism is either *hedonistic*—that is, it conceives that pleasure, variously regarded in terms of the happiness of the individual or of society, is the principal good and proper aim of action—or preaches *liberation* through enlightenment and the destruction of illusion—false perceptions, conceptions, or interpretations, particularly unscientific notions and prescientific prejudices persisting through tradition. In his *Introduction to Weltan-*

schauungslehre (translated as *Dilthey's Philosophy of Existence* by William Kluback and Martin Weinbaum, from Vol. VIII of his *Gesammelte Schriften*, pp. 75-118, Leipzig and Berlin, 1914-36, New York: Bookman, 1957) Dilthey mentions Democritus, Protagoras, Epicurus, Lucretius, Aristippus, Hulme, Feuerbach, Buechner, Moleschott and Comte as representatives of this philosophy.

(2) The second type of *Weltanschauung, the idealism of freedom* is based, Dilthey tells us, on our inner experience of free will, and was "the creative conception of the mind of the philosophers of Athens" (*loc. cit.*, 61). This interprets the world in terms of *personality*; its exponents "are pervaded to the tips of their fingers by the consciousness of totally disagreeing with naturalism" (p. 62). Their basic premise is that there exists in man a moral will which we can know to be free from physical causation; this will is bound, not physically but morally, and therefore freely, to other wills in a society of moral persons. For many of these idealists of freedom the relations between these persons is held to depend upon an absolute free, personal agent, in other words, Deity, God. In religion this *Weltanschauung* appears as Theism, in particular Christian Theism where the fundamental premise of Naturalism, that *ex nihilo nihil fit*, "nothing is made from nothing," that is, *something*, for example, is eternal, is contradicted by the doctrine of creation *ex nihilo*, "out of nothing." In art, and this is what has pertinence for our later study of modern drama from an anthropological perspective, the idealism of freedom emerges as the conception of the world as a "theatre of heroic action," for example, in the works of Corneille and Schiller. Corneille, for example, liked to set up historically true but surprising situations that forced a number of characters into action and in which the individual, through his heroic and magnanimous decisions, his heinous crimes, or his renunciations, proves his powers of transcendency. Corneille favored what is called "the ethics of glory," by which the hero convinces himself and seeks to convince others of his self-possession and superiority of spirit. Freedom of the will appears in the elucidation of the hero's inner conflicts as well as great feats whereby he tries to reconcile his will and his passions in order to achieve his goal. Some heroes rationalize their motives while acting in bad faith—a source of irony. For Schiller the artist's role is to show the moral growth of the individual pitted against the necessities of reality. The idealism of freedom or personality, in Dilthey's view, developed in philosophy from the conception of reason as a formative power in Anaxagoras, Plato, and Aristotle, to the medieval conception of a world governed by the personal providence of God, and thence in Kant and Fichte to the idea of a supersensible world of values, which are real only in and for the infinite will which posits them. Dilthey finds among its modern representatives Bergson, the Neo-Kantians, and the pragmatists.

(3) *Objective idealism*: this third type is based, says Dilthey, on a contemplative and affective attitude to experience. We read our own feelings and

mental activities into the external world, regarding it as a living whole which continually realizes and enjoys itself in the harmony of its parts; we find the divine life of the whole immanent in every part, and rejoice to find ourselves in sympathy with this life. This *Weltanschauung*, he goes on, emerges in the pantheism of Indian and Chinese religion; in art its most notable exponent is Goethe. The epistemology of this third type of philosophy lays emphasis on "intellectual intuition"—the intuitive grasp of the wholeness of things. Dilthey finds examples of it in Stoicism, in Averroes, Bruno, Spinoza, Leibnitz, Shaftesbury, Schelling, Hegel and Schleiermacher.

Dilthey argues in *Die Drei Grundformen der Systeme in der ersten Halfes 19 Jahrhunderts* (G. S., IV, 528-5), that the history of recent philosophy can be described and elucidated in terms of a conflict between the three types. Since *Weltanschauungen* are more than merely cognitive structures, but are ways of looking at the world and life, in which cognitive, affective, and volitional elements are bound up together and are alike primary, they are seldom found in their pure form, often hybridize, and must be seized as lived experience.

But I don't want to become involved in Dilthey's philosophical speculations, only to give you a notion of how his general approach to cultural dynamics provides some reinforcement for my views on the anthropology of performance. As I insisted earlier the truly "spontaneous" unit of human social performance is not a role-playing sequence in an institutionalized or "corporate group" context, it is the *social drama* which results precisely from the suspension of normative role-playing, and in its passionate activity abolishes the usual distinction between flow and reflection, since in the social drama it becomes a matter of urgency to become reflexive about the cause and motive of action damaging to the social fabric. It is in the social drama that *Weltanschauungen* become visible, if only fragmentarily, as factors giving meaning to deeds that may seem at first sight meaningless. The performative genres are, as it were, secreted from the social drama and in turn surround it and feed their performed meanings back into it.

The social drama is an eruption from the level surface of ongoing social life, with its interactions, transactions, reciprocities, its customs for making regular, orderly sequences of behavior. It is propelled by passions, compelled by volitions, overmastering at times any rational considerations. Yet reason plays a major role in the settlement of disputes which take the sociodramatic form. Particularly during the redressive phase—though here again nonrational factors may come into play if rituals are performed (performance here being in terms of regularizing process) to redress the disputes.

In other words, there is a structural relationship between cognitive, affective, and conative components of what Dilthey called lived experience. This is clearly shown in the characteristic sequential structure of the social drama. Although all these psychological processes coexist during every phase of a social drama, each phase is dominated by one or the other. In detailed analysis it would be possible to demonstrate how the verbal and non-verbal symbolic codes and styles employed by the actors correspond to some extent with the primacy of a particular psychological tendency. For example, in the first phase — breach — affect is primary, though an element of cognitive calculation is usually present, and the transgressor's will to assert power or identity usually incites the will to resist his action among representatives of the normative standard which he has infringed. The state of *crisis* involves all three propensities equally, as sides are taken and power resources calculated. Quite often, however, when a social field is divided into two camps or factions, one will proceed under the ostensible banner of rationality, while the other will manifest in its words and deeds the more romantic qualities of willing and feeling. One thinks immediately of the American Civil War, the American and French Revolutions, the Jacobite rebellions of 1715 and 1745, and the Mexican *Insurgencia* of 1810. All these are on the scale of macropolitics, but my studies of micropolitical situations directly among the Ndembu and indirectly from anthropological literature indicate that a similar dichotomy exists on the small scale order. As mentioned, a cognitive emphasis tinges social attempts to remedy disorder, though first will must be applied to terminate the often dangerous contestation in *crisis*. Cognition reigns primarily in judicial and legal redressive action. Where such action fails, however, to command sufficient assent, will and emotion reassert themselves. This reassertion may proceed in opposite directions. On the one hand, there may be reversion to *crisis*, all the more embittered by the failure of restitutive action. On the other hand, there may be an attempt to transcend an order based on rational principles by appealing to that order which rests on a tradition of coexistence among the predecessors of the current community, whether these are conceived as biological ancestors or bearers of the same communal values. This kind of ordering is better regarded as the crystallization of joint experience, handed down in striking or potent cultural forms and symbols and bears rather the character of orexis (feeling and willing) than rational planning. Thus when legal redress fails, groups may turn to activities which can be described as "ritualized," whether these "rituals" are expressly connected with religious beliefs or not. Anti-religious states and societies have their redressive ceremonies, sometimes involving public confession by those held responsible for breaching the norms or transgressing the values of societal tradition. Legal action itself, of course, is heavily ritualized. But in these more fully ritualized procedures what is being introduced into situations of crisis is the non-rational, metaphorically "organic" order of society itself, felt rather than conceived as the axiomatic source of human bonding. It is the "social will." The potency of ritual symbols is well recognized by the antagonists in the phase of *crisis*. In *Dramas, Fields, and Metaphors* I show how, in the Mexican *Insurgencia*, Hidalgo seized the banner of Our Lady of Guadalupe to rally the peasants, while Viceroy Venegas of Spain endowed Our Lady of Remedios with a field marshall's baton to strengthen the loyalty of the people of Mexico City.

In the final stage, the *restoration of peace*, which entails either a reestablishment of viable relations between the contending parties or a public recognition of irreparable schism, cognitive criteria tend to come uppermost again, if only in the sense of a rational acceptance of the reality of change. Every social drama alters, in however miniscule a fashion, the structure (by which term I do not mean a permanent ordering of social relations but merely a temporary mutual accommodation of interests) of the relevant social field. For example, oppositions may have become alliances, and vice versa. High status may have become low status and the reverse. New power may have been channelled into new authority and old authority lost its legitimacy. Closeness may have become distance and vice versa. Formerly integral parts may have segmented, formerly independent parts may have fused. Some parts may no longer belong to the field after a drama's termination, and others may have entered it. Some institutionalized relationships may have become informal, some social regularities become irregularities or intermittences. New norms and rules may have been generated or devised during the attempts to redress conflict; old norms may have fallen into disrepute. Bases of political support may have altered. The distribution of the factors of legitimacy may have changed, as have the techniques (influence, persuasion, power, and so on) for gaining compliance with decisions. These considerations, and many more, have to be rationally evaluated by the actors in a social drama, in order that they may take up the threads of ordinary, regular, custom and norm-bound social life once more.

From the standpoint of relatively well-regulated, more or less accurately operational, methodical, orderly social life, social dramas have a "liminal" or "threshold" character. The latter term is derived from a Germanic base which means "thrash" or "thresh," a place where grain is beaten out from its husk, where what has been hidden is thus manifested. That is why in my first study of social dramas in Ndembu society, *Schism and Continuity*, I described the social drama (p. 93) as "a limited area of transparency on the otherwise opaque surface of regular, uneventful social life. In the social drama latent conflicts become manifest, and kinship ties, whose significance is not obvious in genealogies, emerge into key importance . . . . Through the social drama we are enabled to observe the crucial principles of the social structure in their operation, and their relative dominance at successive points in time." Manifestation, to revert to the "thrashing" metaphor, is the "grain" and "husk" of social life, the values and anti-values, the relationships of amity and enmity, which are revealed in the often passionate action of the social drama, and thus becomes part of a community's reflexive store, its knowledge of itself, stored in the bins of legal precedent, common knowledge, and even ritual symbolism—if the drama is redressed by ritual means.

Let me make the simple point again that I regard the "social drama" as the empirical unit of social process from which has been derived, and is constantly being derived, the various genres of cultural performance. One phase of the social drama in particular deserves attention as a generative source of cultural performances. This is the *redressive phase*, which, as we have seen, inevitably involves a scanning of and reflection upon the previous events leading up to the crisis that has now to be dealt with. I have mentioned legal and judicial processes as having an important place here, and that these are often highly formalized and ritualized. As Sally Moore and Barbara Myerhoff put it in the book they edited, *Secular Ritual* (1977:3): "collective ritual can be seen as an especially dramatic attempt to bring some particular part of life firmly and definitely into orderly control. It belongs to the structuring side of the cultural historical process." Since law is concerned with orderly control, legal and religious ritual have much in common. One difference is that in law cognitive processes assume priority, in religion orectic processes prevail, though both have similar procedures involving repetition, conscious "acting," stylization (as Moore and Myerhoff put it: "actions or symbols used are extra-ordinary themselves, or ordinary ones are used in an unusual way, a way that calls attention to them and sets them apart from other mundane uses" 1977:7), order ("collective rituals are by definition an organized event, both of persons and cultural elements, having a beginning and an end, thus bound to have some order. It may contain within it moments of, or elements of chaos and spontaneity, but these are in prescribed times and places," p. 7), evocative presentation style of "staging" ("collective rituals are intended to produce at least an attentive state of mind, and often an even greater commitment of some kind," p. 7), and have a social "message" and "meaning."

These formal characteristics of collective ceremony or "ritual" are clearly transferrable to other genres, and are shared with, for example, theatre and games. Law and religious ritual, seen as a pair, however, can be distinguished from other kinds of performative genres, Myerhoff argues, in "the area of meaning and effect." She sees collective ceremony (law-ritual) as a container, a vehicle that holds something. It gives form to that which it contains—for ritual is in part a form, and a form which gives meaning (by "framing") to its contents. The work of ritual (and ritual does "work," as many tribal and post-tribal etymologies indicate) is partly attributable to its morphological characteristics. Its medium is part of its message. It can "contain" almost anything, for any aspect of social life, any aspect of behavior or ideology, may lend itself to ritualization, as the late Professor S. F. Nadel argued in *Nupe Religion* in 1954 (p. 99). And as Myerhoff points out, once an event or person or thing has been put into the ritual form and mode recognized by a given culture it has "a tradition-like effect" whether "performed for the first or thousandth time" (Moore and Myerhoff, 1977:8). Her chapter in *Secular Ritual* describes "such a once-and-only event, a graduation ceremony in an urban social center for the aged. The graduation combines many elements from the several cultural backgrounds of the members to make a unique composite ("bricolage") . . . .

Though performed only once it is supposed to carry the same unreflective conviction as any traditional repetitive ritual, to symbolize for the participants all that they share in common, and to insist to them that it all fits together by putting it together as one performance" (pp. 8-9). Here I would take mild issue with Myerhoff's term "unreflective"—I would see such a ritual, which the context of her recent book shows to have been itself a phase in a communal social drama, as involving *reflection* on the past myths and history of the group's culture (Judaism and Yiddishkeit). The "tradition-like" ceremony was, in terms of her own analysis, "an effort to have that past make sense in the situation of their peculiar collective present" (Myerhoff, 1977:9).

Both religious ritual and legal ceremony are genres of social action. They confront problems and contradictions of the social process, difficulties arising in the course of social life in communities, corporate groups, or other types of social fields. They are concerned with breaches of regular norm-governed relationships, involving action of the sort we would call in our culture crime, sin, deviance, offense, misdemeanor, injury, tort, damage, and so forth. In addition to the redress of immediate issues, the reconciliation of the parties involved, and, in extreme cases, the condign punishment, elimination, or ostracism of inveterate offenders, legal and religious rituals and ceremonies are what Moore calls "a declaration against indeterminacy" (1977:16). Through "form and formality they celebrate man-made meaning, the culturally determinate, the regulated, the named, and the explained . . . . Ritual is a declaration of form *against* indeterminacy, *therefore* indeterminacy is always present in the background of any analysis of ritual. Indeed there is no doubt that any analysis of social life must take account of the dynamic relation between the formed and "the indeterminate" (pp. 16-17). Of course, what is socioculturally indeterminate may be biologically, even sociobiologically determinate; or an indeterminate phase of social process may result from contradiction between principles or rules, each of which would produce systematic social action if conceded unimpeded validity. Thus being a "good son" may mean being a "bad citizen," if family loyalty obstructs civil justice. When we examine some Icelandic family sagas we will see how confused states of affairs, crises of conscience, arise from sociostructural contradictions.

My contention is that the major genres of cultural performance (from ritual to theatre and film) and narration (from myth to the novel) not only originate in the social drama but also continue to draw meaning and force from the social drama. I use "force" here in the Diltheyan sense. For him, *Kraft*, "force" meant something different in the humanistic studies from what it means in natural science. In the human studies, force means the influence which any experience has in determining what other experiences shall succeed it. Thus a memory has force in so far as it affects our present experience and actions. All the factors which together lead up to a practical decision are forces, and the decision itself is a force in so far as it leads to action. This category, so conceived, is an expression of something we know in our own lives. In natural science, Dilthey argues, it is different. There the concept of force is not drawn from experience of the physical world, but projected into it from our inner life; and it is bound up with the idea of laws of nature and physical necessity, to which the human studies offer no parallel. In other words, in the natural sciences "force" is used metaphorically; in physics the definition of force as "the form of energy that puts an object at rest into motion or alters the motion of a moving object" derives ultimately from human inner experience of acting vigorously and effectively, of controlling, persuading or influencing others.

Thus the "force" of a social drama consists in its being an experience or sequence of experiences which significantly influences the form and function of cultural performative genres. Such genres partly "imitate" (by *mimesis*), the processual form of the social drama, and they partly, through reflection, assign "meaning" to it. What do I "mean" by "meaning" here? I am aware of the formidable ambiguities of this term, and of the controversies surrounding it. To "mean" is, in its simple lexical definition, to have in mind, to have an opinion, to intend, and derives ultimately from the Indo-European base *maino-*, from which are derived, O. E. *maenan*, and German *meinen*, all of which signify "to have an opinion." Broadly speaking, a "meaning" is "what is intended to be, or in fact is, signified, indicated, referred to, or understood." But in the context of the humanistic studies, I would prefer to look at the term, again influenced by Dilthey, somewhat as follows: If a given human collectivity scans its recent or more distant history—usually through the mediation of representative figures, such as chroniclers, bards, historians, or in the liminal lens of performative or narrative genres—it seeks to find in it a structural unity to whose total character every past, culturally stressed collective experience has contributed something. If the relevant agents of reflexivity go further and seek to *understand* (Dilthey uses the term *Verstehen*, around which numerous methodological and theoretical controversies have raged since the late nineteenth century, especially when it has been contrasted with the German term, *Wissen*, "knowing, acquaintance," which is conceived as denoting a form of conceptual activity peculiar to the physical sciences but which sociological positivists believe is also applicable to the data of the social sciences—but let's pass over this thorny topic for the present!) and *interpret* (*deuten*) the structural unity of their past social life, to explore in detail the character and structure of the whole and the contradictions made by its various parts, we must develop new categories to understand the nature of their quest. One is *meaning*, which Dilthey employs in two ways. The first defines the *meaning* of a part as "the contribution it makes to the whole." The "whole" here would seem to be a complex of ideas and values akin to Clifford Geertz's notions of "world view" (itself akin to Dilthey's *Weltbild*) and *ethos* (or moral system). The resultant character of the whole is also said to possess "meaning" (*Bedeutung*) or *sense* (*Sinn*).

Dilthey throws in for good measure the categories of *value* (*Wert*) and *end*

(*Zweck*) or *good* (*Gut*), and relates them along with *meaning* to the three structural "attitudes of consciousness" cognition, affect, volition, mentioned earlier. Thus, the category of *meaning* arises in *memory*, in *cognition* of the *past* (that is, meaning is cognitive, self-reflexive, oriented to past experience, and concerned with negotiating about "fit" between present and past, as the phenomenological sociologists like Garfinkel and Cicourel might say today). The category of *value* arises, according to Dilthey, dominantly from feeling or affect (that is, value inheres in the *affective* enjoyment of the *present*). The category of *end* (goal, or *good*) *arises from volition*, the power or faculty of using the will, which refers to the *future*. These three categories, says Dilthey, are irreducible, like the three structural attitudes, and cannot be subordinated to one another.

Nevertheless, for Dilthey, value, end, and meaning are not of equal value insofar as they may be regarded as principles of understanding and interpretation. He defines value, for example, as belonging essentially to an experience in a conscious present. Such conscious presents, regarded purely as present moments, totally involve the experiencer, to the extent that they have no inner connection with one another, at least of a systematic, cognitive kind. They stand behind one another in temporal sequence, and, while they may be compared as "values" (having the same epistemological status), they do not form, since they are quintessentially momentary, *qua* values, transient, anything like a coherent whole—if they are interconnected, the ligatures that bind them are of another category. As Dilthey sees it, "From the standpoint of value, life appears as an infinite assortment of positive and negative existence—values. It is like a chaos of harmonies and discords. Each of these is a tone-structure which fills a present; but they have no musical relation to one another." Dilthey's view of value phenomena differs, markedly, of course, from that of many contemporary scientists. Robin Williams sums up their position quite well in the *IESS* (Vol. XVI, p. 283): "It seems all values contain some cognitive elements. . ., that they have a selective or directional quality, and that they involve some affective component . . . when most explicit and fully conceptualized, values become criteria for judgement, preference, and choice. When implicit and unreflective, values nevertheless perform *as if* they constituted grounds for decisions in behavior." Williams does not analyze so finely as Dilthey; he gives *value* cognitive and conative attributes which Dilthey reserves to other categories. The advantage of Dilthey's position, it seems to me, resides in the articulating (as well as reflexive and retrospective) character he assigns to *meaning*. The category of *end* or *good*, for example, shares the limitation of *value*, and, indeed, for Wilhelm Dilthey, depends on it. It can show life as a series of choices between ends, but finds no unity in this sequence of choices. Ultimately, it is only the category of *meaning* that enables us to *conceive an intrinsic affinity between the successive events in life*, and all that the categories of value and end can tell us is caught up in this synthesis. Moreover, Dilthey tells us, since meaning is specifically based on the *cognitive attitude of memory*, and "history is memory," meaning is naturally "the category most proper to historical thought" (G. S., VII, 201-2, 236). I would add, to socio-processual thought also.

Now I see the social drama, in its full formal development, its full phase structure, as a process of converting particular values and ends, distributed over a range of actors, into a system (which may be temporary or provisional) of shared or consensual meaning. The redressive phase, in which feedback is provided by the scanning mechanisms of law and religious ritual, is a time in which an interpretation is put upon the events leading up to and constituting the phase of crisis. Here the meaning of the social life informs the apprehension of itself; the object to be apprehended enters into and determines the apprehending subject. Sociological and anthropological functionalism, whose aim is to state the conditions of social equilibrium among the components of a social system at a given time, cannot deal with *meaning*, which always involves retrospection and reflexivity, a past, a history. Dilthey holds that the category of meaning is all-pervading in history. The story-teller, at the simplest narrational level, for example, "gains his effect by bringing out the *significant moments* in a process. The historian characterizes men at significant, turning-points in life [*Lebenswendungen*—what I would call "crises"] as full of meaning; in a definite effect of a work or a human being upon the general destiny he recognizes the *meaning* of such a work or such a human being" (G. S.,VII:234). Meaning is the only category which grasps the full relation of the part to the whole in life. In the category of *value*, or again in that of good or *end*, some aspect of this part-whole relation is of course made visible; but these categories are, as Dilthey insists, abstract and one-sided, and, he holds, we cannot think in terms of them without finally encountering some brute fact, some empirical coexistence of experiences, which these categories do not help us to resolve into a living whole. It is at this point that we should invoke the comprehensive category of meaning, a category by definition inclusive, laying hold of the factors making for integration in a given situation or phenomenon; whereby the whole, the total sociocultural phenomenon becomes intelligible, of which value and end were but aspects. Meaning is apprehended by looking back over a process in time. We assess the meaning of every part of the process by its contribution to the total result.

Meaning is connected with the consummation of a process—it is bound up with termination, in a sense, with death. The meaning of any given factor in a process cannot be assessed until the whole process is past. Thus, the meaning of a man's life, and of each moment in it, becomes manifest to others only when his life is ended. The meaning of historical processes, for instance, "civilizational" processes such as the "decline and fall of the Roman empire," is not and will not be known until their termination, perhaps not until the end of history itself, if such an end there will be. In other words, meaning is retrospective and discovered by the selection action of reflexive attention. This does not, of course, prevent us from making judgments, both "snap" and considered, about the meaning of contemporary events, but every such judgment is necessarily provisional, and relative to the moment in which it is made. It rests partly on the positive and negative values we bring to bear on events from our structural or psychological perspective, and for the ends we have in mind at the time.

The encounter of past and present in redressive process always leaves open the question whether precedent (an ingredient in Moore's "processes of regularization") or the unprecedented will provide the terminal "meaning" of any problem-situation. At every moment, and especially in the redressal of crises, the meaning of the past is assessed by reference to the present and, of the present by reference to the past; the resultant "meaningful" decision modifies the group's orientation to or even plans for the future, and these in turn react upon its evaluation of the past. Thus the apprehension of the meaning of life is always relative, and involved in perpetual change. Of course, cultural devices exist which attempt to "fix" or "crystallize" meaning, such as religious dogmas, political constitutions, supernatural sanctions and taboos against breaking crucial norms, and so on, but, as we said earlier, these are subject to manipulation and amendment.

References

Benamou, Michel, and Charles Caramello, eds. 1977. *Performance in Postmodern Culture.* Madison, Wisconsin: Coda.

Dilthey, Wilhelm. 1914-1936. *Gesammelte Schriften*, vols. 1-12. Stuttgart: Teubner.

Hinde, Robert. 1974. *Nonverbal Communication.* Cambridge: Cambridge University Press.

Hockett, Charles. 1960. "Logical Considerations in the Study of Animal Communication," in W. E. Lanyon and W. N. Tavolga, eds., *Animal Sounds and Communication.* Washington, D.C.: American Institute of Biological Sciences. Pp. 392-430.

Leach, Edmund. 1972. "The Influence of Cultural Context on Nonverbal Communication in Man," in Robert A. Hinde, ed., *Nonverbal Communication.* Cambridge: Cambridge University Press. Pp. 321-322.

MacKay, D. M. 1972. "Formal Analysis of Communicative Processes," in Robert A. Hinde, ed., *Nonverbal Communication.* Cambridge: Cambridge University Press. Pp. 3-25.

Moore, Sally F., and Barbara Myerhoff, eds. 1977. *Secular Ritual.* Amsterdam: Van Gorcum.

Murphy, R. F. 1971. *The Dialectics of Social Life.* New York: Basic Books.

Olney, James. 1972. *Metaphors of Self.* Princeton: Princeton University Press.

Schechner, Richard. 1977. *Essays on Performance Theory, 1970-1976.* New York: Drama Book Specialists.

Schwartz, Theodore. 1978. "Where is the Culture?" in George Spindler, ed., *The Making of Psychological Anthropology.* Berkeley: University of California Press. Pp. 419-441.

Spindler, George, ed. 1978. *The Making of Psychological Anthropology.* Berkeley: University of California Press.

Turner, Victor. 1957. *Schism and Continuity.* Manchester: Manchester University Press.

————— . 1974. *Dramas, Fields, and Metaphors.* Ithaca: Cornell University Press.

Rokujo's Jealousy:

Liminality and the Performative Genres

Members of our species, *homo sapiens*, are peculiarly festooned with prepositions, with relational and functional connectives. If we are, visibly, islands, we
are genetically and culturally linked by ties of love and hate, by the pleasure-
bond, by the pain-bond, by the duty chain, by noblesse oblige, or by innate or
induced needs for dominance or submission. We are for, against, with,
towards, above, below, within, outside, or without one another. If we could
make a psychosomatigram of a member of our species, it would not be
smoothly nude, but, as it were, sprouting with prepositional lines and plugs,
and pitted with prepositional plug-holes. And if this metaphor has bisexual or
androgynous implications, these would be supported by genetic and depth-
psychological findings. The culture which encompasses speech and the speech
which embraces prepositional forms are attributes of a two-sexed species, each
of whose sexes is in a sense a transformation of the other. I do not intend to
follow up this line of inquiry here, however. My present intention is to discuss
what have been varyingly described as performative genres, cultural performances, modes or exhibition or presentation—such as ritual, carnival, theatre,
and film—as commentaries and critiques on, or as celebrations of, different
dimensions of human relatedness. My work as an anthropologist has been the
study of cumulative interactions over time in human groups, of varying span
and different cultures (Ndembu, Gisu, Mexican, and Irish through direct observation; Icelandic, Indian, medieval English, and Florentine through historical
and literary sources). These interactions, I found, tended to amass towards the
emergence of sustained public action, to which, given my Western background,
it was difficult to characterize as other than "dramatic." When the prepositions,
with and against, involved enough people in dichotomous factions, there was a

public outburst of opposition, involving the mounting of symbols of exclusivity and inclusivity, which led to a sequence of stages in public life, where breach of some crucial bond to which the whole group was committed by its written or unwritten constitution to maintaining (made evident by some signal violation, rejection or disregarding of a rule of behavior, moral conduct or etiquette) was followed by a mounting crisis in the group's affairs which, if not pinched off, grew to the point of dividing it in two, instead of leaving it with gradations of opinion. The pinching-off process involved an attempt, whole-hearted or faint-hearted, to get the affair into a law-court or similar redressive assembly of grave elders or responsible representatives of whatever the group might call itself, from village to district to nation to international forum. Sometimes, I found, nothing short of a religious solution was deemed necessary, with ritual procedures instigated to press the antagonists together. Last scene of all, to close this strange history (which is yet a history familiar to all of us), is the outcome of the redressive, reconciliatory, or reconstitutive action: what happens to all those people prepositionally interconnected or divided? Do they stay together in spatial and psychological proximity (with reservations, of course), or does some parcel of them, some sub-group, unable to accept the elders' verdict, "opt out"—seek a new territory, move away a mile or two, or even go to a new continent like the Pilgrim Fathers and those who took them for paradigm?

This processual form, "breach-crisis-redress-outcome," I called, in my *jeunesse*, a "social drama." It was hardly a "natural" form, since it was heavily dependent on the cultural values and rules by which human conduct, as distinct from behavior, was assessed. Often, indeed, it seemed to be a matter of nature *versus* culture, of human drives transgressing cultural commandments. But even more often it was a question of one cultural rule opposing another. Man's "original sin," perhaps, is the plurality of equally valid rules he imposes on himself, so that whatever virtue he may display in obeying one is negated by the fact that he is in all honesty transgressing another. Original sin is perhaps not merely a mistake in logical sorting, but man's status as an *evolving* life form. If man is inveterately "on the move," developmentally, clearly what was appropriate even a mere hundred years ago is no longer appropriate to what man has culturally, let alone biologically, become in the interim. The problem is not so much "cultural relativism" at a given time, as the fact that we *do*, as a global species, learn by experience, and that the experience is somehow, though perhaps always allusively and enigmatically (hence the need for hermeneutics), communicated in the symbolic actions and forms of our varying cultures.

One of the best ways we learn by experience is through our "performative genres." My position here is that in our quotidian life, social dramas, whether in small groups or large, continue to emerge—offspring of both culture and nature—but that the cultural ways we have of becoming aware of them—rituals, stage plays, carnivals, anthropological monographs, pictorial exhibitions, films, etc.—vary with culture, climate, technology, group history, the

demography of individual genius, etc. I began with a linguistic analogy: prepositions. I continue with another: the "moods" of verbs. For language has
something to say about deeply founded human regularities—particularly grammar. After all, we are linked and separated most significantly by coded sounds
and the rules of their arrangement.

Most cultural performances belong to culture's "subjunctive" mood. "Subjunctive" is defined by Webster as "that mood of a verb used to express supposition, desire, hypothesis, possibility, etc., rather than to state an actual fact, as
the mood of *were*, in 'if I *were* you.' " Ritual, carnival, festival, theatre, film, and
similar performative genres clearly possess many of these attributes. The indicative mood of culture, viewed as cultural process rather than as abstract
systems ingeniously derived from social life's flow, controls the quotidian arenas
of economic activity, much of law and politics, and a good deal of domestic life.
The indicative mood, according to Webster, expresses "an act, state, or occurrence as actual, or to ask a question of fact," as in legal or scientific interroga-
tion. It is perhaps significant that, as the *Concise Oxford Dictionary* puts it, "subjunctive = a verbal mood, obsolescent in English, named as being used in the
classical languages chiefly in subordinate or subjoined clauses." The subjunctive
domain of culture has lost its former validity; the verbal mood is waning with
it. Recent developments in the theatre and cinema, however, seem to be aimed
at restoring the fading subjunctivity of these genres.

I would now like to relate cultural subjunctivity to what I have called
"liminality," following Arnold van Gennep, the great French folklorist who
divided rituals associated with passage from one basic human state or status, individual or collective, to another into three stages. These were: separation from
antecedent mundane life; liminality, a betwixt-and-between condition often involving seclusion from the everyday scene; and re-aggregation to the quotidian
world. Such passage rites were of two broad types: (1) those performed to mark
and, in the view of performers, to effect transitions from social invisibility to
social visibility, as in birth rites; from juniority to seniority, as in circumcision
and puberty rites; of sociosexual conjunction, as in nuptial rites; and of the
passage from visible to invisible social existence, as in funerary rites converting
a corpse or ghost into an ancestor; and (2) those marking a whole group's
passage from one culturally defined season to another in the annual cycle,
where solar, lunar, planetary, and stellar cyclicities may be involved. Such rites
may be extended to include collective response to hazards such as war, famine,
drought, plague, earthquake, volcanic eruption, and other natural or man-
made disasters. I have discussed both these main types elsewhere. Here I merely
want to call attention to the relationship of the second type to the genres of
performance which are the main focus of this conference.

Life-crisis rituals usually involve a liminal phase of seclusion from the centers
of quotidian action: novices are initiated into adulthood or into the mysteries
of a cult association in hidden places—caves, lodges sequestered in the forest,

far-off or covered places. Rituals of the second type, public in general orientation from the first, have their liminality in public places. The village greens or the squares of the city are not abandoned but rather ritually transformed. It is as though everything is switched into the subjunctive mood for a privileged period of time—the time, for example, of Mardi-Gras or the Carnival-Carême. Public liminality is governed by public subjunctivity. For a while almost anything goes: taboos are lifted, fantasies are enacted, indicative mood behavior is reversed; the low are exalted and the mighty abased. Yet there are some controls: crime is still illicit; drunken bodies may be moved off the sidewalks. And ritual forms still constrain the order and often the style of ritual events.

Liminality itself is a complex phase or condition. It is often the scene and time for the emergence of a society's deepest values in the form of sacred dramas and objects—sometimes the re-enactment periodically of cosmogonic narratives or deeds of saintly, godly, or heroic establishers of morality, basic institutions, or ways of approaching transcendent beings or powers. But it may also be the venue and occasion for the most radical scepticism—always relative, of course, to the given culture's repertoire of sceptical concepts and images—about cherished values and rules. Ambiguity reigns; people and public policies may be judged sceptically in relation to deep values; the vices, follies, stupidities, and abuses of contemporary holders of high political, economic, or religious status may be satirized, ridiculed, or contemned in terms of axiomatic values, or these personages may be rebuked for gross failures in commonsense. In general, life-crisis rites stress the deep values, often exhibited to initiands as sacred objects, while the commentary on society and its leading representatives is assigned to cyclical feasts and their public liminality. As dramatic genres, tragedy perhaps departs from the former, comedy from the latter—though I am well aware that the matter is far more complex than this simple statement supposes.

Public liminality and subjunctivity lead me to some of Gregory Bateson's most stimulating ideas: metalanguage and metacommunication. Bateson begins with propositions, expressions in which the predicate affirms or denies something about the subject, the predicate being an assertion or affirmation based on given facts. Propositions flourish best in the indicative mood of the cultural process. They depend upon conventions of codification, verbal or nonverbal, most of which lie below the threshhold of conscious awareness of members of a given group, on tacit agreements between speakers that they be true. But some propositions are not *in* these cultural codes but *about* them. They are liminal, in the sense that they are suspensions of quotidian reality, occupying privileged spaces where people are allowed to think about how they think, about the terms in which they conduct their thinking, or to feel about how they feel in daily life. Here the code rules are themselves the referent of the knowing; the knowledge propositions themselves are the object of knowledge. As Mary B. Black has written (1973:533): "Bateson has pointed out that while traditionally science has proceeded by abstracting out one level or another for analysis, ignoring for the moment the effect of context, he has been doing the reverse, and focusing his attention on the relationships and influences between levels." My view is that cultures of the prescientific kinds have, in their liminal settings (predominantly ritual ones), been doing precisely this, and have given us many examples of metacommunication and the learning of metapatterns. Metapatterns are akin to what some call "frames," the metaphorical borders within which the facts of experience can be viewed, reflected upon, and evaluated, though some see frames on experience's level as sorting out different types. A cyclical ritual is a frame within which members of a given group strive to see their own reality in new ways and to generate a language, verbal or nonverbal, which enables them to talk *about* what they normally talk. But it must not be thought that ritual metalanguage is essentially cognitive or philosophical. It is, as D. H. Lawrence said, though here we must use the plural, "a man in his wholeness wholly attending." Plurally this may be rendered, "men and women, of a given group and culture, wholly attending, in privileged moments, to their own existential situation." Emotion and volition, as well as cool cognitiveness, encompass their metasituation. Other scholars use the term "reflexivity" for similar processes. These, again, have ransacked language for its metaphors: a reflexive act implies an agent's action upon himself, indicating the identity of subject and object. When the subject is plural and human, hence a cultural entity, the agents' action is motivated by and with reference to cultural definitions of who it is that acts and to whom action is directed. Since culture is fed by affectual and volitional as well as cognitive sources, and since these may be unconscious in great part, the terms and symbols of plural reflexivity may be suffused with *orexis*, with desire and appetite, as well as involved with knowing, perceiving, and conceiving.

This brings us back to drama. It is in social dramas that plural reflexivity begins. If social drama regularly implies conflict of principles, norms, and persons, it equally implies the growth of reflexivity; for if all principles and norms were consistent and if all persons obeyed them, then culture and society would be unselfconscious and innocent, untroubled by the shadow of a doubt. But few indeed are the human groups whose relationships are perpetually in equilibrium, and are free from agonistic strivings. I have been criticized for assigning the term "drama" to regular courses of events which become publicly visible through some breach of a norm ordinarily held to be binding, and which is itself a symbol of the maintenance of some major relationship between persons, statuses, or sub-groups held to be a key link in the integrality of the widest group recognized to be a cultural envelope of solidary sentiments. This course of events moves on to what I call the phase of crisis, when people take sides or are in the process of being induced, cajoled, or threatened to take sides, by those who face one another across the revealed breach as prime antagonists. Crisis has some of the characteristics of plague; it is extremely "contagious."

Members of a group, whether it be an African village, an American university department, a trade union local, a church club, or the Cabinet of a major nation-state, remember, when crisis strikes, previous crises—where they stood then, how they felt about the positions adopted by other group members; and nonrational considerations become prominent—temperamental hostilities, unconscious sexual attractions, reanimated infantile anxieties, and the like. The cleavage is thus likely to deepen by including more and more grounds of opposition. All that is why the third stage is so often considered necessary—the application of redressive or remedial procedures. Order is threatened; reordering courses of action, the "antibodies" of the group, are produced in response to that group's contact with a sociocultural "antigen," interpreted by the representatives of the group's ideal solidarity and continuity as the "toxins" of particular interest and ambition. This third stage is perhaps the most "reflexive" phase of the social drama. The group, acting through its delegates or representatives, bends or throws itself back upon itself, to measure what its members, or some of its members, have done against its own standards of how they should or ought to have conducted themselves. Processes, mediated by procedures, established ways of doing things, are set in train, the aim of which is to defuse tension, assess irrational deeds against standards of reasonableness, and to reconcile conflicting parties—having convinced them, through showing them the damaging effects of their actions on group unity, that it is better to restore a state of peace than to continue in a state of hostility. The fourth phase is the action initiated by the outcome of the third. My experience in Africa led me to see this as a bifurcation; *either* there was an overt reconciliation of the conflicting parties, *or* there was social recognition that schism was unavoidable and that the best that could be done was for the dissident party or parties to split off, spatially if possible, from the group of the party or parties adjudged to have the better case.

As I mentioned earlier, certain scholars, Raymond Firth among them, have rebuked me for calling this pattern, abstracted from many observations of social processes in relatively well bonded communities, of breach, crisis, attempted redress, and restoration of peace, a "social drama." They would reserve the term "drama" for "theatrical presentations"—for "a portrayal of some aspect or sector of the human condition in a conventional, stylized form, involving selection and abstraction from observation or from an imaginative range of ideas" (*Times Literary Supplement*, Sept. 13, 1974, p. 966). Now my formulation involves "selection and abstraction from observation," for this is precisely what happens in the third, the redressive stage. I should mention that among redressive procedures we should reckon ritual as well as legal (or jural) action. Among the Ndembu of Zambia, "rituals of affliction," performed to placate ancestral spirits or exorcise witchcraft familiars, very often took place precisely in the midst or wake of the second phase of a social drama, "crisis." It was a fact of observation that more people became ill in various ways during crises than when life had an even tenor. In such cases, their kin go to a diviner who tells them, in the course of a more or less elaborate seance, what has caused the affliction and what type of ritual should be performed to remedy it. During the performance of such rituals, persons divided in the factional struggles of the crisis phase are often united by having to cooperate in ritual tasks and by the injunction to cast out of their "livers" any bad feelings they might harbor there against anyone in the ritual situation. Firth's notion of an "imaginative range of ideas" comes into play here, too, for the senior adepts, or "doctors" in such ritual performances, often display individual virtuosity in the symbols they select and the ways in which they control the proceedings and the actors.

My contention is that social dramas are the "raw stuff" out of which theatre comes to be created as societies develop in scale and complexity and out of which it is continually regenerated. For I would assert that the social drama form is, indeed, universal, though it may be culturally elaborated in different ways in different societies. In some societies, crises, for example, may be muted to all appearances, as in Burmese villages; in others, as in many African villages, overt. The degree of force employed may vary; the tempo may be fast or slow; the rhetoric passionate or restrained; the motivation to produce an unambiguous outcome highly variable. Some societies may regularly favor legal, others ritual, modes of redress. Class, gender, status, age variables, as well as cultural traditions, may affect the style as well as the vehemence of social dramas. Types of issues, whether serious matters of communal survival or debate about how to decorate a house, also affect the aesthetic shape of social dramas.

When all is said, however, both the indicative and subjunctive (and perhaps the optative) moods of society, and the reflexive forms, are present in live relationship in the unfolding of the social drama. This is the "natural unit" (in terms of "human nature") of *societas*, seen as a process with some systematic features, rather than as modelled on an abstract organic or mechanical system. The liveliest confrontation of indicative and subjunctive processes occurs during the redressive phase. For the judicial process seeks to establish the facts by means of cross-examinations of witnesses and the assessment of conflicting evidence in terms of "as-if" models. Max Gluckman has pointed out how the standard of the "reasonable man" is used in Africa, as in the West, to determine the virtual truth of a plaintiff's, defendant's, or witness's statement: how would a reasonable man behave if he caught his wife in flagrant delicto with the deceased? Of course, "reasonableness" becomes alloyed with status-role, for evidence is measured by the yardsticks of "reasonable husband," "reasonable father," "reasonable citizen," "reasonable sub-chief," etc. In any case, narratives are placed in such "as-if" frames, in order to move from the subjunctive mood of "it may have happened like this or that" to the quasi-indicative mood of "these would appear to be the facts, m'lud." The subjunctive is even more evident in ritual procedures, from divination to shamanistic or liturgical curative action, in which many invisible causes of visible afflictions are put forward by ritual specialists as they try obliquely to assess the main sources of discord in the communal context of each case of illness or misfortune.

In any event, the social drama is the major form of plural reflexivity in human social action. It is not yet an aesthetic mode, for it is fully embodied in daily living. But it contains the germs of aesthetic modes, both in its jural and ritual operations. Ritual, in tribal society, represents not an obsessional concern with repetitive acts, but an immense orchestration of genres in all available sensory codes: speech, music, singing; the presentation of elaborately worked objects, such as masks; wall-paintings, body-paintings; sculptured forms; complex, many tiered shrines; costumes; dance forms with complex grammars and vocabularies of bodily movements, gestures, and facial expressions. Ritual also contains plastic and labile phases and episodes, as well as fixed and formal ones. It is only by the *sparagmos*, or dismemberment, of tribal ritual that modern religious and neurotic rituals have become specialized out from their multi-dimensional performative original. Whether such an original matrix can ever be restored, short of the extinction of those power sources which sustain complex modern economies—short of, therefore, retribalization—is a moot point. I am not happy about certain attempts to make theatre regress to ritual. For such a regression is at the same time a resynthesis of that which the division of labor has decisively put asunder. And perhaps no man can wittingly do this! Who can "unwind the winding path"? Though our species could easily, unwittingly, bring it about by destroying the economic bases of its civilized structures.

Plural reflexivity, as represented in the genres of performance, including judicial processes, differs from singular reflexivity in that it involves several persons in dramatic interaction. Prince Hamlet could brood on his own motives, but the play *Hamlet* reflects upon the rottenness not merely "in the state of Denmark" but in the early modern world as old feudal values came to stink in new Renaissance nostrils. It is the total set of interactions which constitutes this metacommentary. The pattern of divination-therapy abides throughout the whole brood of genres released by the division of labor from the jural-ritual performative types found in the less complex societies. Drama heals; art cures; music soothes; the novel is therapeutic. Getting to know oneself is to put oneself on the way to healing oneself. The kind of self-knowledge that produces despair is inadequate self-knowledge, and may, indeed, be a crisis of the disease—as Dostoevsky has so repeatedly shown us.

The social drama, then, endures, while the genres which cultural development has detached from it, and thereafter elaborated, multiply in a manner consistent with Kurt Gödel's theorem on the impossibility (under certain circumstances) of formalizing a consistency proof for a logistic system (here in the sense of a system of symbolic logic) *within* that system. Such a proof demands a metalanguage for talking about the system in terms not derived from it.

Similarly, the redressive machinery of spontaneous social drama, judicial and ritual, attains only a limited degree of reflexivity, lying as it does, on the same plane as the agonistic events being scrutinized. Other languages or metalanguages, nonverbal as well as verbal, other scrutinizing procedures are required—particularly when societies advance in scale and complexity, often with sharp increases in the rates of spatial and social mobility. Such languages and procedures have antithetical qualities to the spontaneous dramas which they have to deal with. They have not only to recapitulate the sequence of agonistic events, but also to scrutinize and evaluate them. The reenactment is framed as a performance, but it is a metaperformance, a performance about a performance.

And so we find performances about performances about performances multiplying. Of course, as Goffman and others have shown, ordinary life in a social structure is itself a performance. We play roles, occupy statuses, play games with one another, don and doff many masks, each a "typification." But the performances characteristic of liminal phases and states often are more about the doffing of masks, the stripping of statuses, the renunciation of roles, the demolishing of structures, than their putting on and keeping on. Antistructures are performed, too. But, still within the liminal frame, new subjunctive, even ludic, structures are then generated, with their own grammars and lexica of roles and relationships. These are imaginative creations, whether attributed to individuals or "traditions." These become the many performative genres we have discussed. They are also within what Gregory Bateson has called "the play frame," which is one of the frames found in liminality. It is a frame which, as he justly remarks, encompasses a special combination of primary and secondary processes, and is likely to precipitate paradox. In a primary process, the thinker is unable to discriminate between "some" and "all," and "not all" and "none," while it is of the essence of secondary thinking, a more conscious mental process, that such distinctions are made. In a dream or fantasy, the subject is usually unaware that he is dreaming. But in play he is made aware that "this is play." It is this peculiar union of primary processes, where subjectively the actor is in what M. Csikszentmihalyi calls "flow," where action and awareness are one and there is loss of the sense of ego, and secondary processes, where cognitive discriminations are made, that constitutes the distinctive quality of performative genres. The actors, to do their work well, must be in flow; but the "script," "scenario," or "message" they portray is finally shaped by discriminative reflexive secondary processes—the author's metastatements are powerfully animated by the actors' absorption in primary-process. Whether the script is by an individual playwright or is "tradition" itself, it usually comments on social relationships, cultural values, and moral issues. But the actors do not take part in the formulation of the author's messages; what they do is to activate those messages by the "flow" quality of their performance—a flow that engages the audience as well, impressing on its members the "message" of the total production.

I would like to illustrate this argument by examining not the Western cultural tradition, but the Japanese. It is unimportant that I am no scholar in this literature, since I am concerned with only a few very general variables. Two expressive genres are involved—the novel and the theatre—and I shall also discuss a subtle metacommentary on the actor's art by Zeami Motokiyo (1363-1444), a great actor, writer, and theorizer of the Noh drama. Many of the plots of the Noh drama were taken from what has sometimes been called "the world's first real novel" (though it was not the first Japanese novel), The Tale of Genji. Murasaki Shikibu, a Court Lady of the Heian period, wrote this masterpiece in the few years after her husband's death in 1001—after only two years of marriage and before she entered the Empress's service in 1007. I shall consider a set of episodes in the novel which formed the basis of the plot of the Noh play Aoi no Uye (Princess Hollyhock), ascribed by tradition to Zeami's son-in-law Zenchiku Ujinobu and known to have existed in something like its present form in the middle of the fifteenth century. The novel form and the drama form each represents a frame; each frame encloses not only a narrative or plot but also an explicit and implicit commentary on the social life of the times in which they were written. Murasaki's standpoint is aesthetic rather than religious; that of the Noh play is the reverse—though the stagecraft is supremely aesthetic. But aesthetics and religion both distance the authors from the stream of events they describe and evaluate, and put their scenarios under the sign of reflexivity. Zeami's essay is about how the actor should handle this situation, and still put the audience into a state of flow through the verisimilitude created by his performance.

Since I am convinced that social anthropology should intertwine with history, like the snakes in Hermes's caduceus, wherever sound documentation exists, if I were to make a detailed study of the relationship between the novel and the play, I would contextualize Murasaki's work in what we know of Heian court society, culture, and religion, and set the Noh play in the mid-Muromachi period, that turbulent time of rival Emperors and feudal lords or daimyos, within whose autonomous domains, nevertheless, there was comparative tranquility and prosperity. The artisans and merchants throve under daimyo protection. Diplomatic relations and trade were opened with Ming China. In this age, called sengoku, or "country at war," replete with social "dramas of living" (to use Kenneth Burke's term), yet with many enclaves of high culture, the Noh drama was born, to reflect upon the past and present by means of a vocabulary of concepts drawn largely from Buddhism, to call any "present" into question. In the Muromachi period, the money economy spread everywhere and the more powerful daimyo protected the developing merchant class in their domains. Trading areas became enlarged and many of them encompassed more than one feudal lord's domain. In this period not only did the Noh theatre prosper under the patronage of the Ashikaga shogunate but so also did Chinese studies, pursued by the Zen monks of the five major temples. The tea ceremony and the art of flower arrangement also originated in this period of general restlessness and uncertainty. Such periods in complex cultures often provoke reflexivity.

But time presses and I must *compress*. Murasaki was a member of a cloistered, sophisticated court, in which the powerful Fujiwara family ruled through a powerless emperor at Kyoto (or Heian-Kyo). Court women were peculiarly well cloistered, cut off from fresh new experiences, and thrown back upon their own circles of gossip, elegance, and royal ceremonies. One of the things they busied themselves with was the copying out of pictorial novels, which combined pictures with narrative in long scrolls. They were so many Mesdames Bovary, dissatisfied with real life. But Lady Murasaki was a most singular person—in any age or culture. Her diary tells us that her father, a considerable scholar in Chinese literature, had her elder brother taught to read the Chinese classics. She writes, "I listened, sitting beside him, and learned wonderfully fast, though he was sometimes slow and forgot. Father, who was devoted to study, regretted that I had not been a son, but I heard people saying that it is not beautiful even for a man to be proud of his learning, and after that I did not write even so much as the figure one in Chinese. I grew clumsy with my writing brush. For a long time I did not care for the books I had already read" (D. Keene, 1960:155). Later, such was the obloquy which fell upon bluestockings in the Heian court that we encounter the pathetic spectacle of Murasaki clandestinely teaching the Empress the works of the great Chinese poet Li T'ai Po. Women should be lovely and trivial, not learned. A learned woman in that court was indeed a liminal figure, though many were literate enough to occupy themselves with volumes of romance and fantasy. Escapism was all right, but classical genius all wrong.

However, Murasaki created a reflexive, subjunctive world of characters, who, as she writes at the very beginning of her novel, "lived at the Court of an Emperor (he lived it matters not when)" (*The Tale of Genji*, 1960:7). But unlike the other ladies, she had a theory of the novel which she made explicit in one of its episodes. This theory suggests that the world of fantastic stories is not so far removed from real life as it may appear. By a singular irony, the episode consists of a homily on the pictorial novel delivered by the principal character of Murasaki's novel, Prince Genji, to Tamakazura, who is the daughter of Yugao, who plays a role in the Noh play we will examine. There is additional irony in the fact that Tamakazura considers herself to be Genji's daughter born out of wedlock. Genji, himself an Emperor's bastard, knows that she is the daughter of another court noble, To no Chujo. Yugao, with whom Genji had a brief, passionate love affair in his youth, though of good birth was thought by Genji at the time to have been a woman of the people. Her death, as we shall see, was due to the jealously of one of Genji's lovers, a high-born Court lady, though in a way weirdly deviant from what we would take to be everyday reality—yet Murasaki supposes that this death was part of *Genji's* everyday reality. As you must be beginning to picture, we are already in a hall of reflecting mirrors, some of them distorting mirrors.

Genji, half-enamored of his late inamorata's daughter, now his ward, visits her and finds her copying out a pictorial novel. He exclaims, "What a nuisance! It looks as if ladies were born into this world only to be deceived by others, and willingly too! They surely know there is very little truth in those stories and yet they allow their minds to wander into fantasies and deceits as they read them in the hot, humid weather, even forgetting that their hair is in tangles" (*Makoto Ueda*, 1967:29). Murasaki adds that "he said this to Tamakazura and laughed."

But Genji is no "male chauvinist," though his sarcasm aims at the contemporary stereotype of women as unable to distinguish between fact and fiction. Genji is Murasaki's own vehicle as well as the occasional butt of her (implicit) feminist critique of male behavior. For he goes on to say, with a flash of empathy, "Indeed, without those old tales we would have no way by which to kill our hopelessly tedious hours" (Murasaki, p. 30). But he then goes on to make a powerful case for the "reality" of the subjunctive mood of culture as conveyed in the Japanese tradition of the novel. "Yet among such make-believe things there are some which, having truly convincing pathos, unfold themselves with natural smoothness. We know they are not real, but still we cannot help being moved when we read them" (p. 30). Genji goes on to tell Tamakazura that the way to sift out the "good" from the "bad" novel is that the former "does not simply consist in the author's telling a story about the adventures of some other person. On the contrary, it happens because the storyteller's own experience of men and things, whether for good or ill—not only what he has passed through himself, but even events which he has only witnessed or been told of—has moved him to an emotion so passionate that he can no longer keep it shut up in his heart . . . . He cannot bear to let it pass into oblivion. There must never come a time when he feels, when men do not know about it, . . .clearly, then, it is no part of the storyteller's craft to describe only what is good or beautiful . . . . anything whatsoever may become the subject of a novel, provided only that it happens in this mundane life and not in some fairyland beyond our human ken" (p. 502). The novel is thus concerned with the possible and not the impossible; if not with the factual, the "may be" and "might have been," but not the "may not be" and "never have been." Genji admits that different cultures have "different methods of composition," different "outward forms"—China and Japan, for example. And that there are "lighter and more serious forms of fiction" (p. 502). But he goes on to say that even in Mahayana Buddhism there is a difference between what is called Factual Truth and Adapted Truth, that is, fictional stories about the Buddha. Both fact and edifying fiction aim at teaching the Law which leads to Enlightenment. In the same way, historical truth—such as Genji claims may be found in the Chronicles of Japan (*Nihon Shoki*)—and imaginative truth differ only in the way by which they grasp *reality*. They are the indicative and subjunctive moods, in the terms I

have suggested, of presentational culture. The great aesthetic and ethical issues
are posed in fiction as much as in religion discourse. Real feeling is in the
novelist and he deals with abiding ethical issues, with the codes which assign
meaning in terms of good and evil to deeds. He may invent plots, situations,
characters, scenery; but imaginative truth underlies surface fiction.

I mentioned that Prince Genji was talking to his dead love's daughter. The
lost lady was called Yugao, literally Moonflower, and the tale of her romance
with Genji is perhaps the most poignant episode in the novel. Let us admire
Murasaki's subtle "double-take." Genji, who was himself a protagonist in a tale
of Murasaki's which has "truly convincing pathos," reflects upon the nature of
the novel, which should convey just this quality, in the presence of Yugao's
child. What makes the matter even more complex is Genji's enthusiastic mention of his literary talks with the girl to his wife, whose name is also Murasaki,
and who had been first raised from infancy, then wooed and seduced by Genji
in his palace. Murasaki is annoyed when Genji calls Tamakazura a "woman of
the world" with a "brilliant future before her." I now quote from Arthur Waley's
translation:

> From his manner Murasaki instantly saw that his interest in
> Tamakazura had assumed a new character. "I am very sorry for the
> girl," she said, "She evidently has complete confidence in you. But I
> happen to know what you mean by that phrase, "a woman of the
> world," and if I chose to do so, could tell the unfortunate creature
> what to expect." . . . "But you surely cannot mean that I shall *betray*
> her confidence?" asked Genji indignantly. "You forget," she replied,
> "that I was once in very much the same position myself. You had made
> up your mind to treat me as a daughter; but, unless I am much
> mistaken, there were times when you did not carry out this resolution
> very successfully . . . ." "How clever everyone is!" thought Genji, much
> put out at the facility with which his inmost thoughts were read . . . .
> Murasaki, he reflected, was not judging this case on its merits, but
> merely assuming, in the light of past experience, that events were
> about to take a certain course. . . .To convince himself that Murasaki
> had no ground for her suspicions he frequently went across to the side
> wing and spent some hours in Tamakazura's company (pp. 487-8).

Prince Genji consistently turned his life into a fiction and gave his love affairs
a certain aesthetic style. He framed them in moments of anticipatory beauty
like so many pictures illustrating a novel of the period. There was so often his
pause in the moonlight to watch the cherry blossoms round her door—more
exquisite than her subsequent seduction. But the death of Yugao after a
clandestine tryst had a macabre quality. It followed Genji's vision of a tall and
majestic woman who "made as though to drag the woman from his side."

Yugao became limp and died. The menacing hallucination came again on various occasions to trouble Genji. And it is on this figure that both Murasaki and the Noh dramatist have chosen to concentrate—in ways revelatory not only of differences between the media used but also of life-stances of the authors. Murasaki uses the supernatural for aesthetic and psychological purposes, the Noh play for ethico-religious ends; yet behind both is a pervasive Buddhistic world-view which stresses compassion and enlightenment, rather than condemnation and revenge.

For the supernatural figure is not a ghost in the novel but the apparition of a living woman. In Heian times—and even today in rural areas—in Japanese belief, a sustained vehement passion of love or jealousy could bring about the translocation of the passionate spirit, either to possess the object of its jealousy or to menace the object of its love. In many cultures this would be called "witchcraft." In most cases the afflicting agent is a woman and she is unconscious of her own malevolence. In *The Tale of Genji*, the living ghost is one Lady Rokujo, widow of the Old Emperor's elder brother who died young. Genji, illegitimate son of the Old Emperor, became the target of her ardent feelings long pent-up by premature widowhood. She was seven years older than the young prince, whose beauty and charm made him every woman's favorite in the court circle. For Genji, the affair soon became painful; "the blind intoxicating passion that had possessed him while she was still unattainable had almost disappeared. To begin with, she was far too sensitive, then there was that disparity of their ages, and the constant dread of discovery which haunted him during those painful partings at small hours in the morning. In fact, there were too many disadvantages" (p. 59).

Normally, Genji would have tapered off the affair with his usual charm and consideration that left the lady still his friend. But Rokujo was high-born, proud, and developed a fierce jealousy for all Genji's women. But this was a jealousy she would hardly admit to herself. It took the form of protecting her living ghost against rivals. I am sure that Lady Murasaki used this widespread belief for the purpose of psychological exploration, though she clearly regarded the vengeful spirit as a reality. For example, some time after Yugao's death, Genji's first wife, Aoi, "Princess Hollyhock," is undergoing a protracted labor. Genji has rounded up the Abbott of Tendai and other great ecclesiastics to pray round her bed. Waley's translation takes up the story (p. 165):

> . . .meaning to cheer her, [Genji] said, "Come, things are not so bad as that. You will soon be much better. But even if anything should happen, it is certain that we shall meet again in worlds to come. Your father and mother too, and many others, love you so dearly that between your fate and theirs must be some sure bond that will bring you back to them in many, many lives that are to be! [This was stock Buddhist deathbed comfort talk.] Suddenly she interrupted him: "No, no.

That is not it. But stop these prayers a while. They do me great harm," and drawing him nearer to her she went on, "I did not think that you would come. I have waited for you while all my soul is burnt with longing." She spoke wistfully, tenderly; and still in the same tone recited the verse, "Bind thou, as the seam of a skirt is braided, this shred, that from my soul despair and loneliness have sundered." The voice in which these words were said was not Aoi's; nor was the manner hers. He knew someone whose voice was very like that. Who was it? Why, yes; surely only she—the Lady Rokujo. Once or twice he had heard people suggest that something of this kind might be happening; but he had always rejected the idea as hideous and unthinkable, believing it to be the malicious invention of some unprincipled scandal-monger, and had even denied that such "possession" ever took place. Now he had seen one with his own eyes. Ghastly, unbelievable as they were, such things did happen in real life."

Behind this lies the Buddhist notion of the binding power of passion. Rokujo so coveted Genji's attentions that she dispossessed the souls of his women. Besides, there were status factors involved. Yugao seemed to be a lowborn maiden—actually she was of good birth, but this was unknown both to Genji and Rokujo. In the high-born Princess Aoi's case, Rokujo had fancied herself to be slighted by her at the recently performed Kamo festival at which Rokujo's daughter was to be installed as Vestal Virgin at the Shinto temple at Ise. Aoi's carriage and those of her ladies had been manoeuvered by her grooms into a front-row position, while Rokujo's was pushed back "among a miscellaneous collection of carts and gigs where she could see nothing at all." This was not Aoi's fault—she is portrayed as a very good natured, though, somewhat uninteresting person—but that of her grooms, who, "already the worse for liquor," would not let Rokujo's old-fashioned carriage—mark of "an exalted personage," they thought, "who did not want to be recognized"—move to the front. Later, Rokujo, hemmed in, was partly forced and partly desired to watch a procession of "magnificently apparelled" noblemen ride by, among them Prince Genji. Murasaki writes: "The humiliation of watching all this from an obscure corner was more than Rokujo could bear, and murmuring the lines, 'Though I saw him but as a shadow that falls on hurrying waters yet knew I that at last my hour of utmost misery was come,' she burst into tears. It was hideous that her servants should see her in this state. Yet even while she struggled with her tears she could not find it in her heart to regret that she had seen him in all his glory" (p. 158).

The irony of this situation is as usual poignant in the extreme; Rokujo had come ostensibly to see her unmarried daughter renouncing the world and actually to catch a glimpse of her lover. Her lover's wife, in her view, shut her off from the religious ceremony and compelled her to see Genji in all his glory "from her obscure corner." None of this was the Lady Aoi's fault—she was described as "exquisitely well-bred"—yet she was the victim of Rokujo's rage, spurred on as it was by "the pangs of disprized love." Rokujo, however, was not conscious of her jealousy; "of hostility towards Aoi she could find no trace at all. Yet she could not be sure whether somewhere in the depths of a soul consumed by anguish some spark of malice had not lurked" (p. 163). Murasaki is a great artist; she does not make value judgments, and uses themes and motifs of religion and folk belief for their aesthetic and psychological effect. It is generally agreed that the Buddhism of the late Heian age had become superficial, a matter of ceremony and prestigious participation in rituals presided over by aristocratic priests and abbots. But by the time we come to the Muromachi period, Buddhism has undergone a major revival, and it is in this revitalized frame that the Noh play based on Rokujo's preternatural attack on Aoi in childbirth takes on its central meaning. That meaning is the salvation of Rokujo's soul; she is not condemned as a witch or villainess but is seen as one bound in demonic guise to the karmic wheel by her passionate longing for Genji and her passionate hate of those he loves independently of her.

While Murasaki's novelistic genius had been to create an expressive frame revealing the ethical complexities of the human condition even within the constraints of the Heian court, swinging between boredom and seduction, in full accordance with Kierkegaard's definition of "the aesthetic," the genius of the Noh drama was to consider social and interpersonal process *sub specie aeternitatis*, in the Buddhist salvific mode. But since Japanese culture can never escape the aesthetic entirely, this dimension in its plenitude migrated to the *performative* aspects of the Noh drama—its stage setting, its music, and above all its acting techniques.

A few words about the form of the Noh play are in order. It took its present shape in the fourteenth century as a unique synthesis of several performative genres, including dance, poetry, music, mime, and costume. Some speak of its roots in ritual. In any case, it represents scenes from the ceremonious life of the Japanese feudal aristocracy, and Noh plays were produced at seasons of festival. They were produced in sequences of five Noh plays interdigitated with farcical, popular plays known as Kyogen. Two men, Kan-ami and Zeami Motokiyo (father and son), mentioned earlier, wrote nearly half the plays in the repertory of those produced today. Hardly any of the 240 still seen have been written since 1600.

There are five types of Noh plays, but almost all have the following processual form. They are in two parts: Part One shows the leading character, or *Shite*, in a humble, human disguise; in Part Two, he or she appears as the diety, hero, or heroine he or she really is, though if as a human being, almost always as a ghost. When a ghost, he or she endures penance for a violent action committed in mortal life. By a species of paradox, therefore, this ghost is essentially more "real" than the humble human he or she had pretended to be in Part One. In this manifestation, the ghost remembers and repents of the violent earth-binding passion of love or hate that prevents release. Both Buddhistic and Shinto ideas help to frame the second part and assign meaning to it. This focus on religion in the scenario is counteracted by an extraordinary appeal to aesthetic sensibility in the acting, almost a religion of beauty. Zeami, as we shall see, has striking things to say about this relationship between the religious and the aesthetic.

The stage setting imposes all kinds of constraints which it is the actor's task to surmount—a limited frame for an illimitable "flow," so to speak:

> The stage is a square, nineteen feet, five inches, raised two feet, seven inches, above the floor of the auditorium, into which it projects on three sides. To the rear is a panel on which an aged pine tree is painted. To the left extends a bridgeway, the *Hashigakari*, leading to a curtained doorway, the entrance and exit for the principal characters. The stage is covered with a roof supported by four corner pillars fifteen feet high. Three small trees are stationed at regular intervals along the bridgeway. In a shallow backstage entirely visible to the audience are seated four musicians, from left to right players of the horizontal drum, the large hand drum, the small hand drum, and the flute. The corner of the stage adjoining the front of the bridgeway is known as the station for the *shite*, or principal actor. Beside the pillar diagonally opposite is the station for the secondary actor, or *waki*. The juncture between the rear of the bridgeway and the back of the stage is known as the *kyogen's* seat. This man serves as stage attendant and may speak informally, giving what may be described as program notes between the two parts of the play . . . the ceremony proceeds to formula, from its prelude to its obligatory conclusion. The manner is stylized to the highest possible degree. The *shite* is masked, so are his immediate followers, if there are any such persons. Other actors have mask-like make-up. Costumes are lavish and symbolical. In two-part plays, that of the *shite* is, of course, changed during the brief interval . . . . the play's style is refined and precious almost to the point of being cryptic. Verse is used in the more elevated and lyrical passages, where spiritual and emotional qualities are at their height. Prose serves for the simpler speeches . . . . Much of the dialogue is . . . quoted from Chinese and Japanese classical poetry. Many phrases are repeated. A chorus, seated on the right of the stage, sings, speaks for or as the leading actor, moralizes, and narrates. It commonly sings as the *shite* mimes the imagined action. Often it completes a sentence commenced by the *shite*, or the *shite* concludes a phrase commenced by the chorus. Two or more characters often speak in unison. Thus the text is treated more in the manner of an oratorio than in that of a Western play (Henry W. Wells, 1969:603-4).

This ritualized form has the effect of limiting the expression of individuality and presenting a generalized drama of salvation or damnation. Such a drama has its source in history or literature, where individual characters abound, but its aim is to transcend these and evaluate events and behavior in the light of Buddhist criteria. Thus, in the play *Aoi No Uye* (Princess Hollyhock), Lady Rokujo is no longer treated as a unique person but as a ghost bound upon the wheel (Arthur Waley, *Noh Plays of Japan*, 1960, pp. 179-189). Early in the play she is "made visible" by the chant of a *miko*, a term which may be translated either as a "maiden in the service of a shrine" or as "a witch" (Arthur Waley's choice), and laments:

> This world
> Is like the wheels of the little ox-cart;
> Round and round they go . . . till vengeance comes.
> The Wheel of Life turns like the wheel of a coach;
> There is no escape from the Six Paths and Four Births.
> We are brittle as the leaves of the *basho* [a plant with
>   banana-like leaves whose spirit in feminine form is the
>   subject of another Noh play with the message that "even
>   plants may attain Buddhahood"];
> As fleeting as foam upon the sea.
> Yesterday's flower, today's dream.
> From such a dream were it not wiser to wake? [p. 182].

Imagery of wheels, coaches, and carts pervades the play, and clearly refers to Rokujo's experiences of humiliation in the novel. For not only does the play mention the scuffle between Aoi's and Rokujo's coachmen, but it also alludes to an episode in which Rokujo sees a coach from which all badges and distinctive decorations had been stripped standing before Yugao's door. She learned that this was Genji's on a clandestine visit to his "Moonflower." The wheels associated with her earthly obsession with Genji are identified with the Wheel of Passion which binds ignorant mortals to the earth in an endless sequence of rebirths, unless they learn Buddha's way of release through Enlightenment.

In the play, Rokujo, thus materialized, cannot but relive her hatred for Aoi. Even after admitting that "in this Saha World/that is, of appearances/where days fly like the lightning's flash/None is worth hating and none worth pitying," and that she has "come to clear my hate," she is again overmastered by passion and "strikes" not once but again and again a folded cloak on the stage representing the "bed of Aoi."

She then dons a female demon's mask, grasps a mallet, and is concealed by two attendants behind a robe she has taken off, representing her invisibility. Next a messenger is despatched to the Little Saint of Yokawa of the Tendai sect, probably because its mountain headquarters at Hieizan near Kyoto were the monastic and scholastic headquarters of all Japanese Buddhism in the Heian period, in which the play is set. The Saint is also an adherent of Shugendo, a religious movement organized during and after the Heian period, which emphasized pilgrimages to the mountains and ascetic retreats among them. Its practitioners, or *yamabushi*, were instrumental in spreading the charms and incantations of esoteric Buddhism (mixed with Taoistic charms and Shinto elements) to the people. The saint promptly begins his incantations to exorcize the demonic manifestation of Rokujo. Eventually, when he cites the *Hannya Kyo*, a sutra which is believed to have a particular influence over female demons (also called *Hannyas*), Rokujo suddenly drops her mallet and presses her hands to her ears. For she has heard the words:

> They that hear my name shall get Great Enlightenment;
> They that see my body shall attain to Buddhahood.

The play concludes:

> When she heard the sound of Scripture
> The demon's raging heart was stilled;
> Shapes of Pity and Sufferance,
> The Bodhisats descend.
> Her soul casts off its bonds,
> She walks in Buddha's Way (p. 189).

Here there is a strange mixture of exorcism and conversion—Shinto and Shugendo intermingled.

If we briefly compare the novel and the play, we find that both "frame" behavior, but in different ways; the novel is flexible and closely in tune with the author's feelings and experience, while the play imposes on itself a stylized, even ritualized, form. Both are metacommentaries. But Murasaki seldom moralizes; she lets her tale tell itself. Nevertheless, there is always a subtly ironical presentation of masculine egoism and obtuseness. Murasaki, too, is the reflexive voice of a civilized court and a veiled critique of the alternate boredom and seductiveness of the aesthetic mode when it is allowed to dominate daily life. There is, however, an undercurrent of Buddhistic evaluation, even in the portrayal of beautiful things and people. These mutabilities are sad in their essence. Only the monastic life can prepare the way for that enlightenment which draws the sting of the fleetingness of the world, even when it is lovely; both Rokujo and Genji eventually renounce the world for the religious life. The Noh play, like most members of its genre, is more explicitly religious. This may have been at least partly due to the troubled state of Japan in the Muromachi period; such "liminal" periods in history often direct the public's attention to meaning-conferring (and hence, redressive) institutions, which themselves acquire new forms and contents in reflexive interaction with the turbulent and complex social process. Perhaps, too, the rigid form and allusive content of Noh are dialectically related to the flux and conflict in the political and cultural life on which this type of drama obliquely commented.

Whatever may have been the case, it is certain that the framing of Noh was highly stylized, and that this theatre's rules were minute and precise. The message thus framed had to be presented by the actors in ways that transcended the limits almost ascetically imposed. Zen Buddhism, a product of the even more turbulent Kamakura period (1155-1333) influenced the disciplinary framework. It also influenced the thinking of Zeami, theorist of this theatre, son of Kanami Kiyotsuga, a priest of the Kasuga Temple near Nara (the old capital), who later left the priesthood to take up acting and virtually founded the Noh theatre.

Zeami Motokiyo (1363-1444) wrote and acted in many plays. But he also wrote *about* them, and he was a brilliant theorist. One of his major concepts, set out in several of his twenty essays written at various times in his long theatrical career, is *yugen*, a term which, we will see, contains the notion of mysterious depth as a counterstroke to the external limitations of Noh conventions. *Yugen* is what the Noh actor should primarily seek to convey to the audience. Noh exemplifies what the poet Rilke once described as the "circumspection of human gesture" found in the greatest art.

Makoto Ueda, in *Literary and Art Theories in Japan* (1967:60), derived *yugen* from *yu*, signifying "deep, dim, or difficult to see," and *gen*, "originally describing the dark, profound, tranquil color of the universe [and] refers to the Taoist concept of truth." "Zeami perceived mysterious beauty in cosmic truth; beauty was the color of truth, so to speak" (p. 61). Since human life is fleeting, like cherry blossoms, man's destiny is sad, from the viewpoint of this world. The skill of the actor is to embody not only the elegant beauty but also the pathos of life in time. Zeami quotes a poem which, in his view, creates this effect:

> Tinted leaves begin to fall
> From one side of the forest
> As it rains in the evening
> And drenches a deer
> Lonesomely calling for its mate (p. 62).

But the supreme skill of the Noh actor is to transcend this impermanence which envelops the world. Zeami, being of a systematic cast of mind, classified all theatrical effects into nine categories (pp. 64-67). These are in three groups of three. The first three, which he calls respectively (1) Roughness and Aberrance; (2) Strength and Roughness; and (3) Strength and Delicacy, lack the quality of *yugen*. *Yugen* begins with the fourth style, Shallowness and Loveliness, and the true Noh actor should begin right there. It is when he masters the rest up to the ninth that he should come down and master the first three which can only be made interesting when a great actor who knows *yugen* performs them. In the fourth style, loveliness implies *yugen*, though still of only a shallow kind. But when the actor grasps the fifth style, Broadness and Minuteness—that is, depth and versatility—he is farther along the Way—and Zeami likens *yugen* for the actor to *Tao* for the man or woman of religion; it is his "Way of ways [which is] not an ordinary way" (p. 65). At this point the actor can tell through his performance of a role "all about the heart of the object he is impersonating" (p. 66).

"The Style of a Right Flower" is the highest of the middle ranks of acting skills. "Flower" means here an impressive theatrical effect, a moment of deep or dazzling beauty in an actor's performance. Zeami uses a poetic metaphor for this: "The spring haze brightens in the setting sun. All mountains in sight are gleaming in crimson." The "flower" is perhaps the aesthetic summit of acting.

But beyond it are the three ranks which Makoto Ueda calls "sublime," quintessential *yugen*. Here the Zen view that it is quiet, subdued beauty, as in the Tea Ceremony, which is truly sublime, prevails. The Style of a Calm Flower is the lowest of the final triad. Its essence, Zeami wrote, is in the Zen saying, "Snow is piled in a silver bowl" (p. 66). As opposed to the earlier flower, this is a flower without color—one might almost say an "anti-structural flower"—the beauty of pure whiteness. Snow, the purity of nature, is held within silver, the beauty of culture. Art and nature are united virginally in this austere style, harmony unblemished.

The eighth style is called the Style of a Profound Flower. Zeami again refers to a Zen saying: "Snow has covered thousands of mountains. Why is it that a solitary mountain towers unwhitened among them?" Everyone must have seen this effect in great mountain ranges—a black peak rising among snow-invested mountains. Something exceptional, unique, aberrant, irrational has happened. As Makoto Ueda writes (p. 67), "The other world has now begun to invade the world of the ordinary senses . . . . [there is] a strange kind of beauty perceptible only to those supreme artists who are endowed with extraordinary sensitivity." An actor who can realize this Flower can put his audience into a kind of trance.

The ninth and supreme style Zeami entitles the Style of a Mysterious Flower. He illustrates it by another Zen epigram: "In Silla the sun shines brightly at midnight." What does this mean? Silla is part of Korea, east of China. While it is still dark in China, the sun is already brilliant in Korea. If someone could overcome the limitations of space and time, he could live in China in darkness and yet be in brightness in Korea. What seems to be a contradiction in space-time is not a contradiction when seen from a higher perspective. A truly great Noh actor, "through the Style of a Mysterious Flower, makes us visualize such a transcendental world, a world of higher reality lying beyond our ordinary senses . . . . At its sight we are struck with the feeling of austerity" (p. 67), that is, the very essence of *yugen*.

With this notion of a transcendental referent, practically everything in Noh becomes symbolic. Actually, Noh is a hyperliminal form. Its protagonists are often deities, spirits, ancestors, and ghosts who have seen the other world as well as this one. Where a Western tragedy would end—with the death of the protagonist (the *shite*)—a Noh play begins. The transcendental being, materialized in some way, recounts the history of the passion which does not allow him to escape from the limen between the worlds. His confession becomes an analysis, and the analysis an evaluation in which he is assisted by the deuteragonist (the *waki*), who is often a Buddhist monk or saint. Sometimes the protagonist appears to the monk in a dream. Here I would like to recall to you what I have said about the liminal being largely in the subjunctive mood. A whole world of wishes and hopes is opened up, as well as a world of moral reflexivity, in which the protagonist's actual behavior is related to how he ought to have acted. But there is a subtle interfusion of the indicative ("normal") and subjunctive (aesthetic) moods in Noh drama. Where these fuse, we find magic; where the "might have been" is conceded to have indicative power, we have performative acts or magical spells. Thus the Little Saint's incantation is portrayed as having an actual effect on Rokujo, releasing her from her demonic obsession.

However, it is the art of the actor which communicates these metamessages embodied in the scripts and scenarios of Noh. This art is the source of the apparently spontaneous "flow" which catches up both actors and audience into itself. The sensorily perceptible symbols and images which convey the "message"—the colorful manifold of scenery, costume, dance, music, singing, poetic utterance, gestural language—must emerge from the actor's limpid singleness of being, something only attainable by much study of his craft and by experience of life as well as art. Zeami puts all this supremely well:

> The seed of the flower that blossoms out in all works of art lies in the artist's soul. Just as a transparent crystal produces fire and water, or a colorless cherry tree bears blossoms and fruit, a superb artist creates a moving work of art out of a landscape within his soul. It is such a person that can be called a vessel. Works of art are many and various, some singing of the mood and the breeze on the occasion of a festival, others admiring the blossoms and the birds at an outdoor excursion. The universe is a vessel containing all things—flowers and leaves, the snow and the moon, mountains and seas, trees and grass, the animate and the inanimate—according to the seasons of the year. Make those numerous things the material of your art, let your soul be the vessel of the universe, and set it in the spacious, tranquil way of the void. You will then be able to attain the ultimate of art, the Mysterious Flower [pp. 68-69].

Zeami is referring specifically to the actor's art here. The actor is the "crystal vessel"—the "Non-Being," in Buddhist language—which brings to life, even engenders, the "heterogeneous matters" of fire and water, contraries which underly the active manifold and manifest of "Being." Noh theatre, in consonance with this stress on what lies beyond, is deeply musical; all the lines are recited in rhythmical speech, with the accompaniment of orchestral music. Zeami even said once that "music is the soul of Noh." The auditory symbols assist the limpid flow of the visual action and drives the religious message in deep.

To show precisely how Murasaki's novel and the Noh play *Aoi No Uye* represent metacommentaries on the social processes of their respective core communities would require detailed study of historical documents. But we might be able to make a few programmatic suggestions here. One would be to stress the contrast between the Heian and Muromachi periods (good material for this may be found in P. Duus, *Feudalism in Japan*, New York: 1969). Both novel and play are refined art forms intended for an elite class. But the former, written by a woman, with a male protagonist, uses material drawn directly from her observations, while the latter, probably written by a man (Zenchiku, Zeami's son-in-law) who has played female roles and advised on how they should be played by male actors, uses material drawn from myth, historical chronicles, and classical literature. Murasaki writes for and about the royal court at Kyoto; the Noh dramatists for the localized landed warriors who were supplanting the once powerful and wealthy court aristocracy. Indeed, there were "two rival Mikados, one in the north and one in the south, who held impotent and dwindling courts" (Waley, 1920:19). The real power was in the hands of the young *Shogun*, or Generalissimo, whose family held absolute power. This man, Ashikaga Yoshimitsu, regarded himself as a patron of the arts and letters, and was also influenced by the recently introduced (from China) Zen form of Buddhism. He loved the theatre and even gave a fief in Yamato to Zeami's father, Kanami. The combination of feudal militancy with Zen spiritual discipline (Kanami was once a monk) probably had much to do with the Noh theatre's use of stirring battle scenes from the preceding even more turbulent Kamakura Period (1185-1333) as its main narrative staple. The past had two uses: on the one hand it represented a model of ideal conduct—men were more chivalrous, women more virtuous than in the present age; on the other hand, the segmentary oppositions of the present—for example, the contemporary division between the two Mikados and the contradiction between the Mikado's status and that of the Shogun (*rex* versus *dux*, in De Jouvenal's terms) were displaced on to the quasi-legendary struggles between the mighty Minamoto and Taira clans (who, between them, ended militantly the relative, if decadent, peacefulness of the Heian age).

Thus Murasaki's metacommentary on her time was, like Jane Austen's, a psychological one—an ironical portrait of court people, and especially men, within the purview of her restricted physical experience—while the metacommentary of the Noh plays was a politico-religious one, responding to changes in the major social structures of Japanese society. The former was made by a woman, the latter by men. The galling problem, from the male perspective, is that Murasaki's commentary was made by a universal genius, while Kanami's and Zeami's perspectives were elaborated by wonderfully talented representatives of a great, but particular culture.

Inveterately an anthropologist, I become addicted to the particular culture, (any particular culture), as the Japanese painter Santo Kyoden (1761-1816) may be said to have become addicted to the spirit of the Yoshiwara, the Nightless City, of Edo (now Tokyo), which framed the "Floating World," the illicit domain where courtesans and artists provided the living counter stroke to the frozen quasi-feudal bureaucracy of the Tokugawa period—in which samurai were transmogrified into civil servants.

To escape this, let me return, in concluding, to my view that any society which hopes to be imperishable must whittle out for itself a piece of space and a while of time, in which it can look honestly at itself. This honesty is not that of the scientist, who exchanges the honesty of his ego for the objectivity of his gaze, son regard. It is, rather, akin to the supreme honesty of the creative artist who, in his presentations on the stage, in the book, on canvas, in marble, in music, or in towers and houses, reserves to himself the privilege of seeing straight what all cultures build crooked. For all generalizations are in some way skewed, while artists with candid vision "labour well the minute particulars," as Blake knew. This may be a "metalanguage," but all this means is that the "meta" part of it is not at an abstract remove from what goes on in the world of "getting and spending," but sees it more crystallinely, whether more passionately or dispassionately is beside my present point. Whether anthropology can ignore this incandescent objectivity and still lay claim to being "the study of man" I gravely doubt.

References

Black, Mary B. 1973. "Belief Systems," in J. J. Honigmann, ed., Handbook of Social and Cultural Anthropology. Chicago: Rand McNally. Pp. 509-577.

Duus, Peter. 1964. Feudalism in Japan. New York: Knopf.

Firth, Raymond. 1974. "Security and its Symbols." Times Literary Supplement, Sep. 13. Pp. 965-6.

Keene, Donald. 1955. An Anthology of Japanese Literature. New York: Grove Press.

Murasaki, Lady (c. 1000-1007). The Tale of Genji, tr. A. Waley. New York: Random House, Modern Library, 1960.

Ueda, Makoto. 1967. Literary and Art Theories in Japan. Cleveland, Ohio: Press of Western Case Reserve University.

Waley, Arthur. 1920. The No Plays of Japan. New York: Grove Press.

Wells, Henry W. 1969. "Noh." J. Gassner and E. Quinn, eds. The Reader's Encyclopedia of World Drama. New York: Crowell.

Zeami Motokiyo (putative author; 1363-1444). "Aoi No Uye," in A. Waley, ed., tr., The No Plays of Japan. New York: Grove Press, 1920. Pp. 180-189.

Carnaval in Rio:

Dionysian Drama in an Industrializing Society

Medieval European carnival had its roots in the pagan past with affinities to the Roman Saturnalia and Lupercalia. But it found a place in the calendar of the church year and was normally performed during the four days before Lent. Folk etymology connected carnival with the medieval Latin phrase "carne vale," (flesh farewell), since it marked a period of feasting and revelry just before Lent, when meat-eating fell under interdict. Being connected with a moveable fast, carnival—notably Mardi Gras—"Fat Tuesday," its climax, just before Ash Wednesday, became a moveable feast. Unlike such civic celebrations as Independence Day, July Fourth, *Cinco de Mayo*, and others, carnival is set in a cosmological calendar, severed from ordinary historical time, even the time of extraordinary secular events. Truly, carnival is the denizen of a place which is no place, and a time which is no time, even where that place is a city's main plazas, and that time can be found on an ecclesiastical calendar. For the squares, avenues, and streets of the city become, at carnival, the reverse of their daily selves. Instead of being the sites of offices and the conduits of purposive traffic, they are sealed off from traffic, and the millions who throng them on foot, drift idly wherever they please, no longer propelled by the urges of "getting and spending" in particular places (see Da Matta, 1984:209-212).

What we are seeing is society in its subjunctive mood—to borrow a term from grammar—its mood of feeling, willing and desiring, its mood of fantasizing, its playful mood; not its indicative mood, where it tries to apply reason to human action and systematize the relationship between ends and means in industry and bureaucracy. The distinguished French scholar, Jean-Richard Bloch, lamented in the title of his book, written in 1920, *Carnival est mort: Premiers essais pour mieux comprendre mon temps*, and the Spanish ethnologist Julio Caro

Baroja, approvingly echoed him in 1965, "*el Carnaval ha muerto.*" "Carnival is dead," indeed! They said as much of pilgrimage when my wife and I set out to study this great mass phenomenon in 1970. We found that literally millions and millions of people were still on the pilgrimage trail of all the world's major religions, and, indeed, that many so-called "tourists" were really closet pilgrims. Certainly, *Carnaval* is by no means dead in Brazil, and rumors of its decease elsewhere are greatly exaggerated. One thinks immediately of Trinidad, New Orleans, and *Fastnacht* in many a German town.

But carnival, though a world-wide phenomenon—I am thinking of Japanese and Indian festivals such as the Gion *Matsuri* in Kyoto, or the *Holi* festival in northern India—has become in Brazil something fundamentally and richly Brazilian. I say this despite Brazilian criticism by certain middle-class elements that it is vulgar, by Marxists that it diverts the energies of the workers from political activity and blurs class lines, and by those in the higher clergy who look upon it as pagan and scandalous. The way people play perhaps is more profoundly revealing of a culture than how they work, giving access to their "heart values." I use this term instead of *key* values for reasons that will become clear, for the heart *has* its values, as well as its reasons.

The Varieties of Playful Experience

I am going to throw in a *soupcon* of theory into this *bouillabaisse* of carnival-esque impressions, since one of my recent concerns is the constant cross-looping of social history with the numerous genres of cultural performance ranging from ritual, to theatre, the novel, folk-drama, art exhibitions, ballet, modern dance, poetry readings, to film and television. Underpinning each type of performance are the social structures and processes of the time; underlying the social drama or "dramas of living," the Dreyfus cases and Watergates, are the rhetorics and insights of contemporary kinds of performance—popular, mainstream and avant-garde. Each feeds and draws on the other, as people try to assign meaning to their behavior, turning it into conduct. They become reflexive, at once their own subject and object. One of the modes in which they do this is play—including games and sports, as well as festivals.

Play, paradoxically, has become a more serious matter with the decline of ritual and the contraction of the religious sphere in which people used to become morally reflexive, relating their lives to the values handed down in sacred traditions. The play frame, where events are scrutinized in the leisure time of the social process, has to some extent inherited the function of the ritual frame. The messages it delivers are often serious beneath the outward trappings of absurdity, fantasy, and ribaldry, as contemporary stage plays, some movies and some TV shows illustrate. Clearly, carnival is a form of play. Current theories of play formulated by anthropologists and others may give us some clues as to what carnival is about.

The main pioneer in this field is Dutch medieval historian Johan Huizinga, rector of the University of Leyden in 1933, and author of the celebrated book, *Homo Ludens* ("Man at Play," or "Man the Player"). Huizinga defined play as follows:

> Summing up the formal characteristics of play we might call it a free activity standing quite consciously outside 'ordinary life' as being 'not serious,' but at the same time absorbing the player intensely and utterly. It is an activity connected with no material interest, and no profit can be gained by it. It proceeds within its own proper boundaries of time and space according to fixed rules and in an orderly manner. It promotes the formation of social groupings which tend to surround themselves with secrecy and to stress their difference from the common world by disguise or other means (1950:13).

Play, then, according to Huizinga, is a "free activity," which nevertheless imposes order on itself, from within and according to its own rules. He grasps the connection between play and the secret and mysterious, but cannot account for the fact that play is often spectacular, even ostentatious, as in parades, processions, Rose Bowls, Superbowls, and Olympics. One might even say that the masks, disguises and other fictions of some kinds of play are devices to make visible what has been hidden, even unconscious—for example, the Demon Masks of Sri Lankan and Tibetan exorcism rituals—to let the mysteries revel in the streets, to invert the everyday order in such a way that it is the unconscious and primary processes that are visible, whereas the conscious ego is restricted to creating rules to keep their insurgence within bounds, to frame them or channel them, so to speak. Huizinga is also surely wrong when he sees play as divested of all material interest. He forgets the important role of betting and games of chance in, for example, gambling houses, casinos, race tracks and lotteries. These may have important economic effects, even though playing for money remains completely unproductive, since the sum of the winnings at best only equals the losses of other players, and the entrepreneur, the bank, is the only ultimate winner; ironically he is perhaps the only one who takes no pleasure in gambling.

A later, more complex, theory of play has been developed by the French scholar, Roger Caillois. He uses some exotic terms, but defines them clearly. For example, he says that play has two axes or "poles," which he calls *paidia* and *ludus*. *Paidia*, from the Greek word meaning "child," stands for "an almost indivisible principle, common to diversion, turbulence, free improvisation, and carefree gaiety . . . uncontrolled fantasy" (1979:13). This anarchic and capricious propensity characteristic of children is countered by *ludus*, from the Latin word meaning "a play, a game," which Caillois sees as binding *paidia* "with arbitrary, imperative, and purposely tedious conventions, [opposing it] still more by ceaselessly practising the most embarrassing chicanery upon it, in order to make it more uncertain of attaining its desired effects" (*Ibid*). *Ludus*, in fact, represents how, in the space/time of the subjunctive mood of cultural action, human beings love to set up arbitrary obstacles to be overcome as in mazes, crossword puzzles or the rules of chess, which are both a general training for coping with obstacles in the day-to-day world and also a means of totally engrossing the player in a world of play framed and enclosed by its intricate rules.

Caillois has four additional concepts for understanding play (see Table 1, below). These are *agôn*, Greek for "contest" or "competition"; *alea*, a dice game, extended to chance, randomness and gambling in general; mimicry, from the Greek *mimos*, an imitator or actor; and *ilinx*, for "whirlpool," which "consists of an attempt momentarily to destroy stability of perception and inflict a kind of voluptuous panic upon an otherwise lucid mind" (p. 23). Caillois uses these categories to explain the structure of games of strength, chance, or skill, and of play-acting—all these being in the world of "make-believe" (whereas ritual is in the world of "we do believe," see Handelman, 1977:187).

Each category contains games and sports that move from the pole of *paidia*, childhood play (in which he includes "tumult, agitation, and immoderate laughter") to the pole of *ludus* ("purposive innovation"). For example, the category *agôn* or competition describes a whole group of games "in which an equality of chances is artificially created in order that the adversaries should confront each other under ideal conditions, susceptible of giving precise and incontestable value to the winner's triumph . . . Rivalry (usually) hinges on a single quality (such as speed, endurance, strength, memory, skill, ingenuity, and the like) exercised, within defined limits and without outside assistance, in such a way that the winner appears to be better than the loser in a certain category of exploits" (p. 14). Agonistic games range from unregulated racing and wrestling, at the *paidia* end, to organized sport (boxing, billiards, baseball, fencing, chess, Olympic Games, and so on) at the *ludus* end.

Alea or "chance" presides over "games that are based on a decision independent of the player, an outcome over which he has no control, and in which winning is the result of fate or destiny rather than triumphing over an adversary" (p. 17). For this reason, games of change have often played an important role in ritual contexts, as indicative of the will of the gods, as in the great Indian epic, the *Mahabharata*, where the oldest of the Pandava hero-brethren gambles away the rights of all the brothers to the throne and to their joint wife Draupadi; the brothers pay the penalty of exile for thirteen years. In our culture, *alea*, chance, ranges from counting out rhymes (*eeny meeny miney mo*), and spinning a coin, at the *paidia* pole, to betting and roulette, to simple or complex continuing lotteries.

Mimicry or simulation involves the acceptance if not of an illusion (the very word is derived from the Latin *in-lusio*, "the beginning of a game"), at least of a "closed, conventional and, in certain respects, imaginary universe" (p. 19). Through mimicry one can become an imaginary character oneself, a subject who makes believe or makes others believe that he/she is someone other than him/herself. At the *paidia* pole, we have children playing at being parents or other adult roles, or cowboys and Indians, or spacemen and aliens. We progress through charades to various kinds of masking and costuming and disguises until at the *ludus* pole we are fully into theatre, masquerade, and, in the popular sphere, pageants, processions, parades, and other types of spectacle. Even the audience at great sports events, such as Superbowls, is under the spell of mimicry. The athletes who perform for them are dominated by *agôn*, but for the audience, as Caillois writes, "A physical contagion leads them to assume the position of the contestants in order to help them, just as the bowler is known to unconsciously incline his body in the direction that he would like the bowling ball to take at the end of its course. Under these conditions, paralleling the spectacle, a competitive mimicry is born in the public, which doubles the *agôn* of the field or track" (p. 22). This is easily observed in a crowd at a football or baseball game. Anticipating somewhat, we shall see how the two-four samba beat sweeps up those who watch the Rio *Carnaval* into mimicry of the *sambistas*, the members of the samba schools who compete with one another for the first prize in each year's glowing *Carnaval*.

The concept *ilinx* or vertigo involves all games which try to create disequilibrium or imbalance, or otherwise to alter perception or consciousness by inducing giddiness or dizziness, often by a whirling or gyrating motion. These range from such children's games as "Ring around the rosy," (Ashes, ashes, we all fall down!) and musical chairs to waltzing, to horseriding, to the intoxication of high speed on skis, waterskis, motorcycles, sports cars, to riding on rollercoasters, carousels, or other vertigo-inducing contraptions. Dancing comes under the sign of *ilinx*, as Caillois says, "from the common but insidious giddiness of the waltz to the many mad, tremendous, and convulsive movements of other dances" (p. 25). I would add, not least the samba! *Ilinx* shows that there is not only cosmos but chaos in the scheme of things.

Caillois sees an evolutionary development, as civilization advances in rationality from the unholy combination of mimicry and *ilinx*, which characterize the games and other cultural performances of societies he calls "primitive" or "Dionysian," which are ruled "by masks and possession"—to the rational sweetness and light of *agôn* plus *alea*, represented by such "civilized" societies as the Incas, Assyrians, Chinese, and Romans. According to Caillois, these are "orderly societies with officers, careers, codes, and ready-reckoners, with fixed and hierarchical privileges, in which *agôn* and *alea*, that is, merit and heredity (which is a kind of chance), seem to be the chief complementary elements of the game of living. In contrast to the primitive societies, these are 'rational' " (p. 87).

Thus Caillois's scheme sees society solely from the positivist perspective of social structure, it fails to take into account the dialectical nature, which moves from structure to antistructure and back again to transformed structure; from hierarchy to equality; from indicative mood to subjunctive mood; from unity to multiplicity; from the person to the individual; from systems of status roles to *communitas*, the I-thou relationship, and Buber's "essential We" as against society regarded as "It."

Antonin Artaud understood at least this: that without a theatre of mask and trance, of simulation and vertigo, the people perish — and this is as true of the most complex and large-scale society as it is of the most obscure aboriginal band. We would do well to value Caillois's conceptual analysis of play but avoid his evolutionist argument, for it disprizes the nonelitist societies that now have perhaps most to give to the general stream of human culture — rationality having ruined many of our natural resources in the name of procuring material comfort.

Great industrial nations such as Brazil and Japan have not despised their public festivals but elevated them to the scale of their secular achievements — all this without destroying the vertigo and theatricality at their liminal heart. We can learn much from their experience.

Classification of Games

	Agon (competition)	Alea (chance)	Mimicry (simulation)	Ilinx (Vertigo)
PAIDIA	Racing Wrestling etc. Athletics	Counting-out rhymes	Children's imitations Games of illusion	Children "whirling" Horseback riding
Tumult Agitation	(not regulated)	Heads or tails	Tag, Arms Masks, disguise	Swinging Waltzing
Immoderate laughter				
	Boxing, billiards	Betting		Volador
Kite flying	Fencing, checkers	Roulette		Traveling carnivals
Solitaire	Football, chess			Skiing
Patience				Mountain climbing
Crossword puzzles	Contests, Sports in general	Simple, complex and continuing lotteries	Theatre Spectacles in general	Tightrope walking
LUDUS				

Note: In each vertical column games are classified in such an order that the *paidia* element is constantly decreasing while the *ludus* element is ever increasing.
Source: Roger Caillois, *Man, Play and Games* (1979)

Aphrodite on the Half Shell

Perhaps the best way of approaching *Carnaval* is to consider how the Cariocas, the true inhabitants of Rio de Janeiro, describe it. Here is the first part of the lyric of a samba composed by the major *sambista* of the renowned samba school, Estação Primeira de Mangueira.

Quando uma luz divinal	When a light divine
Iluminava a imaginação	Illuminated the imagination
De um escritor genial	Of a writer of genius
Tudo era maravilha	All was miracle
Tudo era sedução	All was seduction
Quanta alegria	How much happiness
E fascinação	And fascination . . .
Relembro . . .	I remember
Aquele mundo encantado	That enchanted world
Fantasiado de doirado	Clad in the golden dress of fantasy
Oh! Doce ilusão	Oh! Sweet illusion
	[remember that illusion means entry into play]
Sublime relicário de criança	Sublime shrine of childhood
Que ainda guardo como herança	Which I still keep as a heritage
No meu coração	In my heart

To savor this simple lyric one has to imagine it sung by a *puxador*, which means, surprisingly, a "puller." In *Carnaval* the word refers to a singer who rides ahead of an entire samba school on a float with a voice amplifier, pulling the school behind him, as it were. Some schools consist of many thousands of *sambeiros* who dance, mime, leap, gyrate, and sing choruses in his coruscating wake. He manages somehow to be at once stentorian and tender, tremendous and nostalgic, epic and romantic. His huge brazen voice is charged with *saudade*, an untranslatable Portuguese term, which is far more than the sum of "longing, yearning, ardent wish or desire, homesickness, affectionate greetings to absent persons, hankering for a lover or a homeland," as various Portuguese-English dictionaries describe the meaning.

The last few lines give the clue to a basic feature of *Carnaval*. It is propelled by *paidia* (childhood play). Freud once said that each of us is at once and successively a man, a woman and a child. The child is the player in us, and we are at times homesick for childhood's golden land, "sublime shrine of childhood, which I still keep as my heritage." Even the evident sexuality, the visible *libido*, of *Carnaval* has an infantine quality, like Baudelaire's "paradis parfumé." One could use, I suppose, such barbarous, infelicitous neologisms as "narcissistic display," "polymorphous perversion," and "fantasies about the primal scene," and so on, but this would be to endow the hummingbird lightness, deftness and butterfly-wing color of *Carnaval* play with a heavy northern seriousness, a puritanical spirit of gravity—"denaturing" it, some would say. Heaven help them!

The child is the epitome of antistructure, and perhaps this is why Jesus said, "Except ye become as little children, ye shall not enter into the kingdom of heaven," the un-kingdom beyond social structure. One of the favorite types of *entitades*, as the invisible beings who incorporate themselves with mediums in such Brazilian cults as Candomblé and Umbanda are called, is the line (*linha*) or legion of *crianças* (children). A medium possessed by a child-guide takes a diminutive name, Pedrinho, Joaozinho, and the like; speaks in a childish treble; and receives little treats such as candies from the congregation. The child-image is one link between Afro-Brazilian religious rituals which involve vertigo and trance, and *Carnaval* which involves mimicry, costuming and the enactment of a libretto or plot (*enredo*). Each samba school has its own plot, currently drawn by government edict from Brazil's patriotic past, a rule which makes it difficult but not impossible to slip in some sly digs at the generals' political preference. All this would make of *Carnaval* a "primitive" performance in Caillois's terms.

But we also find within the carnivalesque frame much *ludus* (complicated rules and regulations), *agôn* (competition) and *alea* (chance and gambling). We see that the apparent and real "childlike" is impregnated with a vast irony; the vertigo is tinctured by sophistication. *All* Caillois's components are sparking away furiously at once, like the plugs in a racing car or the wheels of Ezekiel's chariot. We find that everything human is being raised to a higher power, the cognitive along with the emotional and volitional. For the spontaneity and freedom of *Carnaval* can *only* reach their uninhibited height in the four days before Lent, *if* there has been a full year of organizing, plotting, and planning behind the scenes and a set of rules to channel the extravagant tide of song, dance, and generalized Eros.

Let us look at the growth of the samba schools in Rio and how they have been the response of an ever-young, ancient cultural genre to modernity. *Carnaval* has always been a many-leveled, as well as many-splendored, thing. Today there is not only the centrally organized street carnival of samba schools competing in leagues in downtown Rio and the internal carnival of the club balls on Mardi Gras itself, but there are also the locally organized processions of groups known as *blocos*, with their own songs and sambas, often subversive of the regime and not at all respecters of its persons. In addition, countless people dressed in their "private fantasies" stroll, flirt, get drunk, and make love in streets and squares from which business, commerce, and motorized traffic have been summarily banished.

During *Carnaval*, those centers of Brazilian hierarchy—the house, office, and factory—are emptied and closed. The whole city becomes a symbol of Brazilianity, of a single multicolored family brought into the open, which is transformed into a home. *Carnaval* may, indeed, invade the sacred homestead itself, as masked revelers swarm through it and out again. Women, no longer under the *patria potestas* of fathers or the *manus* of husbands, as in ancient Rome, become the very soul of the samba in street and club. In a sense, the whole city worships Aphrodite on the half-shell. Here Aphrodite is a *mulata*, extolled in every song, and appearing in person, in the tiniest of bikinis, on many a float, and reveling with many a tamborinist in groups of two men and one woman, known as *passistas*. The archetypal *mulata* was an eighteenth-century "lady," Xica da Silva, who became a provincial governor's mistress, and dominated men by her lambent, even heroic, sexual prowess. Many movies and TV series have been made about her.

Blacks and mulattos form the very core of *Carnaval*, since they provide the central organization of every samba school, while white celebrities clamor to be allowed into the *desfile* (pageant), as the total procession of *sambistas* and *sambeiros* is called. The anthropologist Da Matta (1984:223) calls this kind of organization "a comet-like structure." The permanent head of the comet is the "Palacio do Samba," the large building located in a mainly black *favela* (slum), where the organizing committee of the samba school has its offices — a bureaucratic structure matching in complexity those of government and business. It is also the site of intense rehearsals which begin almost as soon as the previous *Carnaval* is over. The floating "tail" of the comet consists of the "one-day trippers" who wish to form part of the parade on the Great Night and participate in its glory, together with the upper-class Brazilian *Brancos* (whites) and foreign notables. This type of grouping, which cuts across class and ethnic divisions, Da Matta regards as typical of Brazilian social organization. (The famous soccer clubs are similarly organized.) It is encouraged, Da Matta argues, by the military oligarchy ruling this hierarchical system, where, nevertheless, uncontrollable industrial growth exerts a mounting pressure in the direction of liberalization, for aggressive capitalistic business is hostile to red tape and rigid bureaucratic controls. It is clear that such comet-like structures retard the emergence of explicitly political groups with a single class basis, that is, political parties, contending with the establishment for real power and influence.

On the other hand, one might regard the samba school, with its multitudinous organizational problems and decisions made daily, as a school in governance and administration wherein countless blacks learn the skills of politics at the grass-roots level. And since a great samba school such as Mangueira or Portela represents a sizeable constituency in itself, it can be expected to be wooed by local, even national politicians and administrators.

There is also an intimate connection between the leadership of Rio samba schools and the operators of the illegal kind of lottery known as *jogo do bicho*, a numbers game involving animal symbols. At the Niteroi *Carnaval* across the bay from Rio, my wife and I found ourselves, with Da Matta's help, in the mayor's box or cabin, along with novelist Jorge Amado. We discovered that a samba school had taken for its plot the entire body of Amado's work based on life in the state of Bahia, which always has a romantic glow for Brazilians, and dedicated its samba to him. The group in the box pointed out to me a number of "mobsters" who were deep in the numbers game, and who had contributed munificently to the expenses of the occasion and to particular samba schools. One of these took as its plot or theme "The Wheel of Fortune," with each of its segments, floats, and samba libretto proclaiming the praises of Brazilian games of chance, cards, roulette wheels, *jogo do bicho*, betting on the races, and so on. One mobster was on the best of terms not only with dignitaries of the local government but also with officials and leading role-players of the samba schools as they passed the booths where their performances were given marks according to traditional criteria. Here is a clear association between competition and chance, *agôn* and *alea*, in the parlance of Roger Caillois! As a matter of fact, Caillois himself remarked half-approvingly that "in Brazil gambling is king. It is the land of speculation and chance" (1979:159).[1] Of course, the games/school link is pragmatic as well as symbolic, and many cultural connections are at once instrumental and expressive, and symbols arising in a "play world" are often manipulated to serve political interests and purposes.

If one could say that "antistructure" were merely vertigo and mimicry, one could agree with Maria Goldwasser at the University of Rio de Janeiro when she describes "the crystallization of antistructure," the basic idea which explained for her the functioning of the Mangueira samba school.

> Antistructure is represented here by Carnaval, and is defined as a transitional phase in which differences of (pre-Carnaval) status are annulled, with the aim of creating among the participants a relationship of *communitas*. Communitas is the domain of equality, where all are placed without distinction on an identical level of social evaluation, but the equivalence which is established among them has a ritual character. In *communitas* we find an inversion of the structured situations of everyday reality marked by routinization and the conferment of structural status. The status system and communitas—or structure and antistructure (which also possesses its own systematic character)—confront one another as two homologous series in opposition.
>
> The carioca Carnaval is the exemplary representation of antistructure. "To make a Carnaval" is equivalent "to making a chaos," where everything is confused and no one knows where anything is. In Carnaval, men can dress as women, adults as babies, the poor as princes and, even more, "what means what" becomes an open possibility by a magical inversion of real statuses and a cancellation or readjustment of the barriers between the social classes and categories. (1975:82-3)

---

[1] An article in the *Los Angeles Times* (10 May, 1981) discloses how in 1975 the wealthy Rio *banquiero*, Anix Abrahao David "took over the Beija Flor samba school (holder of a record three first-place trophies), and pumped hundreds of thousands, if not millions, of dollars into the operation."

Yet Goldwasser found that Mangueira, or *"Old Manga,"* the name by which the school is everywhere known, is complicatedly organized and structured. She presents a chart of the organization which resembles that of a major firm or government department. Briefly, it is divided into the directory of the school, whose function is mainly administrative, and the *Carnaval* commission, which operates in the artistic realm. The first is subdivided into three parts: (1) the Wing of the Composers (of the year's main samba and other musical items which deal with the technical supplies and emoluments of the composers themselves; (2) the Wing of the Battery, divided again between artistic and administrative spheres; the *bateria* is the awe-inspiring, compact mass of drummers and other percussion instrumentalists who bring up the rear of a samba school; by law, only percussion instruments can be used in a school's grand parade on the second day of *Carnaval*; some schools are known for their *bateria* which earns them high marks from the judges. Then there is (3) the Committee of the Combined Wings, whose job is to integrate the numerous components of the school's parade. Under the battery officials are the *ritmistas*, the drummers themselves, who are also partly organized by the composers' officials. The *puxadores* and "crooners" also come under the wing of the composers.

In addition to this pattern of technical control, there is a parallel hierarchy in the artistic sphere which attends to such matters as overall design, the plot or libretto and its apportionment among the various components of the parade: the synchronization of dance, song, music, and miming; the tastefulness of the whole presentation; the designing and decoration of floats, costuming and coiffeuring, and the rest. It takes a great amount of order to produce a "sweet disorder," a great deal of structuring to create a sacred play-space and time for antistructure. If "flowing"–*communitas* is "shared flow"–denotes the holistic sensation when we act with total involvement, when action and awareness are one, (one ceases to flow if one becomes aware that one is doing it), then, just as a river needs a bed and banks to flow, so do people need framing and structural rules to do their kind of flowing. But here the rules crystallize out of the flow rather than being imposed on it from without. William Blake said a similar thing using the metaphor of heat: "Fire finds its own form." This is not dead structure, but living form; Isadora Duncan, not classical ballet. The "structure" described by Goldwasser is akin to the rules of sport, and belongs to the domain of *ludus*, not to the politico-economic order.

The Palace of Carnaval

The competition between samba schools, indeed their very existence in their present form, is a fairly recent *Carnaval* phenomenon. The first school, named *Deixa Falar* ("Let 'em talk"), was formally constituted on 12 August, 1928 in Estacio, a city ward which was–and still is–a traditional stronghold of *Carnaval*. Until about 1952, according to de Moraes (1958), *Carnaval* was a rather brutal revel, the heir of the Portuguese *entrudo* (Shrovetide), chiefly consisting of a vulgar battle in which pails of water were thrown about indiscriminately at people in the streets and plazas. Such customs die hard, for I saw fraternity brethren doing exactly the same thing, at the University of Minnesota during the University Carnival! My wife saw Cambridge University students throwing flour in the 1930s on Shrove Tuesday. The wide diffusion of similar carnival customs is perhaps due first to the spread of the Roman Empire which introduced such antistructural rites as Saturnalia and Lupercalia to its distant provinces, and secondly to the spread of the Catholic Church which took with it around the world not only a common liturgy and liturgical year, but also a host of popular feasts and customs representing in some cases "baptised" circum-Mediterranean pre-Christian rituals.

Entrudo drenching was banned by an edict of 1853 and there succeeded a number of new forms of merrymaking. The popular inventiveness of *Carnaval* is limitless; a constant mutation in the type and scope of the revels abounds. Space prohibits mentioning most of them, but one should note the *rancho* of the early 1900s, a group of masqueraders which included a band and a chorus, specializing in the so-called *marchas-rancho*, which have a markedly slow cadence in *choros*, a sentimental musical form, and later in sambas. The *ranchos* opened up the carnival to young women. Their costumes became richer and more luxurious, with a profusion of silks, velvets, spangles, plumes, and sequins. Usually the *ranchos'* names were rather flowery: "Flower of the Avocado," "Solace of the Flowers," "Pleasurable Mignonette."

But in the twenties and thirties the tempo of life changed and the young rejected the sugariness of the *rancho* style, desiring a lighter and different flow of rhythm and shorter, less elaborate lyrics. The samba came into its own, and the units that played it were, first, the *blocos*, and soon after, the samba schools. *Bloco* is a genus, applying originally to any informal group of carnival participants, usually from the lower and humbler social strata.[2] In the film *Dona Flora and Her Two Husbands* the carnivalesque first husband had a fatal heart attack while dancing in a *bloco*. A species of this genus is the *bloco de sujos* ("bloc of the dirty ones"), designating either a loosely organized band of ragamuffins, or a group of revelers that paint their faces with charcoal and rouge and dress in loud colors in artless fashion. These groups have a chaotic, disarrayed appearance, and seem to portray best the "vertigo" component of carnival play. Another species is called *bloco de arrastão* ("bloc of the fishing net"), for as the group moves along, the seduction of its rhythmic chanting and the dancing of its members proves irresistible to spectators, who, totally unable to resist, are "pulled in" to sing and dance.

---

[2]Julie Taymor informs me that today there seems to be a resurgence of "spontaneous" *Carnaval*, in protest against commercial celebrations, both by humbler and middle-class strata. These contemporary *blocos* are particularly typical of the latter, if not of both.

Hundreds of *blocos* still exist in Rio. They rejoice in such names as *Vem Amor* ("Do Come, Love"), *Vai Quem Quer* ("Come Who Will"), *Namorar Eu Sei* ("In Loving, I Know"), *Suspiro da Cobra* ("Sigh of a Snake"), *Canarios das Laranjeiras* ("Canaries from Larenjeiras"—a ward of Rio), and *Bloco do Gelo* ("Ice Block"). New *blocos* come into being with each carnival, while older ones disappear. What usually happens is that a large and well-organized *bloco* eventually establishes a samba school. Like the schools, large *blocos* have detailed regulations and by-laws, are governed by a board of directors, democratically elected by all the members at a general assembly, have adopted heraldic colors of their own, and appear at carnival time wearing uniform costumes which have been especially made for the occasion. Lastly, some of the better-off *blocos*—like the major samba schools—are the proprietors of the clubhouse where they have their headquarters and of the place where they hold their rehearsals.

The samba schools are organized into three leagues, with demotion of the last two schools in the first and second leagues and promotion of two schools from the second and third to replace them. An awards committee judges them. Although their numbers fluctuate, informants suggest that there are now nine jurors. One evaluates the guild's flag, since each "school" is officially a guild (*gremio*) and the line of its officials is known as the *comissão de frente*, usually numbering fifteen, who march at the head of the parade, often in frock coats and top hats. The second evaluates the performance of the flag-bearer, the *porta-bandeira*, and the major-domo, or *mestre-sala*; usually the flag-bearer is the most beautiful woman of the school and the best dancer—always she appears in the dress of an eighteenth-century lady. At every carnival the school presents a different, beautifully embroidered flag, showing on one side the emblem of the guild and on the other some design indicating the plot which is presented in that particular pageant. Until 1967 the flag itself was awarded points, but not subsequently. The major-domo is also called *baliza*, literally a signpost or land-mark. This is apt for he is really the pivot round which the choreography revolves. He is usually tall and slim, agile and graceful. He appears either in seventeenth-century attire, with short cape and plumed hat—like one of Dumas's musketeers—or in the silk and satin knee-length coat of the eighteenth century, with powdered wig in the style of Louis XV. He carries a small fan in his left hand, or a lace handkerchief, and with his right he holds his partner's hand or her waist, as the dance may require. They dance together and then separate. She then gyrates swiftly, the silk of the flag sighs as it cuts the air, while he dances round her, inventing complicated steps, kneeling, bowing as gracefully and delicately, as if he were in Versailles in the days of Louis-le-Beinaimé. While these blacks from the poor slums display the elegance of a vanished feudalism in their liminality, the white "beautiful people" in the restricted indoor *Carnaval of the Clubs* revert to the almost naked barbarism of the night revels of the *La Dolce Vita*. Whites dress down, and blacks dress up.

The third judge evaluates the school's current plot and the lyrics of the samba, which always refer to the plot and indeed create its emotional tone. The fourth judge evaluates the appearance of the school as a whole and the choreography of the ensemble: the main components are the *alas* (wings), consisting of 10 to 30 persons, often of the same sex, who are organized around a subplot, which must conform to the school's main plot. In addition to the *alas*, there are the *destaques* or *figuras de destaque*, "the stand-outs" or individual items. These are persons wearing sumptuous and magnificent costumes and plumes, who strut down the avenue in solitary, solar, lunar, or rainbow splendor. Quite often, they are transvestites with silicone implants to caricature femininity, or commonly well-known Rio socialites. Floats are also a carnival component, limited by regulation to four per school, including the float that spearheads the pageant, known as the *abre-alas* (literally "wings-opener or usher"). Its purpose is to proclaim the name of the school and the title of its plot for the year. An *abre-alas* may represent an open book, a large portal, or a baroque cartouche (like those that appear in old maps and charts). By tradition, the text used is as follows: "G.R.E.S. [an acronym for Gremio Recreativo Escola de Samba] Mangueira pays its compliments to the people of Rio, presents [here follows the plot's title], and requests permission to pass through." Some of the floats are unbelievable. It is recorded that the *Portela* school, in 1965, exhibited a float that was an exact replica of the library of Princess Isabel in which she signed the Act of Abolition of Slavery! (Another example of black Brazilian elegance.) Some floats are in rank bad taste, however, and some schools have substituted for them painted panels and screens and a series of *gonfalons* (standards with two or three streamers) and *oriflammes* (red silk banners split at one end) carried by members of the school.

The fifth judge evaluates the tunefulness and musical texture of the samba and the performance of the *bateria*. The number of bandsmen may vary greatly. The incomparable *bateria* of the *Academicos de Cubango* took the avenue by storm at the *Carnaval* I attended. We were all swept away on the great tide of the samba played on drums by hundreds of *ritmistas*. As mentioned earlier, only percussion instruments are permitted, but they include large and small drums such as *cotixa*, the military drum, and many others; friction drums (*cuicas*) which can make several sounds at once in syncopation; *agogos*, derived from African hunting bells; tambourines; *pandeiros* or timbrels; polished saucepans; and many more. Smaller instruments are played by *passistas*, dexterous leapers and contortionists, who often cavort, two men to one girl, in the sexiest of postures. We all fell in behind the *ritmistas* and *passistas* in a Dionysiac abandonment I have never experienced before or since.

What is it like to be a *sambista* or *sambeiro*? One journalist, Sergio Bitencourt, writing in the *Correio da Manha*, claims that the *Carnaval* is "a mission, a mandate, a supreme moment of deliverance and self-sufficiency." He adds: "The drops of perspiration which cover the face of the *sambista* have the savor of drops of blood." Here we have what Huizinga calls "the deep earnestness in play," even a hint of the *Via Dolorosa*, the Way of the Cross. Festival, at times, is not too far from its ritual origins and can give its participants something akin to a religious experience—Ash Wednesday is not too far behind Mardi Gras. Death is implicitly present; in the movie *Black Orpheus* he appeared in the guise of *Exu* of the cemeteries, the chaos deity of the Umbanda religion, *Exu sem Luz*.

The sixth juror evaluates the masquerades and the individual floats. Their mimicry is magnificently complex. No anthropologist has yet done an adequate study, either aesthetic or semiotic, of the costumes, masks, disguises, ritual nakedness, color, symbolism, and the structural oppositions and mediations among all these, that can be found in any Rio carnival.

To round off my tally of the jurors, three are placed at different locations on the parade route to assign negative votes as penalties for any delays caused by willful negligence. There is further anthropological material in the politicking that surrounds the awards committee, and the hostility, often leading to violence—even homicide and suicide—which greets their final assessment of the various schools' performances. The jurors are drawn from the ranks of professional artists or art critics; dress designers; newspaper persons; television personnel; professional ballet dancers, choreographers, musicians, and composers. But umpires and referees are seldom popular in any of the fields of play we have been talking about. When play makes serious statements about the human condition, people take its outcomes seriously.

It is a Brazilian point of honor that if one is going to wear a costume, or *fantasia*, it must communicate one's most private or intimate fantasy in the most artistic way possible. Repression must be lifted. One might even talk about the aestheticization of the repressed, making the very private very public in the mode of beauty. The secret of Brazilian culture perhaps lies in this, that it has created a "palace of *Carnaval*," a place of samba, out of fantasies suppressed through the rest of the year by immersion in industrial labor, by submission to an autocratic regime, by tenacious vestiges of feudal attitudes in the relations between men and women, young and old. Even more, Brazilian culture has raised a traditional ritual of reversal to the scale of a great industrial nation, in every way equivalent, in its subjunctive mood and at the unconscious and preconscious levels, to the complex modern industrial nation that is Brazil's indicative mood and conscious reality. *Carnaval* is made to serve as a kind of paradigm, or model, for the whole modern and postmodern world. *Carnaval* is no Aldous Huxleyan "orgy porgy," for its ironical, whimsical, urbane, and genial touch dispels such a thought. Rather it is the creative anti-structure of mechanized modernity. *Carnaval* is the reverse of fiction or fake: it demands validity of feeling, sad or glad. It is mostly glad, and there is no mistaking the authenticity of radiant joys that pour out of faces and songs, and make the samba live up to one of its names, *arrasta-pé* (netter or snarer of feet). No one can feel embarrassed in the many-dimensioned world of carnival. "Shame is absent from *Carnaval*," the saying goes. It is a world oblivious of original sin, as its own lyrics dare to say in a Christian country . . . *Aquele mundo encantado* ("that enchanted world"). The Golden Age really does return. Naturally, there are many Brazilians who are skeptical, regarding *Carnaval* as "opium for the people" (though "speed" would perhaps be a better metaphor). Again, at *Carnaval* time the roads leading from Rio are choked with the cars of the middle class, fleeing the revelries of the streets, dreading the carnivalesque reversal of their hard-won bourgeois values.

What has Caillois and his theories of play to do with all this? Only that *Carnaval* engulfs all his categories in a dynamic, many-leveled, liminal domain of multiframed antistructures and spontaneous *communitas*. *Paidia, ludus, agôn, alea*, mimicry and *ilinx* are spun together indistinguishably in the spangled tapestry of the nocturnal parade of the Carioca samba schools. As the poet, Cassiano Ricardo, put it: "A bit of Brazil in the hearts of angry men—wouldn't it be a solution?"

Performing Ethnography

with Edie Turner

Anthropological literature is full of accounts of dramatic episodes which vividly manifest the key values of specific cultures. Often these are case-histories of conflicts between lineages or factions, spreading into feuds, vendettas, or head-hunting expeditions. Frequently they describe how criminal behavior is defined and handled. Other accounts describe how illness and misfortune are ascribed to witchcraft or ancestral affliction and reveal tensions and stresses in the social structure. Such descriptions are richly contextualized; they are not flat narratives of successive events for they are charged with meaningfulness. The actors commonly share a world-view, a kinship network, economic interests, a local past, and a system of ritual replete with symbolic objects and actions which embody a cosmology. They have lived through hard times and good times together, Culture, social experience, and individual psychology combine in complex ways in any "bit" or "strip" of human social behavior. Anthropologists have always favored the long-term, holistic study of a relatively small society, examining its institutions and their interconnections in great detail, locating the links among kinship, economic, legal, ritual, political, aesthetic and other sociocultural systems. When they study, say, a particular performance of ritual, they are on the look-out for expressions of shared cultural understandings in behavior, as well as for manifestations of personal uniqueness.

Nevertheless, while it may be possible for a gifted researcher to demonstrate the coherence among the "parts" of a culture, the models he presents remain cognitive. Cognizing the connections, we fail to form a satisfactory impression of how another culture's members "experience" one another. For feeling and will, as well as thought, constitute the structures of culture—cultural experience, regarded both as the experience of individuals and as the collective experience of its members embodied in myths, rituals, symbols, and celebrations. For several years, as teachers of anthropology, we have been experimenting with the performance of ethnography to aid students' understanding of how people in other cultures experience the richness of their social existence, what the moral pressures are upon them, what kinds of pleasures they expect to receive as a reward for following certain patterns of action, and how they express joy, grief, deference, and affection, in accordance with cultural expectations. At the University of Virginia, with anthropology students, and at New York University, with drama students, we've taken descriptions of strips of behavior from "other cultures" and asked students to make "playscripts" from them. Then we set up workshops—really "playshops"—in which the students try to get kinetic understandings of the "other" sociocultural groups. Often we selected either social dramas—from our own and other ethnographies—or ritual dramas (puberty rites, marriage ceremonies, potlatches, etc.), and asked the students to put them in a "play frame"—to relate what they are doing to the ethnographic knowledge they are increasingly in need of, to make the scripts they use "make sense." This motivates them to study the anthropological monographs—and exposes gaps in those monographs in so far as these seem to depart from the logic of the dramatic action and interaction they have themselves purported to describe. The actors' "inside view," engendered in and through performance, becomes a powerful critique of how ritual and ceremonial structures are cognitively represented.

Today, students of social science are familiar with Bateson's concept of "frame," and Goffman's, Handelman's and others' elaborations on it, including Goffman's notions of "framebreaking," "frame slippage," and "fabricated frames." To frame is to discriminate a sector of sociocultural action from the general on-going process of a community's life. It is often *reflexive*, in that, to "frame," a group must cut out a piece of itself for inspection (and retrospection). To do this it must create—by rules of exclusion and inclusion—a bordered space and a privileged time within which images and symbols of what has been sectioned off can be "relived," scrutinized, assessed, revalued, and, if need be, remodeled and rearranged. There are many cultural modes of framing. Each of them is a direct or indirect way of commenting on the mainstream of social existence. Some use special vocabularies, others use the common speech in uncommon ways. Some portray fictitious situations and characters which nevertheless refer pointedly to personages and problems of everyday experience. Some frames focus on matters of "ultimate concern" and fundamental ethics; these are often "ritual" frames. Others portray aspects of social life by analogy, including games of skill, strength, and chance. Other modes of "play" framing are more elaborate, including theatre and other performative genres. Some social events are contained in multiple frames, hierarchically arranged, frame within frame, with the ultimate "meaning" of the event shaped by the dominant, "encompassing" frame. Frames, in other words, are often themselves "framed." But let's not speak of "meta-frames," except in a play frame! Nevertheless, ribaldry may be the most appropriate "metalanguage" for today's play frames – as Bakhtin argued in his great defense of Rabelais and the "Rabelaisian language" he drew from "the people's second world" – in order to reinstate human good sense in a literature bedeviled by the cognitive chauvinism of intellectual establishments, secular and sacred.

Framing frames perhaps makes for intensified reflexivity. In 1981, one of our Virginia graduate students, Pamela Frese, who has been studying marriage (culturally, structurally, and in terms of social dynamics) in the Charlottesville area – usually in the official role of photographer – elected to cast the entire anthropology department as participants in a simulated or fabricated contemporary Central Virginian wedding. Edith and Victor Turner, for example, were the bride's mother and father, and the bride and groom were identified primarily because they were not in the least a "romantic item." The rest obtained kinship or friendship roles by drawing folded strips of paper from a hat – each slip describing a role: bride's sister, groom's former girl friend, groom's father's father, bride's drunken uncle, and so on. A Department of Religious Studies graduate student was cast as the minister. Both faculty and students were involved. A "genealogy" of the families was pinned up in the department office several weeks before the event. Almost immediately people began to fantasize about their roles. One of the faculty members declared, as father of the groom, that his "side" of the wedding represented $23 million of "old New England money." This figure, he remembered, was what the heiress whom he nearly became engaged to at Yale was alleged to be worth. Victor Turner was an old proletarian Scots immigrant who made vulgar money by manufacturing a cheap, but usable, plastic garbage can, and who quoted Robbie Burns, often irrelevantly. The Lévi-Straussian principle of "binary opposition" was clearly in evidence.

The "wedding" took place in the large basement of our house at Charlottesville – the "kiva," some called it. Afterwards, there was a "reception" upstairs with a receiving line, real champagne and festive foods. At subsequent sessions students were asked to describe, or if they wished, to write down their impressions – partly as seen from their own "real" viewpoint. The data is still coming in. Several people took photographs of the different stages of the event. Others taped conversations and registered variations in the decibel level of the group during the reception. All the materials would add up to several full length papers. Pam Frese, the original researcher, will "write up" the whole enterprise. Here, let's consider just the "nesting" of "frames" involved.

(1) The encompassing frame is a *pedagogical* one – "everything within this frame is data for anthropological analysis." The formula is "let us learn."

(2) Within (1) nests a play frame, with Batesonian "metamessages." (a) The messages or signals exchanged in play are in a certain sense untrue or not

meant; and (b) that which is denoted by these signals is non-existent. The formula is: let us make believe.

(3) Within (1) and (2) nests a ritual-script—the preparations for the wedding and a Christian form of the wedding service. If this frame had not itself been framed by the override "all this is play," the ritual frame would have had its wider cultural "moral function." Ritual says "let us believe," while play says, "this is make-believe." Without the play frame there would have been a real danger that, in terms at least of Catholic theology, a real marriage would have taken place, for here it is the couple who are the ministers of the sacrament of marriage, not the priest, whose basic role is to confer the blessings of the Church on the couple. Since ritual is "transformative," the couple would have transformed their relationship into that of spouses by the performative utterances of the nuptial liturgy. Truly to "play at" performing a ritual drama is, without suitable precautions being taken, to play with fire. But it was clear that the "serious" ritual frame was being desolemnized and demystified by its own containment in the wider play frame. A reminder of play was the reciting of a poem—an epithalamion by Sappho, in fact—before the service proper began, by a stranger to the group, though a close friend of the "bride." Of course, in a real marriage the couple's intentions are all-important. They must seriously "intend wedlock."

(4) Within this frame of fabricated marriage ritual was the frame of the parapolitical structure of the University of Virginia's Department of Anthropology. This frame was covert but genuine, fabricated like the other frames. At the "wedding reception" it was clear in the behavior of the pretended kin and friends of the groom and bride what the extant pattern was of cleavages and alliances, oppositions and coalitions, between and among faculty and students—a delicate situation we won't dwell on here. However, these artificial rufflings were minor indeed, hardly troubling a genial group of scholars. But under the protection of the play frame and simulated wedding frame, in words, gestures, conversational style, and dress, in reversals of "real-life" roles and manners, one saw everyday departmental politics as a "projective system."

As the evening progressed, frame slippage occurred more and more frequently, and people reverted to their ordinary "selves," though for a few "peak moments"—for example, when the champagne cork popped—there was the sort of "ecstasy" that E. D'Aquili and C. Laughlin in *The Spectrum of Ritual* (1979) write about—the simultaneous "firing" of cerebral and autonomic nervous systems, right brain and left brain, sympathetic and parasympathetic. It was interesting, too, to observe which persons "stayed in role" longest and who could or could not suspend disbelief in order to play their roles properly. Some, it became clear, thought there was something sacrilegious, some profanation of their own cherished values, in enacting what for them was a religious sacrament. Others, atheists or agnostics, introduced a note of parody or irony into the ritually framed episodes. We were surprised at the wholeheartedness with

1. Everything inside this frame is pedagogic, and data for anthropological analysis

2. Everything inside this frame is not meant, is play

3. Everything inside this frame is ritual; over-ridden by (2)

4. Everything inside this frame is the reality of the department of anthropology, seen as a "projective system" under the protection of (2)

which some anthropology students played their conventional roles—for example, the "bride," who in real life was having reservations about her own marriage, sewed her own bridal gown. We were also astonished at how well the students understood what phenomenological sociologists would call the "typifications" of American culture, how almost "instinctively" and "automatically" they "knew what to do next" and how to do it, in fact, how "natural" many people find it to act "ritually" given the proper stimuli, motivations, and excuse. It was interesting, too, for us to observe how some participants were almost shocked into recognizing buried aspects of themselves. Others were taken over, "possessed" by what Grathoff and Handelman have called "symbolic types"—priest, bride, bridegroom, and so on, in the domain of ritual liminality; Drunken Uncle, Pitiful Lean and Slippered Pantaloon in the play domain (the "bride's grandfather"—a student played this senile type; in the middle of the service he shouted, "Battlestations! Battlestations!" reliving old wars.)

A few comments on this performance: in practice, the hierarchical nesting of frames was overridden by the subjective responses of the actors, who evidently selected one or another of the frames as dominant. For example, the "bride" caught herself on numerous occasions following the performance talking about her "wedding" as though it was real. Others remained resolutely within the play frame; enacted creative fantasies pivoted on their chosen cultural roles. One woman remained consistently "dotty" throughout the whole ceremony, denouncing the sexual innuendoes of Solomon's *Song of Songs* in loud tones, and remaining generally objectionable during the subsequent reception and "wedding breakfast." Others kept on shifting frames, both during the performance and for some weeks afterwards; some remained "in frame" for several months and continued to call each other by kinship terms derived from the fabricated genealogy. Most participants told us that they understood the cultural structure and psychology of normative American marriage much better for having taken part in an event that combined flow with reflexivity. Some even said that the fabricated marriage was more "real" for them than marriages in the "real world" in which they had been involved.

The fabricated marriage was not our first attempt to "play" ethnography. At the University of Chicago, in seminars we ran in the Committee on Social Thought, our students put on several performances. One was a simulation of the midwinter ceremony of the Mohawk Indians of Canada, directed by David Blanchard, which involved the use of "False Face" masks, "dreaming," trancing, and prophesying. Another "ritual" was a deliberate construct of our students, led by Robert Abernathy, using van Gennep's *Rites of Passage* and Victor Turner's *Ritual Process* and *Forest of Symbols* as "cookbooks" or "how-to" protocols. This "ritual" expressed in terms of symbolic action, symbolic space, and imagery, the anxieties and ordeals of Chicago graduate students. It was divided into three stages, each occupying a different space. Each participant brought along a cardboard box in which he/she had to squat, representing his/her constricted, inferior social status. There were episodes, of a sado-masochistic character, representing registration, in which the actors were continually referred between different desks, monitored by sinister rhadamanthine bureaucrats, who constantly found fault with the registrants. Another scene, using multi-media, portrayed a typical student, being harangued from a lectern by an "anthropology professor" spouting technical gobbledygook (actually excerpts from published texts), while he was typing his dissertation to the accompaniment of a series of rapid slides of familiar architectural details of the University of Chicago. Finally he "died," and was solemnly buried by a group of his peers clad in black leotards. The scene then shifted from a room in the students' activities hall to a yard in the campus, where the constraining boxes were placed so as to represent a kind of Mayan pyramid which strongly resembled the new Regenstein Library, scene of so many painful graduate attempts at study. The whole group danced around the pyramid, which was set on fire. This "liminal period" was followed by a final rite in another room of the hall, where student papers that had been unfavorably commented upon by faculty were cremated in a grate; the ashes were then mixed with red wine, and two by two the students anointed one another on the brow with the mixture, symbolizing "the death of bad vibes." Finally, all joined together in chanting "Om, Padne, Om," representing a "communitas of suffering." This production involved music, dancing, and miming, as well as dialogue. Many of the participants claimed that the performance had discharged tensions and brought the group into a deeper level of mutual understanding. It had also been "a lot of fun."

There was one curious further "real-life" development. Victor Turner was contacted by a notorious dean in charge of student discipline, who inquired whether a series of small harmless fires, started in odd corners of the Regenstein Library, could have resulted from the "ritual." He even suggested that some of the participants should be hypnotized by a university psychiatrist to elicit information about "wild-looking" people who participated in the fire dance around the symbolic Regenstein Library. Turner said it was unlikely that one of the actors was to blame for the small fires, since ritual theory suggested that such "rituals of rebellion" (in this case, a "play" rebellion) were cathartic, discharging tensions and allowing the system to function without serious contestation. He then invited the dean to the next seminar, which was an explanation by a Benedictine nun of a new script she had devised for the clothing ceremony of a postulant who would be taking her final vows. This evidently proved too much for the Irish American dean, who no doubt disapproved of Vatican II and all its "liberating" consequences including taking liberties with the script of traditional ceremonies. Turner never heard from him again.

We have described, in some detail, in a *Kenyon Review* article, "Dramatic Ritual/Ritual Drama: Performative and Reflexive Anthropology" (1980:80-93) how we experimented with the performance of a social drama described in Victor Turner's books, *Schism and Continuity* (Manchester University Press, 1957) and *The Drums of Affliction* (Oxford: Clarendon, 1968), with a mixed group of drama and anthropological students at New York University. This was our contribution to an intensive workshop devoted to exploring the interface between ritual and the theatre, between social and aesthetic drama. In subsequent sessions at NYU, we have experimented, mainly with drama students, in performing Central African and Afro-Brazilian rituals, aided by drummers drawn from the appropriate cultures or related cultures.

These ventures emboldened us to experiment further at the University of Virginia with the rendering of ethnography in a kind of instructional theatre. Our aim was not to develop a professional group of trained actors for the purposes of public entertainment. It was, frankly, an attempt to put students more fully inside the cultures they were reading about in anthropological monographs. Reading written words kowtows to the cognitive dominance of written matter and relies upon the arbitrariness of the connection between the penned or printed sign and its meaning. What we were trying to do was to put experimental flesh on these cognitive bones. We were able, fortunately, to do more than this, for we could draw upon the recent first-hand experience of returning fieldworkers. We therefore cast in the roles of director and *ethnodramaturg* anthropologists fresh from immersion in fieldwork in, for example, New Ireland and the American Northwest Coast. Students were encouraged to read available literature on these areas, and were then given roles in key ritual performances of the cultures recently studied by their returned colleagues.

One of the performances we tried to bring off was the Cannibal (Hamatsa) Dance of the sacred winter ceremonials of the Kwakiutl Indians. Here the director was Dr. Stanley Walens, an authority on the Northwest Coast, whose book, *Feasting with Cannibals: An Essay on Kwakiuti Cosmology* (1981), was published shortly after the performance. Walens condensed the long series of rituals composing the Hamatsa ceremony into a short script (see Appendix). My students prepared the ceremonial space, which, again, formed part of the extensive cellarage of my house. Under Walens's guidance they made props, and improvised costumes and body decoration, including face-painting. For speeches, invocations, homilies, myth-telling, ridicule songs, and occasional bursts of competitive dialogue, Walens used Franz Boas's translations of Kwakiutl texts. Walens acted as narrator, chorus, and coordinator throughout.

A similar format was used by Mimi George, the ethnographer who had just returned from her study of Barok ritual in New Ireland. We have no space to discuss these performances in detail, but it might be useful for those who contemplate doing something similar to quote from comments made subsequently by Walens and others. Both, we think, indicate the high reflexive potential of ethnographic performance as a teaching tool, essentially as a means of raising questions about the anthropological research on which they are based, but which the performances transform in the process of dramatic action.

First, then, Walens's commentary:

> The most obvious aspect of putting on the cannibal ritual was perhaps the continual feeling that it was play. The actual ritual must have been far more serious, more cataclysmic in its experiential effect on native observers than it could possibly be on non-natives. The ideas behind the ritual are so cosmic that without the associations that a native makes between those overweening social and cosmic forces, the symbols and actions of the ritual must lose much of their impact.

At the same time, the reactions of the students to the ritual did seem to imply that they picked up on the tenor and timbre of the actual ritual. The sense of aggressiveness, conflict, the controlled display of hostility and destructiveness did come across despite the constant messages from the actors that these were amateurs playing. Of course, there is a dual element of seriousness and play in all drama; one might even wonder about the use of the word "play" to refer to dramatic presentations. Indeed, rituals often seem to focus on the revelation that reality is merely a fiction, a presentation that humans make for one another. Vast secrets are revealed as being mere mechanical tricks; the spirit in the mask turns out to have the same birthmark behind his left knee as does Uncle Ralph. We may marvel at the technical ability of an Uncle Ralph or a Laurence Olivier to make us temporarily suspend belief that we are watching them (indeed that may be the most cogent marvel of drama as a whole) and for a moment to see only a Hamlet, or a cannibal bird, or a Willie Loman. We might ask why that most cosmic of modern plays, *Waiting for Godot*, seems to be one in which the action consists solely of play activity, activity in which all the conventional dramatic moments are negated by statements of their irreality. Contrast how Beckett handles suicide with the way Chekhov or Ibsen do.

In short, the problems encountered in putting on an ethnographic performance are not by nature different from those that an opera or drama director would face. In fact, while preparing the Kwakiutl ritual, I was continually made aware of just how much preparation, training, rehearsal, how many years of stockpiling the paraphernalia, the foods for the feast, the validating gifts, how much patience in achieving the requisite status, must have gone into such native ceremonies. Kwakiutl ceremonies are long—the winter ceremonial season lasts as long as four months, consisting of daily ritual activities in hundreds of varieties, all complexly interrelated, and all of which alter the statuses of the participants so that subsequent rituals must take account of the newly acquired or divested statuses of everyone else in the society. We prepared only a minimal amount of food and paraphernalia, and had only the merest mote of performance, yet the amount of preparation time and rehearsal time was tremendous. The amount of camaraderie that arose among us was also astounding; I was not particularly friendly with the people who helped with the preparations before the class, but since then have felt much closer toward them. Perhaps one of the most important aspects of dramatic presentation is the way in which the mutual performance of a fiction unites all its creators.

Another matter is that of performers versus audience. In one sense, we were all the audience for this ritual. The Hamatsa ritual now exists only in a printed form; we tried to approximate this form as much as possible. It was therefore quite unlike the production of a play, where there is a movement toward breathing new life into a form. By nature, living rituals seem to be ever changing. To perform a ritual the same way twice is to kill it, for the ritual grows as we grow, its life recapitulates the course of ours. It becomes the symbol for the society itself. Just as the experimental theatre directors of the sixties and seventies rebelled against the strictures of our society by contravening those strictures in their performance texts, so do Kwakiutl see the cannibal ritual as a symbol of the life and death of their culture, and mourn the demise of their culture in mourning the demise of its ceremonies. Our play presentation then can be seen as a representation of the modern view of primitive ritual as a whole—that it is slightly if not completely foolish, that it is primarily a social act, that it is play-acting.

We imagine our own view of the Kwakiutl is the same as their view of themselves. The meaning of the ritual for them is forever unapproachable by us. We experience only the ritual we perform, the one that actually takes place between a group of students, colleagues, and friends in the basement of a house in Charlottesville in December 1981. If we rejoice in our common experience, well and good. We have put on a play, we compare notes, and wait for the reviews. As in any play, we reaffirm, through this particular fiction communally performed, truths communally experienced. We must also question the validity of *that* experience. The situation is not unlike that in which a Plains Indian presents his vision, gained on a solitary quest, to a committee of elders who review it and give it their stamp of approval, or when a ritual of fecundity is given validity through subsequent bestowal of approval by the relevant deific elders. The reviews are important, as important as the production itself, for they define the commonality of the experience.

I wonder if I would have asked these questions about the nature of performance if I hadn't had to put one on. I certainly feel much more aware of the nature of performance *per se* than I did before. It becomes easy to see the messages embedded in rituals that remind the audience that this is a performance—the little skits in the cannibal ritual, or the overblown speeches, the constant revelations by dancers of their human identities. There is an interesting paradox here—in Western drama, the performer's technique should be so good that he conveys through the maximum of artifice the greatest amount of naturalness to his stage character. Both poor mastery of technique and overpresentation of the emotions themselves ("hamming") detract from the illusion of balance between contrivedness and spontaneity that makes for convincing dramatic presentation. Since stage gestures bear no relation to everyday gestures, having by nature to communicate over distances far greater than those normally used in gestural communication, the illusion of naturalness is possible only with carefully controlled artifice. In the cannibal dance too there must be this balance—the cannibal dancer must convey through the balanced use of gesture and action the feeling that he is going to destroy the people in the room. He must make them fear for themselves—is this not the purpose of all drama—by striking a balance between natural human motion and alien motion.

I have often wondered how to convey to my classes an emotion that would be similar in character and degree to that which the audience at a cannibal dance might feel when the cannibal first appears. How do you convey to people that the instrument of their own deaths is present in the room? My classes know me as a cream puff, so I could never begin to pretend to be the type of psychopathic villain that might, in our society's mythology, strike fear into their hearts; I have not prepared them to expect it from me, nor do I possess the acting ability to convey it to them. I think this the most important facet of the cannibal dance—the confrontation each person has with his own death in a living embodiment—and can only feel that it was not conveyed in our play ritual. Douglas Dalton, one of the participating students, giving a somewhat different view, wrote: "As the ceremony progressed I felt not so much the antagonistic rivalry that was overtly expressed in the ceremony between the bear clan and the killer whale clan, but the fact that we were collectively doing something really important—something essentially correct. There was so much power flowing all over the place in the longhouse (the Charlottesville basement) that night! The spirits were really at work that evening and we had to keep everything in line so all that power wouldn't destroy everything!" The Kwakiutl used to enhance the destructiveness of cannibal dancers, putting on demonstrations of death by using masks, bladders full of blood, and the like. To the audience these must have been very effective; and of course, there were times when people were really killed.

I keep coming back to this one issue—the nature of artifice and fiction in play performance. I think this is what people in the seminar were most aware of, a universal of drama, not the particular ritual we performed. I also think the questions that lie at the foundation of theatre and theatrical performance lie at the foundation of ritual and ritual performance—questions about the relationship of actors to text, of actors to audience, or fiction to fictive reality, and so on. I have no doubt that the students see some of the dramatic nature of the cannibal ritual—dramatic in both senses of the word: it is effective and it is theatre—and that they can now read ethnography and introject those feelings of theatre into the dry accounts of dances and songs and spirit names which anthropologists have written down. I have breathed life into Kwakiutl ritual just as a director breathes life into a play—but I have done it independently of the intentions of the Kwakiutl authors, just as a play production is independent of the intentions of the play's author.

One has the feeling that rituals are magical, that for some reason as yet unknown to science they can communicate to people, not despite their artificiality, but because of and through their artificiality. Rituals are efficacious and we wonder how. Just as we know that a good stage magician is performing tricks—that is, really not levitating that elephant or sawing that woman in half—we still marvel at the beauty of the illusion and the mastery with which it is presented; so we marvel at the mastery of illusion in ritual while we reaffirm its illusionary nature.

It's obvious from all this that I've been thinking about the question of doubt, in an Augustinian sense, as the basis of ritual. In the chart of frames, each of the inner levels presents more doubt of the outer levels, each contravenes and obviates the outer levels. It is not that religion is so much a statement of belief but that at its most effective it enables us to suspend disbelief in the things that are larger than ourselves, whether they be deities or nature or history or the sacred corpus of anthropological theory. Just as at a ritual we may have a momentary inkling that there was something greater present than simply a bunch of people playing at ceremony, so in our acting of the cannibal dance we have an inkling of something which transcends the limitations of a particular moment in the history of the anthropology department at the University of Virginia. Compare this finale with Dalton's leap into what he took to be the Kwakiutl view of the Hamatsa ceremony: "The ritual ended, in fact, with the assurance that the Kwakiutl would continue to keep the world in order in a pledge for next year's ceremony. The bitter rivalry that was expressed in the early parts of the ceremony gave way to a final reconciliation and a true feeling of oneness with the forces of the universe." Perhaps this is the critical difference between aesthetic theatre and ritual—the actors on stage must always seem to be the characters they portray or they have failed; the ritualist must always seem to be nothing other than what he is, a frail human being playing with those things that kill us for their sport. Stage drama is about the extrapolation of the individual into alien roles and personalities; ritual drama is about the complete delimitation, the total definition of person.

Unlike Walens, Mimi George insisted that the participants in the Barok initiation ritual were not to be instructed in the culture and social structure, but rather assigned ritual roles without preparation. This, in the words of one of the participants, Jean-Jacques Decoster, "provided the feeling of magic that prevailed most of the evening . . . We went through a rite, and didn't just enact a 'savage ritual.' When I went home that evening and my housemates asked me about the stripes painted on my face, my answer was: 'I have just been initiated.' " Mimi George, the director, dramaturg, and fieldworker who prepared the scenario, told us that despite the alienness of the context, the students were "caught up into the meaning and worth of the ritual." Indeed, she was surprised by the similarity of their performance to its Papuan original. However, she felt that she had not given the actors sufficiently detailed guidance, and was continually beset by the cry, "What do I do now?" What this ritual did bring off was a kind of existential "double-take." At one point the "initiands" beat the Tubuan masked figure. It was then revealed that inside it was merely a human being (in this case Victor Turner). But later, in the garden, in darkness and simulated firelight, the Tubuan glided in unexpectedly to the beat of drums. The demystified "spirit" was dramatically remystified. Decoster notes, "The moment of greatest intensity was the outdoor ceremony . . . I felt definitely uneasy when we initiands were lined up and facing away from the entity, and it was not Eric (the dancer within the Tubuan) I was turning my back upon, but truly the Tubuan, an unknown and decidedly scary being. In a curious way, the ritual flogging (administered to the initiands by the 'elders') worked as a tension reliever." Other "initiands" commented on how close they felt to one another as against the uninitiated and already initiated.

We have a thick file of such comments on these and other performances of rituals in other cultures. On the whole they are enthusiastic and encouraging, though not a few echo Waltens's skepticism about whether any culture can be adequately translated into the action-language of another. For our own part, we have not reached any definite conclusions as to the merits of this performative approach to ethnography. Whenever our classes have performed scripts based on our own fieldwork among the Ndembu of Zambia in Central Africa we have undoubtedly learned something about that culture that we failed to understand in the field. For example, when we enacted the girl's puberty ceremony (in which the novice is wrapped completely in a blanket, laid at the foot of the symbolic "milk tree," and is compelled to remain motionless for a long period of time, while a large group of initiated village women dance and sing around her), we were later presented with the following account of her subjective impressions by Linda Camino, the student taking the role of *Kankang'a* (novice, initiand, literally, "guinea fowl").

> Around and around they danced, again and again with punctuated cries and claps. Beneath the blanket I lay still and quiet, firm and

"cool," patiently awaiting the next stage, which I knew would be to escort me to my seclusion hut. Then a strange thing happened. Time lengthened, expanded, and my wait seemed interminable, for as the singing and cries of the women grew lustier, as the pulsation of their feet and hands quickened to the driving beat of the insistent drums, I began to fear that they had quite forgotten all about me, guinea fowl. They were having fun; I was not. The drums beckoned me. Their wrenching beats filled my muscles with tension, demanding a response, a response I could not give as guinea fowl. The women's enthusiasm and boisterous cheers challenged me to spring out from the blanket to join them. At this point, a desire to be like those other women, a desire to move my body freely to the sounds of the drums overwhelmed me. I longed to be a woman—alive, vital, responding, moving; not a dull guinea fowl, still before a tree, unseen, stationary, alone.

We were aware of the ambivalence with which pubescent girls had regarded the passage to adult social status, but Camino's comments suggested a hypothesis about how the ritual might have motivated a real Ndembu novice not merely to accept but to strongly desire her new status-role and membership in a community of wives and mothers. Such a hypothesis would have to be tested out, of course, in further field research, but the fact that a simulated ritual could raise it is at least one persuasive argument in favor of performed ethnography. In our experience the most effective kind of performed ethnography is not the simulation of a ritual or a ceremony torn from its cultural context, but a series of "acts" and "scenes" based on detailed observations of processes of conflict.

Rituals, like law cases, should not be abstracted from the frameworks of the ongoing social process in which they were originally embedded. They have their source and raison d'etre in the ceaseless flow of social life, and in the social dramas within which communities seek to contain that life. By posing the functionally familiar against the culturally exotic in the dynamics of social drama, we can make our students vividly aware both of innate commonalities and cultural differences in relation to a wide range of human societies. Our recommendation, then, is this: If we attempt to perform ethnography, let us not begin with such apparently "exotic" and "bizarre" cultural phenomena as rituals and myths. Such an emphasis may only encourage prejudice, since it stresses the "otherness of the other." Let us focus first on what all people share, the social drama form, from which emerge all types of cultural performance, which, in their turn, subtly stylize the contours of social interaction in everyday life. In practice, this means setting apart a substantial block of time to familiarize students with the culture and social system of the group whose dramas they will enact. Such instruction should be interwoven with what Richard Schechner might call "the rehearsal process." The resultant instructional form could be a kind of synthesis between an anthropological seminar and a postmodern theatrical workshop. The data should be scripted; costumes, masks, stage settings, and other props should be made carefully, with an eye to cultural authenticity (though heavy-handed realism may not be appropriate). It is highly desirable, whenever possible, to bring in a member of the group studied as a dramaturg or director—or someone in the group who has done fieldwork should be dramaturg or director. We have found that students greatly enjoy these detailed, technical preliminaries. We have also found that nearly all the rituals we have performed involve at least one episode of feasting. If possible, the foods used in the original setting should be provided, cooked in the traditional ways. Foods, food taboos, and ways in which food is shared and exchanged make up a kind of cultural grammar and vocabulary which often give clues, when their symbolism is decoded, to basic attitudes and values of the group and to its social structure.

At least one session should be allocated to a close review of all aspects of the performance seen in retrospect. This should include subjective statements by the actors, the director, the dramaturg, and members of the audience if an audience was thought necessary. Much of the emphasis will be found to be on cultural differences, and the difficulties and delights of playing roles generated by cultures often far different from our own. In these occasions of intercultural reflexivity, we can begin to grasp something of the contribution each and every human culture can make to the general pool of manifested knowledge of our common human condition. It is in dramatics and dynamics most of all that we learn to coexperience the lives of our conspecifics, "our brother man and sister woman," to quote the great bard of Victor Turner's own Scottish culture, Robert Burns.

Appendix

Hamatsa (cannibal) ceremony

Meals and covenantal songs

Cries and whistles heard from woods (hamatsas and all helpers)

Ghost dancer appears
mentions death, excites old hamatsas and spirit retinue

Hatmatsas enter from all over—dance four times around fire
new initiate appears—enters excitedly, circles fire four times; he is now very wild,
dressed only in hemlock, with no restraining clothes;
comes from upper level

People try to encircle hamatsa; he is too wild, enters sacred room, sheds some hemlock branches — burned

Discussion of why hamatsa has escaped
  confession of sins and analysis of ceremonial errors; must be corrected by pledging potlatches, becoming a hamatsa's victim, or becoming an initiate; records are kept of who agrees to be a victim.

Adjournment — repurification through smoke

Setting of trap for hamatsa
  hemlock neckring made; all carry hemlock old man put in center as bait hamatsa escapes three times — on fourth time all join hands and he is captured all sing taming songs

Family of hamatsa is on steps of house — acknowledge their pledges

Hamatsa will not enter house — women dance before him enticingly to no avail, entice him with bones and mummified flesh

Screen is set up — hamatsa goes to sacred room

Hamatsa returns
  goes counterclockwise four times around fire, each time holding a victim's arm in his mouth and pulling him along; more taming songs, unsuccessful

All hemlock removed, burned

Distribution of property; display of coppers
All spirits appear to dance — faces black; eagle down in their hair and put around the room (carried in dishes like food)

Hamatsa appears
  dances around fire — reappears dressed in cedarbark clothing, a new piece added each time he reappears

House is totally shut up, no chinks or light from outside

Burning of cedar bark
  smoldering bark passed over head of dancer; everyone says "hoip, hoip"; much loud drumming, very rhythmic

Hamatsa dances, squatting and turning

Four more days of ceremony follow, during which time no one enters
or leaves the house; no food is served; there is constant singing of
power songs

Hamatsa appears wearing cedar bark only
 a simulacrum of him is washed and ritually treated, then smoked

Hamatsa still trembles
 women sing their most powerful songs simultaneously while men sing
 songs of wildness

A bloody menstrual napkin from the hamatsa's mother is burned
 he is made to inhale the smoke; he immediately collapses and has
 to be carried from the room

Someone has to pledge next year's ceremonials

The ceremonials end

References

d'Aquili, Eugene, C. Laughlin, and John McManus, eds. 1979. *The Spectrum of Ritual*. New York: Columbia University Press.

Turner, Victor. 1957. *Schism and Continuity*. Manchester: Manchester University Press.

————. 1968. *The Drums of Affliction*. Oxford: Clarendon.

————. 1980. "Dramatic Ritual/Ritual Drama: Performative and Reflexive Anthropology." *Kenyon Review*. 1. 3. Pp. 80-93. Reprinted in *From Ritual to Theatre* by Victor Turner. New York: Performing Arts Journal Publications, 1982.

Walens, Stanley. 1981. *Feasting with Cannibals*. Princeton: Princeton University Press.

Body, Brain, and Culture

BODY, BRAIN, AND CULTURE

The present essay is for me one of the most difficult I have ever attempted. This is because I am having to submit to question some of the axioms anthropologists of my generation—and several subsequent generations—were taught to hallow. These axioms express the belief that all human behavior is the result of social conditioning. Clearly a very great deal of it is, but gradually it has been borne home to me that there are inherent resistances to conditioning. As Anthony Stevens has recently written in an interesting book which seeks to reconcile ethological and Jungian approaches: "Any attempt to adopt forms of social organization and ways of life other than those which are *characteristic of our species* must lead to personal and social disorientation" (italics added; Stevens, 1982:24). In other words, our species has distinctive features, genetically inherited, which interact with social conditioning, and set up certain resistances to behavioral modification from without. Further, Robin Fox has argued: "If there is no human nature, any social system is as good as any other, since there is no base line of human needs by which to judge them. If, indeed, everything is learned, then surely men can be taught to live in any kind of society. Man is at the mercy of all the tyrants who think they know what is best for him. And how can he plead that they are being inhuman if he doesn't know what being human is in the first place?" (1973:13). One of those distinctive human features may be a propensity to the ritualization of certain of our behaviors, from smiling and maternal responsiveness onwards.

THEORIES OF RITUALIZATION

In June 1965, I took part in a discussion on "ritualization of behavior in animals and man" organized by Sir Julian Huxley for the Royal Society and held—perhaps appropriately—in the lecture hall of the Zoological Society of London, near the Mappin Terraces, where the monkeys revel. The "hard core" of the conference consisted of zoologists and ethologists, Huxley, Konrad Lorenz, R. A. Hinde, W. H. Thorpe, Desmond Morris, N. M. Cullen, F. W. Braestrup, I. Eibl-Eibesfeldt, and others. Sir Edmund Leach, Meyer Fortes, and I spoke up for British anthropology in defining ritual, but by no means as unanimously as the ethologists did in defining ritualization. Other scholars represented other disciplines: psychiatrists included Erik Erikson, R. D. Laing, and G. Morris Carstairs. Sir Maurice Bowra and E. H. Gombrich spoke about the ritualization of human cultural activities, dance, drama, and art. Basil Bernstein, H. Elvin and R. S. Peters discussed ritual in education and David Attenborough shared his ethnographic films on the Kava ceremony in Tonga and land-diving in Pentecost, New Hebrides.

The nonethologists generally accepted Leach's position that "it cannot be too strongly emphasized that ritual, in the anthropologist's sense, is in no way whatsoever a genetic endowment of the species" (Leach, 1966:403). I took up no public position at that time, since I was secretly, even guiltily impressed by the ethologist's definition of "ritualization" which seemed to strike chords in relation to human ritual, summed up by Huxley as follows: "Ritualization is the adaptive formalization or canalization of emotionally motivated behavior, under the teleonomic pressure of natural selection so as: (a) to promote better and more unambiguous signal function, both intra- and inter-specifically; (b) to serve as more efficient stimulators or releasers of more efficient patterns of action in other individuals; (c) to reduce intra-specific damage; and (d) to serve as sexual or social bonding mechanisms" (Huxley, 1966:250). Actually, much of Huxley's definition is better applied analogically to those stylized human behaviors we might call "communicative," such as manners, decorum, ceremony, etiquette, polite display, the rules of chivalry (which inhibit the infliction on one another of damage by conspecifics) than to ritual proper.

In various publications I have suggested that ritual was "a *transformative* performance revealing major classifications, categories, and contradictions of cultural processes." In these respects it might conceivably fulfill Huxley's fourth function, that of "serving as sexual or social bonding mechanisms," by transforming social and personal life-crises (birth, initiation, marriage, death) into occasions where symbols and values representing the unity and continuity of the total group were celebrated and reanimated. The cultural rituals which seem most to embody something resembling Huxley's definition of "ritualization" are "seasonal, agricultural, fertility, funerary, and healing ones, because they make explicit the interdependence of people with their physical environments and bodies" (Grimes, 1982:34). But as I have written elsewhere, ritual is not necessarily a bastion of social conservatism; its symbols do not merely condense cherished sociocultural values. Rather, through its liminal processes, it holds the generating source of culture and structure. Hence, by definition ritual is associated with social *transitions* while *ceremony* is linked with social *states*. Performances of ritual are distinctive phases in the social process, whereby groups and individuals adjust to internal changes and adapt to their external environment.

Meyer Fortes, William Wyse Professor of Anthropology and Archaeology at Cambridge, influenced by Sigmund Freud, defined ritual at the London conference as "procedure for prehending the occult, that is, first, for grasping what is, for a particular culture, occult (i.e., beyond everyday human understanding, hidden, mysterious) in the events and incidents of people's lives, secondly, for binding what is so grasped by means of the ritual resources and beliefs available in that culture, and thirdly, for thus incorporating what is grasped and bound into the normal existence of individuals and groups" (1966:411). This formulation might well identify psychoanalytical clinical procedure as ritual process. Fortes makes his Freudian affiliation quite clear when he goes on to write that "ritual is concerned with prehending the unconscious (in the psychoanalytic sense) forces of individual action and existence, and their social equivalents, the irreducible factors in social relations (e.g., the mother-child nexus, at one end of the scale, the authority of society at the other). By bringing them, *suitably disguised*, or symbolized in tangible material objects and actions, into the open of social life, ritual binds them and makes them manageable" (italics added, 1966:413).

Unlike Leach, Fortes sees ritual more as the handling of otherwise unmanageable power than the communication of important cultural knowledge. For Fortes irreducible ambiguities and antinomies are made visible and thus accessible to public and legitimate control—a position to which with important modifications I myself have subscribed—while for Leach the emphasis in ritual is cognitive and classificatory. As he writes, "it is characteristic of many ritual and mythical sequences in primitive society that the actors claim to be recapitulating the creation of the world and that this act of creation is mythologized as a list of names attached to persons, places, animals, and things. The world is created by the process of classification and the repetition of the classification of itself perpetuates the knowledge which it incorporates" (1966:405). Ritual's multicoded redundancies inscribe its "messages" on the minds of the participants. Clearly, the main difference between anthropologists of the Leachian persuasion and the ethologists in their concept of ritualization or ritual lay in the emphasis of the former on ritual as learned, culturally transmitted behavior, intrinsically linked with the development of language, and of the latter on ritual as genetically programmed behavior with important nonverbal components.

THE NEUROBIOLOGY OF THE BRAIN: CULTURETYPE AND GENOTYPE

The years passed. I continued to treat ritual essentially as a cultural system. Meanwhile exciting new findings were coming from genetics, ethology, and neurology, particularly the neurobiology of the brain. I found myself asking a stream of questions more or less along the following lines. Can we enlarge our understanding of the ritual process by relating it to some of these findings? After all, can we escape from something like animal ritualization without escaping our own bodies and psyches, the rhythms and structures of which arise on their own? As Ronald Grimes has said, "They flow with or without our conscious assent; they are uttered-exclamations of nature and our bodies" (1982:36). I also asked myself many of the questions raised by Ralph Wendell Burhoe—especially, following Edward O. Wilson, what is the nature of the alleged "chain," and how long is it, by which genes hold cultural patterns, including ritual patterns, to use the idiom of sociobiology, "on leash"? This, it seemed to me, is where the neurobiology of the human brain begins to be relevant.

We shall have occasion to look at the findings of Paul MacLean, the neuroanatomist, again later, but something should be said now about his work on what might be called "archaic" structures of the human brain. His early work dealt with what is called the limbic system, an evolutionarily ancient part of the brain concerned with the emotions, cradled in or near the fringes of the cortex. In a 1949 paper he suggested that the limbic system is "the major circuit that would have to be involved in psychosomatic diseases, such as gastrointestinal ulcers caused by social or psychological stress, a now widely accepted hypothesis since it has been demonstrated that this system controls the pituitary gland at the base of the brain and the autonomic nervous systems, which in turn control the viscera (quoted in Konner, 1982:47). He further proposed in 1952 that the frontal lobes of the cerebral hemispheres, shown to be "the seat of the highest human faculties, such as *foresight and concern for the consequences and meaning of events,* may have these functions and others *by virtue of intimate connections between the frontal lobes and the limbic system*" (italics added, ibid.). Here we see that the highest and newest portion of the cerebral cortex has by no means detached itself from an ancient, "primitive" region, but functions as it does precisely "by virtue of its relationship to the old emotional circuitry" (ibid.). Later, Walle Nauta, a celebrated neuroanatomist, has referred to the frontal lobes as "the neocortex of the limbic system" (1971:167-87). As Melvin Konner concludes: "Just as other parts of the cortex have been identified as the highest report-and-control centers for vision, hearing, tactile sensation, and movement, so the frontal lobes have emerged as the highest report-and-control center for the emotions" (Konner, 1982:147).Thus evolutionarily recent and archaic patterns of innervation interarticulate, and the former is pliant to conditioning while the latter is quite resistant.

Paul MacLean's work, and related studies by Jason Brown, raise the question neatly formed by Burhoe: What is the role of the brain as an organ for the appropriate mixing of genetic and cultural information in the production of mental, verbal, or organic behavior? Burhoe raises further important questions: To what extent is the lower brain, including the limbic system and its behavior (to continue the metaphor), "on a very short leash" under the control of the genotype? (Konner uses the term genetically "hard wired.") In other words is genetic inheritance a definitive influence here? The corollary would seem to run as follows: To what extent is the upper brain, especially the neocortex, which is the area responsible in mammals for coordination and for higher mental abilities, on a longer leash in terms of control by the genotype or genome, the fundamental constitution of the organism in terms of its hereditary factors? Does socioculturally transmitted information *take over* control in humankind and, if so, what are the limits, if any, to its control? Does the genotype take a permanent back seat, and is social conditioning now all in all? The picture thus built up for me was of a kind of *dual control* leading to what Burhoe calls a series of symbiotic coadaptations between what might be called culturetypes and genotypes. MacLean's hypothesis about the anatomical relations of the frontal lobes to the limbic system is certainly suggestive here. Subsequently MacLean went further and gave us his model of the "triune brain." (As we shall see later, J. P. Henry and P. M. Stephens, 1977, have recently argued that the dominant or left cerebral hemisphere represents a fourth and phylogenetically most recent system peculiar to our species.) According to his model, MacLean sees us as possessing three brains in one, rather than conceiving of the brain as a unity. Each has a different phylogenetic history, each has its own distinctive organization and make-up, although they are interlinked by millions of interconnections, and each has its own special intelligence, its own sense of time and space, and its own motor functions (MacLean, 1976). MacLean postulates that the brain evolved in three stages, producing parts of the brain which are still actively with us though modified and intercommunicating.

The first to evolve is the *reptilian brain*. This is the *brain stem*, an upward growth of the spinal cord and the most primitive part of the brain, which we share with all vertebrate creatures and which has remained remarkably unchanged throughout the myriads of years of evolution. In lizards and birds this brain is the dominant and controlling circuitry. It contains nuclei which control processes vital to the sustenance of life (i.e., the cardiovascular and respiratory systems). Whereas we can continue to exist without large portions of our cerebral hemispheres, without our reptilian brain we would be dead! What MacLean did was to show that this "structure" or "level," as some term the reptilian brain, whether in reptiles, birds, or in mammals, is not only concerned with control of movement, but also with the storage and control of what is called "instinctive behavior"—the fixed action patterns and innate releasing mechanisms so often written about by the ethologists, the genetically preprogrammed perceptual-motor sequences such as emotional displays, territorial defense behaviors, and nest-building. According to Brown, reptilian consciousness at the sensory-motor level is centered on the body itself and not differentiated from external space; yet it constitutes, I suppose, a preliminary form of consciousness. The reptilian brain also has nuclei which control the reticular activating system, which is responsible for alertness and the maintenance of consciousness. It is a regulator or integrator of behavior, a kind of traffic control center for the brain. Reptiles and birds, in which the *corpus striatum* seems to be the most highly developed part of the brain, have behavorial repertoires consisting of stereotyped behaviors and responses: a lizard turning sideways and displaying its dewlap as a threat, or a bird repeating again and again the same territorial song. I am not suggesting that mammals have no such behavior—clearly many have much—but rather that birds and reptiles have little else.

MacLean's "second brain" is the one he calls the *paleo-mammalian* or "old mammalian brain." This seems to have arisen with the evolution of the earliest mammals, the monotremata, marsupials, and simpler placentals such as rodents. It is made up of those subcortical structures known as the midbrain, the most important components of which are the limbic system, including the hypothalamus (which contains centers controlling homeostatic mechanisms associated with heat, thirst, satiety, sex, pain and pleasure, and emotions of rage and fear), and the pituitary gland (which controls and integrates the activities of all the endocrine glands in the body). The old mammalian brain differs from the reptilian brain generally in that it is, as the neuroanatomist James Papez defines it, "the *stream of feeling*," while the older "level" is the "*stream of movement*." The hypothalamic and pituitary systems are homeostatic mechanisms *par excellence*; they maintain normal, internal stability in an organism by coordinating the responses of the organ systems that compensate for environmental changes. Later, we shall refer to such equilibrium-maintaining systems as "trophotropic," literally "responding to the 'nourishing' (*trophe*) maintenance of organic systems," "keeping them going," as opposed to the "ergotropic" or aroused state of certain systems when they do "work" (*ergon*), "put themselves out," so to speak. These trophotropic systems, In Stevens's words,

> not only maintain a critical and extremely sensitive control of hormone levels [hormones, of course, being substances formed in some organ of the body, usually a gland, and carried by a body fluid to another organ or tissue, where it has a specific effect], but also balance hunger against satiation, sexual desire against gratification, thirst against fluid retention, sleep against wakefulness. By this evolutionary stage, the primitive mammalian, the major emotions, fear and anger, have emerged, together with their associated behavioral responses of

flight or fight. Conscious awareness is more in evidence and behavior is less rigidly determined by instincts, though these are still very much apparent. The areas concerned with these emotions and behaviors lie in the limbic system, which includes the oldest and most primitive part of the newly evolving cerebral cortex—the so-called *paleocortex* . . . . In all mammals, including man, the midbrain is a structure of the utmost complexity, controlling the psycho-physical economy and many basic responses and attitudes to the environment. An animal deprived of its cerebral cortex can still find its way about, feed itself, slake its thirst, and avoid painful stimuli, but it has difficulty in attributing function or "meaning" to things: a natural predator will be noticed, for example, but not apparently perceived as a threat. Thus, accurate perception and the attribution of meaning evidently requires the presence of the cerebral hemispheres.

The *neo-mammalian* or "new mammalian" brain, the third in MacLean's model, corresponds to "the stream of thought" proposed by Papez and achieves its culmination in the complex mental functions of the human brain. Structurally, it is the *neocortex*—the outer layer of brain tissue or that part of the cerebrum which is rich in nerve-cell bodies and synapses. Some estimate there to be 10,000 million cells. Functionally, it is responsible for cognition and sophisticated perceptual processes as opposed to instinctive and affective behavior.

Further questions are triggered by MacLean's model of the triune brain. For example, how does it fit with Freud's model of the id, ego, and superego, with Carl Jung's model of the collective unconscious and archetypes, with neo-Darwinian theories of selection, and especially with cross-cultural anthropological studies and historical studies in comparative religion? One might further ask with Burhoe: to what extent is it true that human feelings, hopes, and fears of what is most sacred are a necessary ingredient in generating decisions and motivating their implementation? This question is connected with the problem of whether it is true that such information is necessarily filtered through the highly genetically programmed areas in the lower brain, the brain stem and the limbic systems. Further questions now arise. For example, if ritualization, as discussed by Huxley, Lorenz, and other ethologists, has a biogenetic foundation, while meaning has a neocortical learned base, does this mean that creative processes, those which generate new cultural knowledge, might result from a coadaptation, perhaps in the ritual process itself, of genetic and cultural information? We also can ask whether the neocortex is the seat of programs largely structured by the culture through the transmission of linguistic and other symbol systems to modify the expression of genetic programs. How far, we might add, do these higher symbols, including those of religion and ritual, derive their meaning and force for action from their association with earlier established neural levels of animal ritualization? I will discuss this later in connection with my field data on Central African ritual symbols.

HEMISPHERIC LATERALIZATION

Before I examine some recent conjectures about the consequences for the study of religion of a possible coadaptation of cultures and gene pools, I should say something about the "lateralization" (the division into left and right) of the cerebral hemispheres and the division of control functions between the left and right hemispheres. The work of the surgeons P. Vogel, J. Bogen, and their associates at the California Institute of Technology in the early sixties, in surgically separating the left hemisphere from the right hemisphere to control epilepsy by cutting the connections between the two, particularly the inch-long, quarter-inch thick bundle of fibers called the *corpus callosum*, led to the devising of a number of techniques by R. W. Sperry (who won a Nobel Prize in 1981), Michael Gazzaniga, and others, which gained unambiguous evidence about the roles assumed by each hemisphere in their patients. In 1979, an important book appeared, *The Spectrum of Ritual*, edited and partly authored by Eugene d'Aquili, Charles D. Laughlin, and John McManus. In an excellent overview of the literature on ritual trance from the neurophysiological perspective, Barbara Lex summarizes the findings of current research on hemispheric lateralization. She writes: "In most human beings, the left cerebral hemisphere functions in the production of speech, as well as in linear, analytic thought, and also assesses the duration of temporal units, processing information sequentially. In contrast, the specializations of the right hemisphere comprise spatial and tonal perception, recognition of patterns—including those constituting emotion and other states in the internal milieu—and holistic, synthetic thought, but its linguistic capability is limited and the temporal capacity is believed absent. Specific acts involved complementary shifts between the functions of the two hemispheres (1979:125). Howard Gardner, following Gazzaniga, suggests that

> at birth we are all split-brained individuals. This may be literally true, since the corpus callosum which connects the hemispheres appears to be nonfunctional at birth. Thus, in early life, each hemisphere appears to participate in all of learning. It is only when, for some unknown reason, the left side of the brain takes the lead in manipulating objects, and the child begins to speak, that the first signs of asymmetry are discernible. At this time the corpus callosum is gradually beginning to function. For a number of years, learning of diverse sorts appears to occur in both hemispheres, but there is a gradual shift of dominant motor functions to the left hemisphere, while visual-spatial functions are presumably migrating to the right. . . . The division of labor grows

increasingly marked, until, in the post-adolescent period, each hemisphere becomes incapable of executing the activities that the other hemisphere dominates, either because it no longer has access to its early learning, or because early traces have begun to atrophy through disuse (Gardner, 1975:386).

D'Aquili and Laughlin hold that both hemispheres operate in solving problems via a mechanism of mutual inhibition controlled at the brain stem level. The world "is approached by a rapid functional alternation of each hemisphere. One is, as it were, flashed on, then turned off; the second flashed on, then turned off. The rhythm of this process and the predominance of one side or the other may account for various cognitive styles [one thinks of Pascal's contrast between 'l'esprit de geometrie' and 'l'esprit de finesse'], from the extremely analytic and scientific to the extremely artistic and synthetic" (d'Aquili and Laughlin, 1979:174). These authors and Lex then make an interesting attempt to link the dual functioning of the hemispheres with W. R. Hess's model of the dual functioning of what are termed the ergotropic and trophotropic systems within the central nervous system, as a way of exploring and explaining phenomena reported in the study of ritual behavior and meditative states (Hess, 1925). Let me explain these terms. As its derivation from the Greek *ergon* ("work") suggests, ergotropic is related to any energy-expending process within the nervous system. It consists not only of the sympathetic nervous system, which governs arousal states and fight or flight responses, but also such processes as increased heart rate, blood pressure, sweat secretion as well as increased secretion of catabolic hormones, epinephrine (a hormone secreted by the medulla of the adrenal gland, which stimulates the heart and increases muscular strength and endurance) and other stimulators. Generally speaking, the ergotropic system affects behavior in the direction of arousal, heightened activity, and emotional responsiveness, suggesting such colloquialisms as "warming up" and "getting high." The trophotropic system (*trophé*, in Greek, means nourishment—here the idea is of system-sustaining) includes not only the parasympathetic nervous system, which governs basic vegetative and homeostatic functions, but also any central nervous system process that maintains the baseline stability of the organism, for example, reduction in heart rate, blood pressure, sweat secretion, pupillary constriction as well as increased secretion of insulin, estrogens, androgens, and so on. Briefly, the trophotropic system makes for inactivity, drowsiness, sleep, "cooling down," and trance-like states (Gellhorn and Kiely, 1972).

Developing the work of Hess, d'Aquili and Laughlin propose an extended model, "according to which the minor or nondominant hemisphere [usually the right hemisphere] is identified with the trophotropic or baseline energy state system, and the dominant or major hemisphere [usually the left] that governs analytical verbal and causal thinking is identified with the ergotropic or energy-expending system" (d'Aquili and Laughlin, 1979:175). They present evidence which suggests that when either the ergotropic or trophotropic system is hyperstimulated, there results a "spillover" into the opposite system after "three stages of tuning," often by "driving behaviors" employed to facilitate ritual trance. They also use the term "rebound" from one system to the other; they find that when the left hemisphere is stimulated beyond a certain threshold, the right hemisphere is also stimulated. In particular, they postulate that the rhythmic activity of ritual, aided by sonic, visual, photic, and other kinds of "driving," may lead in time to simultaneous maximal stimulation of both systems, causing ritual participants to experience what the authors call "positive, ineffable affect." They also use Freud's term "oceanic experience," as well as "yogic ecstasy," also the Christian term *unio mystica*, an experience of the union of these cognitively discriminated opposites, typically generated by binary, digital left-hemispherical ratiocination. I suppose one might also use the Zen term *satori* (the integrating flash), and one could add the Quakers' "inner light," Thomas Merton's "transcendental consciousness," and the yogic *samadhi* (Mandell, 1978:80).

D'Aquili and Laughlin believe that though the end point of simultaneous strong discharge of both the ergotropic and trophotropic systems is the same in meditation and ritual, the former begins by intensely stimulating the trophotropic system through techniques for reducing thought and desire in order to maintain "an almost total baseline homeostatis" (d'Aquili and Laughlin, 1979:176).This results in "spillover" to the ergotropic side, and eventually to strong excitation of both systems. Ritual, on the other hand, involves initial ergotropic excitation. The authors have previously speculated that *causal* thinking arises from the reciprocal interconnections of the inferior parietal lobule and the anterior convexity of the frontal lobes, particularly on the dominant, usually left side, and is an inescapable human propensity. They call this brain nexus "the causal operator" and claim that it "grinds out the initial terminus or first cause of any strip of reality" (*ibid.* p. 170). They argue that "gods, powers, spirits, personified forces, or any other causative ingredients are automatically generated by the causal operator" (*ibid.*). Untoward events particularly cry out for a cause. Hence "human beings have *no choice* but to construct myths to explain their world," to orient themselves "in what often appears to be a capricious universe." Cause-seeking is "inherent in the obligatory functioning of the neural structures." We are, indeed, back, via neurobiology it would seem, to Aristotle's "first cause that is uncaused" or "Prime Mover unmoved"! We humans cannot do otherwise than postulate first causes to explain what we observe. They write, "since it is highly unlikely that humankind will ever know the first cause of every strip of reality observed, it is highly probable that humankind will always create gods, powers, demons, or other entities as first causes" (p. 171).

Myths present problems to the verbal analytic consciousness. Claude Lévi-

Strauss has made us familiar with some of these problems: life and death, good and evil, mutability and an unchangeable "ground of being," the one and the many, freedom and necessity, and a few other perennial "posers" (Levi-Strauss, 1963a, 1962b, 1964). Myths attempt to explain away such logical contradictions, but puzzlement remains at the cognitive left-hemispherical level. D'Aquili and Laughlin argue that *ritual* is often performed situationally to resolve problems posed by myth to the analytic verbalizing consciousness. This is because like all other animals, man attempts to master the environmental situation by means of motor behavior, in this case ritual, a mode going back into his phylogenetic past and involving repetitive motor, visual, and auditory driving stimuli, kinetic rhythms, repeated prayers, mantras, and chanting, which strongly activate the ergotropic system. Ergotropic excitation is appropriate because the problem is presented in the "mythical" analytical mode, which involves binary thinking, mediations, and causal chains arranging both concepts and percepts in terms of antinomies or polar dyads. These are mainly left-hemispheric properties and connect up, in the authors' view, with the augmented sympathetic discharges mentioned earlier: increased heart rate, blood pressure, sweat secretion, pupilary dilation, increased secretion of catabolic hormones, and so on. If excitation continues long enough the trophotropic system is triggered too, with mixed discharges from both sides, resulting often in ritual trance. Lex writes that "driving techniques [also] facilitate right-hemisphere dominance, resulting in gestalt, timeless, nonverbal experiences, differentiated and unique when compared with left-hemisphere functioning or hemisphere alternation" (1979:125). One solution, if it can be so termed, of the Sphinxian riddles posed by myth, according to d'Aquili and Laughlin, is that "during certain ritual and meditation states, logical paradoxes or the awareness of polar opposites as presented in myth appear simultaneously, *both* as antinomies and as unified wholes" (italics added, 1979:177). TThere is an ecstatic state and a sense of union, belief in ritual, prolonged meditation, where culturally transmitted techniques and intense personal discipline sustain the peak experience. One is aware of paradox, but rejoices in it, reminding one of Soren Kierkegaard's joyous celebration of the paradox of the cross as the heart of Christianity.

The problem therefore is resolved in d'Aquili and Laughlin's view not at the cognitive, left-hemispheric level but directly by an experience which is described by the authors as ineffable, that is, literally beyond verbal expression. Presumably the frequent embodiment or embedment of the myth in the ritual scenario, either verbally in prayer or song, or nonverbally in dramatic action or visual symbolism, continues to arouse within the ritual context the "cognitive ergotropic functions of the dominant hemisphere" (*ibid.*). If the experiences of participants have been rewarding—and ritual devices and symbolic actions may well tune a wide range of variant somatic, mental, and emotional propensities in a wide range of individuals (amounting to the well-known redundancy of ritual with its many sensory codes and multivocal symbols)—faith in the cosmic and moral orders contained in the myth cycle will obviously be reinforced. A. J. Mandell argues in "Toward a Psychobiology of Transcendence" that "transcendent consciousness, suggested by William James to be the primary religious experience, is a neurochemically and neurophysiologically definable state, an imperturbable hypomania . . . blissful, empathic, and creative" (1978:1)

PLAY

It is clear that all this refers to the serious work of the brain, as distinct from "play." Full ergotropic, left-hemisphere behavior tends to be dramatic, agonistic behavior. I am not too happy about some authors' tendency to localize mental functions somewhat specifically in cortical regions rather than in interrelational networks, but there does seem to be, broadly speaking, something in the division of labor between the hemispheres, in the different work they do. The term "ergotropic," as we have seen, is derived from the Greek *ergon*, "work" and *tropos*, "a turn, way, manner." It represents the autonomic nervous system in the mode of work, as a sympathetic subsystem, whereas the trophotropic system (from the Greek *trophe*, "food, nourishment") represents the autonomic nervous system in the mode of sustenation, as a parasympathetic subsystem responsible for producing a balance of functions and of chemical composition within an organism. This too is a kind of diffused work, less focused and mobilized, less intense than the ergotropic functions. But where does "play" play a part in this model? One seldom sees much mention of play in connection with brain neurophysiology. Yet play is a kind of dialectical dancing partner of ritual and ethologists give play behavior equal weight with ritualization. D'Aquili and Laughlin hardly mention the word.

The hemispheres clearly have their *work* to do, and the autonomic nervous system has its *work* to do. The one makes for social dramas, the other for social routines. Whether normally functioning or intensely stimulated, the components of the central nervous system seem to have clearly assigned, responsible, interdependent roles to perform. One might speculate that at the neurobiological level play might have something to do with the sensitization of neural structures of an interface type, like the limbic system at the core of the brain, which is known to be intimately associated with the expression of emotion, particularly with the experience of pleasure, pain, and anger. We will return to this later.

As I see it, play does not fit in anywhere particular; it is a transient and is recalcitrant to localization, to placement, to fixation—a joker in the neuroanthropological act. Johann Huizinga, Roger Caillois, and many afterwards have commented on the enclosure of playing within frames of "arbitrary, imperative, and purposely tedious conventions" (Caillois, 1977:189). Playfulness is a volatile, sometimes dangerously explosive essence, which cultural institutions seek to bottle or contain in the vials of games of competition, chance, and strength, in modes of simulation such as theatre, and in controlled disorientation, from roller coasters to dervish dancing—Caillois's "ilinx" or vertigo. Play could be termed dangerous because it may subvert the left-right hemispheric regular switching involved in maintaining social order. Most definitions of play involve notions of disengagement, of free-wheeling, of being out of mesh with the serious, "bread-and-butter," let alone "life-and-death" processes of production, social control, "getting and spending," and raising the next generation. The neuronic energies of play, as it were, lightly skim over the cerebral cortices, sampling rather than partaking of the capacities and functions of the various areas of the brain. As Don Handelman and Gregory Bateson have written, that is possibly why play can provide a metalanguage (since to be "meta" is to be both beyond and between) and emit metamessages about so many and varied human propensities, and thus provide, as Handelman has said, "a very wide *range* of commentary on the social order" (1977:189). Play can be everywhere and nowhere, imitate anything, yet be identified with nothing. Play is "transcendent" (to use Edward Norbeck's term), though only just so, brushing the surfaces of more specialized neural organizations rather than existing apart from them or looking down from a godlike height on them. Play is the supreme *bricoleur* of frail transient constructions, like a caddis worm's case or a magpie's nest in nature. Its metamessages are composed of a potpourri of apparently incongruous elements: products of both hemispheres are juxtaposed and intermingled. Passages of seemingly wholly rational thought jostle in a Joycean or surrealist manner with passages filleted of all syntactical connectedness. Yet, although "spinning loose" as it were, the wheel of play reveals to us (as Mihaly Csikszentmihalyi has argued, 1975) the possibility of changing our goals and, therefore, the restructuring of what our culture states to be reality.

You may have guessed that play is, for me, a liminal or liminoid mode, essentially interstitial, betwixt-and-between all standard taxonomic nodes, essentially "elusive"—a term derived from the Latin *ex* for "away" plus *ludere*, "to play"; hence the Latin verb *eludere* acquired the sense of "to take away from someone at play," thus "to cheat" or "to deceive." As such play cannot be pinned down by formulations of left-hemisphere thinking—such as we all must use in keeping with the rhetorical conventions of academic discourse. Play is neither ritual action nor meditation, nor is it merely vegetative, nor is it just "having fun"; it also has a good deal of ergotropic and agonistic aggressivity in its odd-jobbing, *bricolage* style. As Roger Abrahams has remarked, it makes fun of people, things, ideas, ideologies, institutions, and structures; it is partly a mocker as well as a mimic and a tease, arousing hope, desire, or curiosity without always giving satisfaction. It is as much a reflexive interrupter as an inciter of what Csikszentmihalyi has described as flow states. Like many Trickster figures in myths (or should these be "antimyths," if myths are dominantly left-hemisphere speculations about causality?) play can deceive, betray, beguile, delude (another derivation of *ludere* "to play"), dupe, hoodwink, bamboozle, and gull—as that category of players known as "cardsharps" well know! Actually, Walter Skeat derives the English verb "play" itself from the Anglo-Saxon *plegian*, "to strike or clap"; the Anglo-Saxon noun *plega* means not only "a game, sport," but also, commonly, "a fight, battle" (here again with ergotropic implications).

Play, as stated earlier, draws its materials from all aspects of experience, both from the interior milieu and the external environment. Yet, as Handelman writes, it has no instrumental potency; it is, we might put it, a "shadow warrior," or *Kagemusha*. For this very reason, its range of metacommunication is great; nothing human escapes it. Still, in its own oxymoronic style it has a dangerous harmlessness, for it has no fear. Its lightness and fleetingness protect it. It has the powers of the weak, an infantine audacity in the face of the strong. To ban play is, in fact, to massacre the innocents. If man is a neotonic species, play is perhaps his most appropriate mode of performance.

More than that, it is clear, as Konner points out, play is educative. The most intelligent and long-lived mammals have developed it most fully—the primates, the cetacea, and the terrestrial and aquatic carnivores. "It serves the functions of exercise, of learning about the environment and conspecifics, and, in some species, of sharpening or even acquiring fundamental subsistence and social skills." Opportunity for observation of a task in the frame of "play" while or before trying to do it has been "shown to improve the rate of learning it in a number of mammals in experimental settings" (Konner, 1982:246-47). Play, then, is probably related to the higher cerebral centers—not forgetting its connection also with arousal and pleasure—particularly in rough and tumble games, where the limbic system is clearly engaged. Yet serious violence is usually controlled objectively and culturally by rules and subjectively by inhibitory mechanisms of perhaps a different type from the Freudian superego or ego-defense mechanisms, although perhaps play does defend consciousness from some of the more dangerous unconscious drives.

Finally, play, like other liminal phenomena, is in the subjunctive mood. What does this mean? The subjunctive designates a verb form or set of forms used in English to express a contingent or hypothetical action. A contingent action is one that may occur but that is not likely or intended. Subjunctivity is possibility. It refers to what may or might be. It is also concerned with supposition, conjecture, and assumption, with the domain of "as-if" rather than "as-is." (Hence, there must be a good deal of left-hemispheric activity in play, linguistic and conceptual activity, but done for its own sweet sake.) "As-is" refers to the world of what culture recognizes as factuality, the world of cause and effect, expressed in the "indicative mood"—which indicates that the denoted act or condition is an objective fact. This is *par excellence* the world of the left cerebral hemisphere. The world of the right hemisphere is, nevertheless, not identical with the world of play either, for its gestalt grasp of things holds for it the sense of a higher reality, beyond speculation or supposition. Play is a light-winged, light-fingered skeptic, a Puck between the day world of Theseus and the night world of Oberon, putting into question the cherished assumptions of both hemispheres, both worlds. There is no sanctity in play; it is irreverent and is protected in the world of power struggles by its apparent irrelevance and clown's garb. It is almost as though the limbic system were itself endowed with higher intelligence, in a kind of carnivalesque reversal of the indicative system.

However, since play deals with the whole gamut of experience both contemporary and stored in culture, it can be said perhaps to play a similar role in the social construction of reality as mutation and variation in organic evolution. Its flickering knowledge of all experience possible to the nervous system and its detachment from that system's localizations enables it to perform the liminal function of ludic recombination of familiar elements in unfamiliar and often quite arbitrary patterns. Yet it may happen that a light, play-begotten pattern for living or social structuring, once thought whimsical, under conditions of extreme social change may prove an adaptive, "indicative mood" design for living. Here early theories that play arises from excess energy have renewed relevance. Part of that surplus fabricates ludic critiques of presentness, of the status quo, undermining it by parody, satire, irony, slapstick; part of it subverts past legitimacies and structures; part of it is mortgaged to the future in the form of a store of possible cultural and social structures, ranging from the bizarre and ludicrous to the utopian and idealistic, one of which may root in a future reality, allowing the serious dialectic of left- and right-hemispherical functions to propel individuals and groups of individuals from earth to heaven and heaven to earth within a new indicative mood frame. But it was the slippery Trickster who enabled them to do it, and he/she modestly, in Jacques Derrida's ludic words, "erases the trace."

The experiments of James Olds and Peter Milner, at the California Institute of Technology from 1953 onwards, on stimulating by implanted electrodes the hypothalamus of the brains of rats, including the parts radiating from the hypothalamus like spokes (neural pathways to the olfactory and limbic systems, the septal areas, amygdala, etc.) seem to have a bearing on the pleasures of play, but I have not followed up this avenue of inquiry (Olds, 1976).

FURTHER QUESTIONS ON THE BRAIN: RELIGION, ARCHETYPES, AND DREAMING

By indirections we seek out directions. This long digression on hemispherical lateralization, play, and cultural subjunctivity brings me back to some of Burhoe's questions that have been vexing me. How does this picture of brain functioning and of the central nervous system accord with distinctive features of the varied religious systems that have survived to this point in time and exerted paradigmatic influence on major societies and cultures? Here we could profitably compare Eastern and Western religions and their variations. Can some be described as emphasizing in their cosmologies, theologies, rituals, meditative techniques, pilgrimages, and so on, right-hemispherical properties or left-hemispherical dominance? Do some emphasize rituals while others stress modes of meditation and contemplation as their central processes of worship? Again how does this picture fit with descriptions of the varieties of religious experience that have been noted by William James and his successors? Would it be a fruitful enterprise to foster experimental work on the varied genetic and experiential structurings of human brains which might throw light on aspects of religious experience and motivation? We will take a brief look later in this essay at some interesting guesswork by Jungians in relation to this problem. Conversely, can we illuminate, through cross-cultural comparison, the capacity of culturally shaped systems of ritual, symbols, myths, and rational structures to produce viable types of religious experience in the genetically varied population of brains? Here much more detailed descriptive work in the study of different kinds of ritual in a single religious system, as well as cross cultural and transhistorical studies of ritual systems is imperative. So many questions; so few answers. But we can only do fruitful research if we first ask the right questions.

Naturally, the findings of neurophysiologists have provoked many speculations from members of other disciplines not directly concerned with the brain and its workings. The notion of the triune brain propounded by MacLean, for instance, has encouraged Jungian psychologists to claim that a neurological basis has been found for the collective unconscious and its archetypes. One Jungian, Anthony Stevens, has been impressed by the work of P. Flor-Henry and of G. E. Schwartz, R. J. Davidson, and F. Maer (1975). The latter showed that human emotional responses are dependent on neuronal pathways linking the limbic system of the midbrain (the old mammalian brain) with parietal and frontal areas of the right hemisphere. Flor-Henry found that this whole complicated right-hemispheric/limbic affectional system is under the surveillance and control of the left, I repeat, of the *left* frontal cortex. This lends additional testimony to the view that the left hemisphere (via the corpus callosum or the large cable of nerve fibers which connect the two cerebral hemispheres, functioning to transmit information between the hemispheres and to coordinate their activities) can repress or inhibit the activities, especially the emotionally toned activities (which are the vital concern of psychiatrists), of the right. In my discussion of the possible neuronal base of play, you will recall, I guessed at a connection between the midbrain and human upper brain. If Flor-Henry is correct in supposing a left-hemisphere inhibiting effect, might not the propensity to play result from a temporary relaxation of the inhibitory effect, perhaps through the focused cultural means of framing and arousal?

All this leads Stevens to speculate rather interestingly about the relationship of various psychical processes recognized by depth psychology to what is known about the neurophysiology of the brain. His views also bear on the questions I have been raising about the possible nature of religion as at once a supergenetic and a superindividual agency developed from the coadaptation or integration of two semiautonomous systems. These are, in Burhoe's terms, first, basic genetic information and its biological expression, particularly in the lower levels of the brain, whose genetic programs are not so very different from those in protohuman hominids, and, second, the specifically human generation of a living sociocultural system where the learning powers of the upper brain radically modify the common human gene pool, resulting in enormous cultural and phenotypical variation, that is, variation in manifest characteristics. Stevens argues, "While it may well be that psychic processes belonging to the personal 'Freudian' unconscious proceed in the right hemisphere, it seems probable that Jung was right when he guessed that the archetypal systems, if they could be given a local habitation and a name, must have their neuronal substrate located in the phylogenetically much older parts of the brain (1982:265:66).

For those who are unfamiliar with Jungian terminology, archetypes (according to Stevens's definition) are "innate neuropsychic centers possessing the capacity to initiate, control, and mediate the common behavioral characteristics and typical experiences of all human beings irrespective of cultural differences" (p. 296). Jung himself, who rejected the view that humankind was a blank slate or *tabula rasa* on which experience was prenatally and postnatally inscribed, held that our species is *born* with numerous predispositions for perceiving, feeling, behaving, and conceptualizing in particular ways. As he put it:

> There is no human experience, nor would experience be possible at all without the intervention of a subjective aptitude. What is this subjective aptitude? Ultimately it consists of an innate psychic structure which allows man to have experiences of this kind. Thus the whole nature of the human male presupposes woman, both physically and spiritually. His system is tuned into woman from the start, just as it is prepared for a quite definite world where there is water, light, air, salt, carbohydrates, etc. The form of the world into which he is born is already inborn in him as a virtual image. Likewise parents, wife, children, birth, and death are inborn in him as virtual images, as psychic aptitudes. These *a priori* categories have by nature a collective character; they are images of parents, wife, and children in general, and are not individual predestinations. [This is perhaps Jung's clearest formulation of what he means by archetypes.] We must therefore think of these images as lacking in solid content, hence as unconscious. They only acquire solidity, influence, and eventual consciousness in the encounter with empirical facts which touch the un-

conscious aptitude and quicken it to life. They are, in a sense, the deposits of all our ancestral experiences, but they are not the experiences themselves. (Jung, 1972:para. 300).

Archetypes manifest themselves subjectively in such things as dreams, fantasies, writing, poetry, painting and objectively in such collective representations as myths, rituals, and cultural symbols—and in many other modalities. Jung speaks of the Family archetype, the Feminine archetype, the God archetype, the Hero archetype, the Mother archetype, the Masculine archetype, the Wise Old Man archetype, using capital letters to distinguish them from the identically named roles occupied by actual, historical individuals.

Stevens thinks it is impossible to locate any of the archetypes in any precise neurological fashion. Each must have "an extremely complex and widely ramifying neurological substrate involving millions of neurons in the brain stem and limbic system (the instinctive or biological pole) and *both* cerebral hemispheres (the psychic or spiritual pole)" (Stevens, 1982:266). However, E. Rossi, another Jungian psychologist, argues that it is the right hemisphere which principally processes archetypal components, since, "Jung's concepts of archetype, collective unconscious, and symbol are more closely associated with the use of the imagery, gestalt, and visuospatial characteristics of right hemispheric functioning" (Stevens, 1982:266). Rossi also insists that, although the archetype is an imprint or pattern—perhaps a "trace"—which exists independently of the conscious ego, it constantly comes under left hemispheric processing in the form of words, concepts, and language. But when this happens the archetypes, he writes, "take their color from the individual consciousness in which they happen to appear" (Stevens, 1982:266). Thus they are, so to speak, superfically denatured and clothed in the vestments provided by individual memory and cultural conditioning.

It is because of the difficulty of translating right-hemispherical processes into the logical, verbal formulations of the left brain that some emissions into ego consciousness of archetypal images are perceived as numinous, awesome and mysterious, or uncanny, preternaturally strange. They seem to be clad in primordial authority undetermined by anything known or learned. Henry and Stephens consider that both hemispheres are able to suppress communication from the limbic system (1977). We have seen how the left hemisphere may inhibit communication from the right. Henry and Stephens believe that psychic health and personality integration depend as much on the maintenance of open communication between limbic system and cortex as on interhemispheric communication. They suggest that the neurophysiological function of dreaming is to facilitate integration of processes occuring in the limbic system with those of the cerebral hemisphere. This would fit well with Jung's views as well as with the French sleep expert Michel Jouvet's findings that the low voltage, high frequency EEG waves characteristic of dreaming sleep originate in the brain stem and spread upward through the midbrain to the cortex—perhaps bringing information from various levels of the unconscious (Jouvet, 1975). Perhaps dreams, like the ritual symbols I have analyzed, are laminated, accreting semantic layers, as they move from brain stem through limbic system to the right hemisphere before final processing or editing by left-hemispheric processes.

THE COMPOSITE BRAIN AND THE BIPOLAR SYMBOL

These findings are interesting when related to my fieldwork among the Ndembu, a matrilineal society of northwest Zambia, during the 1950s. I discovered that what I called dominant or pivotal symbols in their ritual processes were not only possessors of multiple meanings but also had the property of polarization. For example, a tree which exuded a milky white latex was the dominant symbol of the girls' puberty ritual (the novice was laid under a consecrated "milk tree" wrapped in a blanket, where she had to lie motionless throughout a whole long day while initiated women danced around her and the tree). The whole milk tree site, almost *mise-en-scène*, was called *ifwilu*, which means "place-of-dying," for it was there that she died from her childhood. At this point she was separated from her own mother, who took a minimal part in the ritual. But the milk tree (*mudyi*) was intimately connected with motherhood. I pieced together its many meanings from talking to many informants during many performances at which my wife and I were present, and have written about this research in several books, including *The Forest of Symbols* and *The Drums of Affliction*. Briefly, the milk tree was said to "be" (more than merely to "represent") mother's milk, lactation, breasts, and nubility, at what could be called the physiological or orectic pole of its meaning. "Orectic" is a term used by philosophers, and was formerly quite popular among psychologists, meaning "of or characterized by appetite or desire."

But the milk tree also "was" the matrilineage of the girl novice; it was where "the ancestress slept, where they initiated her and another ancestress and then another down to the grandmother and the mother and ourselves the children. It is a place where our tribe (*muchidi*) began—and also the men in just the same way" (Turner, 1967:21). Thus it was more than a particular matrilineage; it was the principle of matriliny itself. It was even the whole Ndembu nation, one of whose distinctive features was its matrilineal organization. At some episodes of the long complex ritual, the milk tree was also said to stand for women and for womanhood. Another meaning, indexical rather than iconic, represented the milk tree as the relationship between the novice and her own mother in that place and at that time. It indicated that the relationship would be transformed by the performative action, since the daughter was no longer a dependent child but would become, like her mother, a married woman after the ritual seclusion and the coming-out rites were over and was potentially a mother herself. I called this more abstract set of meanings the normative or ideological pole, since it referred to principles of social organization, social categories, and values.

The milk tree also has other denotations and connotations, but it has struck me recently that these layers of meaning might well relate to what is being discovered about the functions of the brain. The orectic pole, referring to physical mothering and lactation, and charged with desire – the novice's desire to be fully a woman, the desire of the mature women to add a recruit to their number, the desire of a lineage for replenishment, the future bridegroom's desire for the novice (represented by the insertion of an arrow presented by the bridegroom into the ground among the roots of the milk tree) and many other modalities of desire – the orectic pole, then, surely has some connection with the functions of the limbic system, the old mammalian brain. This system MacLean calls the visceral brain because of its close connections to control centers for drive and emotion. Structures in the limbic system are believed to be the sites of action of many psychotropic drugs, including antipsychotic tranquilizers (e.g., Thorazine) and hallucinogens (e.g., LSD). In the ritual itself, with its powerful drumming and insurgent singing in which the women lampoon and deride the men, we observe ways of arousing the ergotropic system and the left-hemispheric functions of critical, linear thought. We can also see a triggering of the right-hemispheric apprehensions of pattern and holism by finally including the men in the ritual action and making them part of a scenario in which the novice is borne off to a newly made seclusion hut on the margin of the village, where she will undergo liminal instruction by female elders for many months, before "coming out" in a ritual which is also the precursor of her marriage.

Clearly, too, the normative pole of meaning including the references to matriliny, womanhood, tribal unity and continuity, and the mother-child bond, has connections with upper brain activities involving both hemispheres. One might speculate that the Jungian archetype of the Great Mother and the difficulty, resolved among the Ndembu by prolonged and sometimes painful initiation ritual, of separation from the archetypal of the Great Mother is in some way connected with the milk tree symbolism and with the ritual behavior associated with it. It is interesting to me that a dominant symbol – every ritual system has several of them—should replicate in its structural and semantic make-up what are coming to be seen as key neurological features of the brain and central nervous system.

CONCLUSION

Does the new work on the brain further our species' self-understanding? Clearly an extreme ethological view of human society as rigidly genetically determined is as uninformative as an extreme behaviorist view of the human brain as a *tabula rasa* written on by experience. According to the extreme ethologists, we are "innately aggressive, acquisitive, nationalistic, capitalistic, and destructive" (Rose, 1976:351). Some of them announce our doom by overcrowding or urge the space race as a means of channelling aggressiveness. Some even give veiled approval to limited war or natural population control by drought, famine, or plague, as the means of securing ecological balance. While B. F. Skinner would modify and adapt us by environmental manipulation, reminding me irresistibly of H. G. Wells's *First Men on the Moon* in which the Selenites (the original Moonies), an insect species, were quite literally shaped by biological and psychological techniques to perform the labor appropriate to their caste, some ethologists would argue that our genetics damn us, despite our intelligence and will to survive. Regnarokr, not Walden II, will be the end of history. Hence the vogue for doom talk about such inevitabilities as ecocide, population explosion, and innate aggressiveness. Surely, a middle path is possible. Cannot we see those modalities of human perception and conceptualization, the lower brain and the upper brain, the archaic and recent systems of innervation as having been for at least several millions of years in active mutual confrontation?

It seems to me that religion may be partly the product of humanity's intuitions of its dual interiority and the fruitful creative Spirit generated by the interplay of the gene pool, as the Ancient of Days, and the upper brain, as Logos, to use the intuitive language of one historical religion, Christianity. The Filioque principle (the Spirit proceeding from the Father *and* the Son), Western Christians might say! Since culture is in one sense, to paraphrase Wilhelm Dilthey, objectivated and crystallized mentality (*Geist*), it may well be that some cultures reinforce one or another semiautonomous cerebral system at the expense of others through education and other modes of conditioning. This results in conflict between them or repression of one by another, instead of free interplay and mutual support—what is sometimes called love.

As you can see, I have been asking questions and making guesses in this paper rather than coming up with answers. My career focus mostly has been on the ritual process, a cultural phenomenon, more than on brain neuroanatomy and neurophysiology. But I am at least half convinced that there can be genuine dialogue between neurology and culturology, since both take into account the capacity of the upper brain for adaptability, resilience, learning, and symbolizing, in ways perhaps neglected by the ethologists *pur sang*, who seem to stop short in their thinking about ritualization at the more obviously genetically programmed behaviors of the lower brain. It is to the dialectic, and even contradiction at times, between the various semiautonomous systems of the developed and archaic structures of innervation, particularly those of the human brain, that we should look for the formulation of testable hypotheses about the ritual process and its role as performing noetic functions in ways peculiar to itself, as a *sui generis* mode of knowing.

Let me conclude by reassuring those who may have obtained the impression that all I am saying is that ritual is nothing but the structure and functioning of the brain writ large, or that I am reducing ritual to cerebral neurology, that I am really speaking of a global population of brains inhabiting an entire world of inanimate and animate entities, a population whose members are incessantly communicating with one another through every physical and mental instrumentality. But if one considers the geology, so to speak, of the human brain and nervous system, we see represented in its strata—each layer still vitally alive—not dead like stone, the numerous pasts and presents of our planet. Like Walt Whitman, we "embrace multitudes." And even our reptilian and paleomammalian brains are human, linked in infinitely complex ways to the conditionable upper brain and kindling it with their powers. Each of us is a microcosm, related in the deepest ways to the whole life-history of that lovely deep blue globe swirled over with the white whorls first photographed by Edwin Aldrin and Neil Armstrong from their primitive space chariot, the work nevertheless of many collaborating human brains. The meaning of that living macrocosm may not only be found deep within us but also played from one mind to another as history goes on—with ever finer tuning—by the most sensitive and eloquent instrument of Gaea the Earth-spirit—the cerebral organ.

References

D'Aquili, E., Laughlin, C. D., and McManus, J., eds. 1979. *The Spectrum of Ritual.* New York: Columbia University Press.
Brown, J. 1977. *Mind, Brain, and Consciousness.* New York: Academic Press.
Caillois, Roger. 1979. *Man, Play, and Games.* New York: Schocken.
Flor-Henry, P. 1976. "Lateralized Temporal-Limbic Dysfunction and Psychopathology," *Annals of the New York Academy of Science,* vol. 380, pp. 777-97.
Fortes, M. 1966. "Religious Premises and Logical Technique in Divinatory Ritual," in *A Discussion on Ritualization of Behaviours in Animals and Man,* organized by Julian Huxley. *Philosophical Transactions of the Royal Society of London,* Series B, vol. 251, Biological Sciences. London: Royal Society, pp. 409-422.
Fox, Robin. 1973. *Encounter with Anthropology.* New York: Harcourt Brace Jovanovich.
Gardner, Howard. 1975. *The Shattered Mind.* New York: Vintage.
Gellhorn, E. and Kiely, W. F. 1972. "Mystical States of Consciousness: Neurophysiological and Clinical Aspects," *Journal of Mental and Nervous Diseases.* 154, pp. 399-405.
Grenell, R. G. and Gabay, S., eds. 1976. *Biological Foundations of Psychiatry,* Vol. I, New York: Raven.
Grimes, Ronald. 1982. *Beginnings in Ritual Studies* Washington: University Press of America.
Handelman, Don. 1977. "Play and Ritual: Complementary Frames of Metacommunication," in A. J. Chapman and H. Fort, eds. *It's A Funny Thing, Humour.* London: Pergamon, pp. 185-192.
Henry, J. P. and Stephens, P. M. 1977. *Stress, Health, and the Social Environment.* New York: Springer-Verlag.
Hess, W. R. 1925 *On the Relationship Between Psychic and Vegetative Functions,* Zurich: Schwabe.
Huxley, Julian. 1966. Ed. *Introduction to A Discussion on Ritualization of Behaviours in Animals and*

Man. *Philosophical Transactions of the Royal Society of London*, Series B, vol. 251, Biological Sciences. London: Royal Society, pp. 249-271.

Jouvet, Michel. 1975. "The Function of Dreaming: A Neurophysiologist's Point of View," in *Handbook of Psychobiology*, eds. M. S. Gazzaniga and C. Blakemore. New York: Academic Press.

Jung, Carl. 1972. *Collected Works*, vol. 7, "Two Essays on Analytical Psychology." Princeton: Princeton University Press.

Konner, Melvin. 1982. *The Tangled Wing: Biological Constraints on the Human Spirit*. New York: Holt, Rinehart, and Winston.

Leach, E. R. 1966. "Ritualization in Man in Relation to Conceptual and Social Development," in *A Discussion on Ritualization of Behaviours in Animals and Man*, organized by Julian Huxley. *Philosophical Transactions of the Royal Society of London*, Series B, vol. 251, Biological Sciences, London: Royal Society.

Levi-Strauss, Claude. 1963a. *Structural Anthropology*. New York: Anchor.

————. 1963b. *The Savage Mind*. Chicago: University of Chicago Press.

————. 1964. *Mythologiques: Le Cru et le Cruit*. Paris: Plon.

MacLean, Paul. 1949. "Psychosomatic Disease and the 'Visceral Brain': Recent Developments Bearing on the Papez Theory of Emotion," *Psychosomatic Medicine*, 11, pp. 338-53.

————. 1973. *A Triune Concept of Brain and Behaviour*. Toronto: University of Toronto Press.

————. 1976. "Sensory and Perceptive Factors in Emotional Functions of the Triune Brain," in *Biological Foundations of Psychiatry*, vol. 1, eds. R. G. Grenell and S. Gabay. New York: Raven, pp. 177-198.

Mandell, Arnold J. "Toward a Psychobiology of Transcendence," in *The Psychobiology of Consciousness*, eds. J. M. Davidson and J. R. Davidson. New York: Plenum Press.

Nauta, Walle. "The Problem of the Frontal Lobe: A Reinterpretation," *Journal of Psychiatric Research*. 8, pp. 167-87.

Olds, James. 1976. "Behavioral Studies of Hypothalamic Functions," in *Biological Foundations of Psychiatry*, vol. I, eds. R. Grenell and S. Gabay. New York: Raven.

Rose, Steven. 1976 *The Conscious Brain*. New York: Vintage Books.

Rossi, E. 1977. "The Cerebral Hemispheres in Analytical Psychology," *Journal of Analytical Psychology*, 22, pp. 32-51.

Schwartz, G. E., Davidson, R. J., and Maer, F. 1975. "Right Hemisphere Lateralization for Emotion in the Human Brain: Interaction with Cognition," *Science*, vol. 190, pp. 286-88.

Stevens, Anthony. 1982. *Archetypes: A Natural History of the Self*. New York: Morrow.

Turner, V. W. 1967. *The Forest of Symbols*. Ithaca: Cornell University Press.

————. 1968. *The Drums of Affliction*. Oxford: Clarendon Press.

Index

Abernathy, Robert, 144
Abrahams, Roger, 168
Academicos de Cubango Samba School, 136
Actor's Art, 118-121
Advice in Umbanda, 58; see also Consultation
Aesthetic, in Noh Drama, 115, 118-120
Affect and rationality, 90-91
Africanity, in Umbanda, 47, 49, 50, 51, 55, 68, 69
Afro-Brazilian folk ritual, 43
Agôn (contest), 126-130, 132
Alea (gambling), 126-128, 130, 132
Amado, Jorge, 131-132
Amerindian origins of Umbanda, 47, 68
Anthropology: and history, 108; drama as the unit of analysis, 84
Antistructure, 128, 132, 133, 134
Aoi, 112-114, 116
Aoi no Uye, Noh play (Princess Hollyhock), 29, 108, 116-117, 121
Aparecida, Maria, 62-69
Apparition, 112
d'Aquili, E., and C. Laughlin, 163, 164, 166, 167
d'Aquili, E, C. Laughlin, and J. McManus, 142
Archaic structures of brain, 159
Archetypes, 172,; the Great Mother, 175
Aristotelian categories, 27
Arrabal, Fernando, 30
Artaud, Antonin, 29, 128
Artifice, 149
Artist, 87, 122
Ashikaga Yoshimitsu, 121
Atabaque drums, 65
Audience, 147-148
Augusto, 32
Austen, Jane, 121

Babcock, Barbara, 24
Bakhtin, Mikhail, 141
Baroja, Julio Caro, 123-124
Barok ritual, 146, 151
Barth, Fredrik, 78
Bastide, Roger, 49, 50
Bateria, percussion band, 133, 136
Bateson, Gregory, 54, 102-103, 107, 140, 168
Batuque cult, 47, 48, 50
Beckett, Samuel, 28, 30
Bedeutung, meaning, 85, 95
Benamou, Michel, and Charles Caramello, 72
Bento, Dilson, 51-52
Bitencourt, Sergio, 136

Black, Mary B., 102-103
Black Orpheus, 136
Blake, William, 120, 133
Blanchard, David, 144
Bloch, Jean-Richard, 123
Blocos, 130, 134-135
Blood symbol, 75
Bogen, J., 163
Boiadeiro, Cowboy, 51, 59
Boundary ambiguity, 73, 79-80
Brain, 159-177; archaic structures of, 159; composite, 174-175; corpus callosum, 163, 171; interarticulation of recent and archaic patterns, 159; limbic system, 159, 161, 167, 169-170, 175; neomammalian (neocortex), 162; operators, 165; and play, 167-170; and religion, 162; reptilian, 160-161; triune, 160-162
Brazil, 43, 48-49
Breach, 34, 66, 91; as symbolic transgression, 75
Brown, Jason, 160
Buber, Martin, 44, 84, 128
Buddhism, 42, 110, 112-114, 116-117, 121
Burhoe, Ralph W., 159-160, 162, 170
Burke, Kenneth, 108
Burns, Robert, 153

Caboclo, Cowboy, 51, 59
Caboclo Serra Negra, 62
Caillois, Roger, 125-126, 130, 132, 138, 167-168; positivistic, 127-128
Camino, Linda, 151-152
Candomblé, 47, 48, 50, 53, 69, 130
Cannibal dance, Hamatsa, 146-150, 153-155
Carneiro, Edison, 50, 69
Carnival, 26, 29, 48-49, 59, 102, 123-138; alleged death of, 123-124; costume, 137; etymology of word, 123; history of in Brazil, 133-134; judges of, 135-137; lead singer in, 129, 133; organization of, 132-137; percussion band in, 133, 136; seriousness of, 136, 137; severed from ordinary time, 123
Catholic elements in Umbanda, 50
Causal operator, 165
Cemetery, 58, 63
Chicago, University of, 144
Children, 125-130; as Orixá, 52, 130
Chimbanda, officiant at ritual of affliction, 51
Chomsky, Noam, 76-77
Christianity, 166, 176
Chronicle, 35

Cicourel, A. V., 96
Cinema and ritual, 30-31
Civil War, American, 91
Cognition, 162
Cognitive and social structures, 80
Cognitive character of anthropological litera-
ture, 139
Cognitive paradigm, critique of, 56
Commedia dell'Arte, 28, 29, 30
Communitas, 44-45, 84, 128, 145; at Carnival,
132, 133, 138; dynamic nature of, 84; as
shared flow, 133
Competence and performance, 21, 76
Compte, Auguste, 88
Conflict, 152
Consultations in Umbanda, 63, 68
Contagion of crisis, 103-104
Contest of gods, 60
Continuum of action, 22
Corpus callosum, 163, 171
Creative flash, 32
Crisis, 34, 66-67, 91
Crisis, contagion of, 103
Csikszentmihalyi, Mihali, 54, 107, 168
Cultural media, 23
Cultural performance, 42, 81-82, 83-84, 124
Cyclical feasts, 101-103

Daimyo, 108
Dalton, Douglas, 149, 150
Da Matta, Roberto, 48, 123, 131
Darwin, Charles, 162
Decoster, Jean-Jacques, 151
Definitional dramas, 46-47
Deixa Falar Samba School, 133
Demanda, contest, 60-61, 63-69
Derrida, Jacques, 170
Dilthey, Wilhelm, 48, 55, 94-97, 176; on ex-
perience, 84; on force, 94-95; on Weltan-
schauung, 85-90
Director, movie, 31, 32
Discontinuum of action, 22
Distributive model of culture, 36
Dominant genres of cultural performance, 21-
22
Dona Flor and Her Two Husbands, 134
Douglas, Mary, 73
Drama: defined, 27; as ephemeral, 31; etym-
ology of word, 26, 37-38; and film, 31; forms
and movements in the world of, 27-29; origin
of, 27; the unit of analysis in history and an-
thropology, 84
Dreaming, 173-174
Drummers, 133
Drums, 50, 51
Duncan, Isadora, 133
Durkheim, Emile, 34, 41, 77
Duus, Peter, 121

Effervescence, social, 77

Eisenstadt, S. N., 49
Elegba, 51, 52
Elizabethan drama, 27
Engels, Friedrich, 36
English drama, 27
Enlightenment, Buddhist, 117
Entertainment, etymology of word, 41
Entidades, Umbanda gods, 50-53, 130
Ergotropic, etymology of word, 167
Ergotropic system, 164-167, 169, 175
Ethnodramaturg, 146
Ethnography of speaking, 21
Ethologists, 157, 175, 176
Experience, 84; as primary in Umbanda, 56
Expressionism, 28
Exu, Trickster deity, 50-51, 52; appearance in
situation of frame slippage, 54; Caveira, 58;
incorporates with mediums, 56-59, 63; Man-
gueira, 62; subjunctive mood of, 60; of the
Two Heads, 53; without Light, 65, 136

Factions, 35, 91
"False Face" simulated ceremony, 144
Fantasia, carnival costume, 59, 137
Fastnacht, 124
Fazer cabeça, to make the head, 58
Fellini, Federico, 31, 32
Fields, sociosymbolic, 21
Firth, Raymond, 37, 54, 58, 104-105
Flamenco, 49
Floating World, 122
Flor-Henry, P., 171
Flow, 54, 107, 133
Flow/reflexivity dialectic, 55
Fluminense, 49
Fon, 51
Food symbolism, 153
Force, 94-95
Fortes, Meyer, 157, 158
Fox, Robin, 156
Frames, 54, 55, 103, 140-144; nesting of, 141-
143, 150; play, 167-169; slippage, 54, 142, 144
"Frame, Flow, and Reflection," 54
French drama, 27-28
French Revolution, 77, 91
Frese, Pamela, 141
Freud, Sigmund, 83, 129, 158, 162, 165, 169,
172
Freyre, Gilberto, 50
Functionalism, 74, 97
Futebol, soccer, 49

Gaea, 154
Galileo, 37, 73
Gambling, 125, 132
Games, 125-128; classification of, 128
Gardner, Howard, 163
Garfinkel, Harold, 96
Gazzaniga, Michael, 163
Gebser, Jean, 72-73

Geertz, Clifford, 22, 26, 87; on myths and rites, 42; on "unpacking" meaning, 29; on world view, 95
Gemeinschaft and Gesellschaft, 44
Genes, by long and short leash, 159
Genet, Jean, 28, 30
Genetics, 156-159
Genji, Price, 109-113, 116, 117
Gennep, Arnold van, 25, 101, 144
George, Mimi, 146, 151
Ghost, 114-115
Girard, René, 34
Global population of brains, 177
Gluckman, 37, 41, 105
Gödel, Kurt, 106
Goffman, Erving, 74, 75, 76, 81, 107; on frame analysis, 54, 140
Golden Age, 129, 137
Goldwasser, Maria, 132-133
Gongá, altar room, 63
Grathoff, Richard, and Don Handelman, 143
Great and Little Traditions, 22, 23
Greek and Roman drama, 28
Grimes, Ronald, 75
Guadalupe, Virgin of, 91
Guerra de Orixá, 43
Guides, 50, 53, 64, 69

Hamatsa ritual, 146-150, 153-155
Handelman, Don, 52, 140, 143; on play, 126, 168, 169
Hard-wired genes, 160
Hashigakari, Noh bridgeway, 115
Hassan, Ihab, 72
Healing, in Umbanda, 51, 58
Heian period, 108-109, 112, 114, 121
Henry, James P., and P. M. Stephens, 160, 173
Heraclitus, 78, 84
Herbs, 58, 65
Herskovits, Melville, 50
Hess, W. R., 164
Hidalgo, Miguel, 91
Hierarchies, fictitious, 51, 59
Hinde, Robert, 83
History: and anthropology, 108; and meaning, 96-97; drama as the unit of analysis of, 84
Hockett, Charles, 76
Holistic thought, 163, 175
Horse (medium), 51, 68
Huizinga, Johan, 125, 136, 167
Human being, a self-performing animal, 81
Huxley, Julian, 157, 162
Hymes, Dell, 77

Iansã, 53
Iceland, 41, 43
Idioverse, 80
Iemanjá, 51, 53, 59
Ifwilu, place of dying, 174
Il Bidone, 32

Ilinx, dizziness, 126-128, 130, 132, 168
Illness, during crisis, 104-105
Improvisation, 29
Incorporation, see Trance
Indeterminacy, 60, 77-78, 94
India, performance in, 22-23, 28
Indicativization, 61
Ineffable, the, 165
Initiation, 64, 151-152
Interdictions, 59-60
Ionesco, Eugene, 28, 30
I-Thou relationship, 44
Ivins, William M., 73

Jacobite rebellion, 91
James, William, 167, 171
Japanese drama, 27, 28; see also Noh drama
Japanese literature, 29, 42-43, 108-114, 117, 121-122
Jerusalem-Athens-Rome, tradition of, 41
Jesus, 53, 60
de Jouvenal, Bertrand, 121
Jouvet, Michel, 173-174
Judges of carnival, 135-137
Judicial process, 39, 105
Jung, Carl, 156, 162, 171, 172-173

Kagemusha, 169
Kahali, 75
Kamakura period, 118, 121
Kan-ami, 114
Kanami Kiyotsuga, 118, 121
Kankang'a, novice, 151
Kardecism, 47, 50
Keene, D., 109
Kierkegaard, Soren, 114, 166
Kinship, 67
Kluback, William, 89
Konner, Melvin, 159, 160, 169
Kuhn, Thomas, 79
Kwakiutl, 146-150, 153-155
Kyogen, 114

Lateralization, cerebral, 163-176
Law, 93-94, 100
Lawrence, D. H., 84, 103
Leacock, Seth and Ruth, 50
Leash metaphor, in genetics, 159, 160
Left cerebral hemisphere, 163, 170-171, 173-174
Lévi-Strauss, Claude, 23, 165-166
Lex, Barbara, 163, 166
Life crisis ritual, 101-102
Limbic system, 159, 162, 168, 169, 175
Limen, 34
Liminal character of crisis, 34-35
Liminality, 107; elegance of the poor in, 135; and entertainment, 41, public, 32, 102; in rites of passage, 25-26; secret and public, 25; and the subjunctive, 101, 107; of terreiro, 55
Liminoid, 29

Line of deities, 51-53, 130
Little Saint of Yokawa, 116-117
Lived experience, 84
Lorenz, Konrad, 157, 162
Ludic, in Umbanda, 61
Ludus (games), 125-128, 130
Lupercalia, 123, 134
Lyons, J., 77

Mabe, Ann, 43
MacAloon, John, 54
MacKay, D. M., 82-83
MacLean, Paul, 160-162, 171, 175
Macquet, Jacques, 50
Macumba, 50-51
Madness, 61, 63-66, 69
Madras, 23
Mãe de Santo, 53, 55-59, 62-69
Magic: at fusion of indicative and subjunctive, 120; and ritual, 150
Mahabharata, 126
Mair, Lucy, 37
Major-domo, 135
Makoto Ueda, 98-100, 110, 118-120
Malinowski, Bronislaw, 40
Mamãe Oxum, 53
Mandell, Arnold J., 165, 167
Mangueira Samba School, 129, 131, 132
Maracana Stadium, 49
Mardi-Gras, 102, 123
Marina, 63, 64
Mario, in Umbanda, 54, 62, 64, 66
Mater Dolorosa, 53
Matriliny, 174-175
McGrew, Julia H., 43
Meaning, 33, 95-97; assessment only at death, 97-98; definition of, 95; etymology of word, 95; Geertz on, 29
Meditation, 165
Mediums, 53, 55, 56, 64
Merton, Thomas, 165
Metacommunication, 102
Metapatterns, 103
Metaphysics of speech, 29, 30
Mexican *Insurgencia*, 91
Milk tree, 174-175
Milner, Peter, 170
Mimicry, 126-129, 132
Mirrors, 22, 42, 43, 109-110
Modern, the, 73, 76, 80
Molière, 28, 29
Moore, Sally F., 74, 77-79, 80, 86, 98
Moraes, Eneida de, 133-134
Movies, 30-32
Mudyi, milk tree, 174-175
Mulata, carnival woman, 131
Multigenre performance, 31
Murasaki Shikibu, Lady, 29, 42-43, 108-111, 117, 121
Murdock, G. P., 74

Muromachi period, 29, 108, 117-118, 121
Murphy, R. F., 77
Music in Noh drama, 121
Myerhoff, Barbara, 42, 43, 46, 47, 93
Myth, 165-166, 169
Mythologization, 40

Nadel, S. F., 93
Narrative, 37-43, 47
Naturalism, 88
Nature elements in Umbanda, 68
Ndembu, 37, 39, 45, 51; girls' initiation among, 151-152, 174; social dramas among, 37-41, 74-75; villagers and Brazilian Umbandistas contrasted, 46-47
Neomammalian brain (neocortex), 162
Neurobiology, 159-177
New Orleans Mardi Gras, 124
Nicols, Dudley, 31
Niteroi, 131
Noh drama, 28, 29, 42-43, 108, 114-122; classification of theatrical effects, 118-119; music, 121; processual form of, 114-115; stage, 115
Nominalism, 88
Nonelitist societies, 128
Nonverbal signals, 82-84
Norbeck, Edward, 168
Normative pole of symbol, 175
Novel, Japanese, 110-11, 117
Novo Iguaçu, 56, 57
Number Our Days, 46
Numbers game, 131
Nzambi, 51

Obaluae, 63
Occult, 158
Ogum, 52, 58-59
Olds, James, 170
Olney, James, 78
Open and closed domains at carnival, 130
Operator, causal, 165
Orchestrations of media, 23
Orectic pole of symbol, 174-175
Original sin, 100
Orixá, gods, 49, 50, 51-53, 60-70
Oxosse, 51-52

Pai de Santo, 53, 57
Paidia, play of children, 125-129
Palacio de Samba, 131, 133
Paleomammalian brain, 161
Palmer, Richard, 72-73, 80
Papez, James, 161, 162
Paradox, 166
Parasympathetic nervous system, 164
Pascal, Blaise, 164
Passistas, 131, 136
Peak moments, 142

Percussion, 133
Performative acts, spells, 120
Performance: as agency of change, 24; analysis of, 84; in Brazil, 48-49; in cannibal ritual, 148-150; of ethnography, 139-155; and flow, 107; in India, 23; as liminal, 25; and literature, 139; as orchestration of media, 23; plan of study of, 26-29; preparation for, 147; as reflexive, 81; as sacred, 24; and social drama, 94; structure of as process, 80, 84
Perspective, 73, 80
Pervasive factionalism, 35
Phenomenology, 96
Philosopher, 87
Pierrot Grenade, 29
Pinter, Harold, 28, 30
Play, 124-127, 147; etymology of word, 169; function of, 169-170; of genres, 24; of kinship terms, 67; and limbic system, 168, 169, 170; and neurophysiology, 167-170; and Shakespeare's Puck, 170; and spectacle, 125
Play frame, 107, 124, 126
Plot, 130, 133
Polarization of symbol, 174
Pomba-Gira, Whirling Dove, 51, 57, 59
Porta-bandeira, 135
Portela Samba School, 136
Positivism, 88
Possession by god, 54
Postmodern, 72, 76-77, 79-80
Power of the weak, 57
Premodern, 72
Prepositional plugs, 99
President of terreiro, 54, 60, 63-64, 66
Pressel, Esther, 50
Preto-Velho, Old Black, 50, 52, 54, 58-59, 69
Primary process, 125
Process, 74; as performance, 80
Psychological processes, 90-91
Psychotropic drugs, 175
Puck, 170
Public liminality, 21, 32
Pure Land Buddhism, 42
Puxador, song leader, 129, 133

Quakers, 165
Quiumba, Exu without Light, 65

Radcliffe-Brown, A. R., 41
Ramos, Arthur, 50
Realism, 27, 28, 88
Reasonable man, 105
Redfield, Robert, 22
Redressive phase of social drama, 34, 38, 67, 69, 97; as metaperformance, 107; as reflexive, 104; ritualized, 90, 91, 93, 100
Redundancy, 23
Reference groups, 45
Reflexive genres, 22
Reflexive metalanguages, 32

Reflexivity, 25, 38, 55, 103; and aesthetics, 87; defined, 24; and framing, 140-141; and meaning, 96, 97; and performance, 42, 81; in religion, 86; about values, 29
Regularization, processes of, 77-79, 80, 98
Rehearsal process, 152-153
Reintegration, 35, 92
Religion, 48, 86, 162, 170-172, 176
Remedios, Virgin of, 91-92
Reptilian brain, 160-161
Restoration drama, 27
Reversal, 123, 137
Rex versus dux, 121
Right cerebral hemisphere, 163-164, 172-173; linked with limbic system, 163, 171
Rilke, Rainer Maria, 69, 118
Rio de Janeiro, 23, 110-119
Rites of passage, 25, 48, 101
Ritual, 75, 106; and left brain spillover, 165; definitions of, 157-158; and law, 93-94; magic of, 150; as orchestration of genres, 106; as play acting, 148; preparation for, 147; process, 39; western view of, 25, 26
Ritualization: definition of, 157; and meaning, 162
Ritualization of behavior in animals and man, conference, 157-158
Rivail, Leon, 50
Rokuju, Lady, 42-43, 112-114, 116-117
Roots, 59
Rose, Steven, 176
Rossi, E., 173
Russian drama, 28

Saga, 43
St. George, 52
St. Jerome, 51
St. Lazarus, 63
St. Peter, 53
Samba schools, 129-136
Samurai, 29
Sandombu, 75
Santa Barbara, 53
Santos, 50-51
Satan, 53, 60
Satire, 29
Saturnalia, 123, 134
Saudade, nostalgia, 129
Scandinavian drama, 28
Schechner, Richard, 74, 75-76, 153
Schism, 35, 60, 68, 75
Schism and Continuity, 35, 37, 39, 40, 92, 145; Turner's later criticism, 40-41, 75
Schneider, David, 67
Schwartz, G. E., R. J. Davidson, and F. Maer, 71
Schwartz, Theodore, 36, 80-81
Screenplays, 30, 31
Sensory codes, 23
Sessão, session, 51

Shakespeare, William, 27, 28
Shite, Noh actor, 114-115
Shiva, 60
Shugendo, 29
Sickness, in phase structure of social drama, 38
Siegel, A. E., and S. Siegel, 45
Siegel, Bernard, and Alan Beals, 35
Simpson, N. F., 30
Singer, Milton, 21-24
Singer (puxador) leading carnival band, 129, 133
Situational adjustment, 77-79, 80-81
Skinner, B. F., 176
Skull, Exu symbol, 58
Soccer, 49
Social drama, 33-46, 74-75, 100; analysis, 74; critique of the concept, 104; defined, 33; force of, 95; and liminality, 75, 92; and meaning, 97; and performance, 94; phases of, 34-35, 66-67, 74-75, 103-104; phases corresponding to psychological tendency, 90-93; processually structured, 33, 34; and reflexivity, 103, 106; and sickness, 38; and theatre, 75-76, 105; in Umbanda, 61, 66
Social performances, 81-82, 83-84
Social recognition of irreparable schism, 35, 67
Sociosymbolic fields, 21
Sonia, in Umbanda, 64
Spectrum of Ritual, The, 142, 163
Spells, 120
Sperry, R. W., 163
Spillover, interhemispherical, 165, 166
Spindler, George, 73, 80
Spiritism, 47, 50
Spontaneity: in Commedia dell'Arte, 29; and social drama, 33
Star group, 44-47, 60, 69
Stevens, Anthony, 156, 161-162, 171, 173
Story, 33, 35-36
Structural-functionalism, critique of, 40-41, 74
Structure of experience, 48, 55
Structure/process dichotomy, 21, 74, 77, 84
Sturlunga Saga, The, 43
Subjunctive mood, 25, 26, 41, 42, 101-102, 105-106; of carnival, 59, 123, 137; defined, 101; of Exu, 60; in kinship terms, 67; liminality of, 101; and ludus (games), 126; in Noh drama, 120; of play, 169; in The Tale of Genji, 110; of Umbanda and carnival, 59
Sumner, W. G., 44
Suspension of disbelief, 150
Symbol, polarization of, 174
Symbolic transgression, 75
Symbolic type, 52, 70, 143
Symbolist theatre, 28
Sympathetic nervous system, 164

Taboos, see interdictions
Tale of Genji, The, 29, 42, 108-113, 116
Tamakazura, 109, 111

Terreiro, cult center, 43-44, 47-48, 50-51, 54-55, 67; in conflict, 61; da Rua do Bispo, 65, 66; familial atmosphere of, 59; life history of, 60, 62-70; Tenda Espiritu Caboclo Serra Negra, 44, 64, 66
Text: in context, 28; of movie, 31
Theater and Its Double, The, 29-30
Theatre and ritual contrasted, 150
Theatre of Cruelty, 29
Theatre of the Absurd, 28, 29, 30
Theatrical paradigm, 74, 75
Three Screenplays by Fellini, 31
Time, 80
Tönnies, Ferdinand, 44
Toynbee, Arnold, 7u2
Trance, 53, 56-59, 62-66, 119; advice and consultation in, 58; and the brain, 166; disclosures in, 68; healing in, 58
Transvestites, 136
Trickster, 51, 168-169, 170
Trinidad carnival, 29, 124
Triune brain, 160-162
Tropes, 27, 85
Trophotropic, etymology of word, 167
Trophotropic system, 161, 164-166
Tubuan spirit dancer, 151
Tuning, cerebral, 165
Turner, Edith, 56-59, 141
Turner, Victor: an actor in simulated wedding, 141; Dramas, Fields, and Metaphors, 91; The Drums of Affliction, 145, 174; The Forest of Symbols, 144, 174; "Frame, Flow, and Reflection," 54; a patient in Umbanda, 59; The Ritual Process, 144; in role of masked Tubuan, 151; Schism and Continuity, 35, 37, 39, 40, 92, 145

Umbanda, 43-44, 46-70, 130; advice and consultation in, 58, 63, 68; and alcohol, 59; Catholic elements in, 50; conflict in, 60-69; curing in, 51, 58; domestic servants as members of, 57; embraces in, 58; experience of performers as primary, 56; madness of member, 63-64; nature elements in, 68; origins of, 47, 50; trance in, 53, 56-59, 62-66, 68; treatment in, 58

Valéry, Paul, 68
Value, 95-96
Velho, Yvonne Maggie Alves, 43-44, 46, 48, 50, 54, 56-58, 60-69
Venegas, Viceroy, 91
Verstehen, 95
Via crucis, 32, 36, 136
Virgin Mary, 51
Vogel, P., 163

Wagner, Roy, 66
Waiting for Godot, 147
Waki, Noh actor, 115, 120

Walens, Stanley, 146
Waley, Arthur, 111, 116, 121
War of Orixás, 60, 66, 69; see also Demanda
Wedding, simulated, 141-144
Wells, Henry W., 115
Wells, H. G., 176
Weltanschauung, 85-90
Weltbild, 85
Wheel imagery, 113, 116
White, Hayden, 35
White and red clay, 51
Whitman, Walt, 177
Williams, Robin, 96
Wilson, E. O., 159
Witchcraft, 38, 65

Women, bias against, 109
Work of the reflexive genres, 26

Xangô, 50, 58

Yoga, 165
Yoruba, 51
Yugao, 109, 111, 113, 116
Yugen, 118-120

Zambi, 51
Zeami Motokiyo, 29, 108, 114, 118-122
Zen, 29, 42, 118, 119, 165
Zenchiku Ujinobu, 108, 121